LET ME ENTERTAIN YOU

LET ME ENTERTAIN YOU

David Brown

WILLIAM MORROW AND COMPANY, INC.
New York

Grateful acknowledgment is made for permission to reprint from: "Zip" by Lorenz Hart and Richard Rodgers. Copyright © 1979 by Chappell & Co. All rights reserved. Used by permission.

James Harvey excerpt reprinted by permission of *The New York Review of Books.* Copyright © 1988 by Nyrev, Inc.

Library of Congress Cataloging-in-Publication Data
Brown, David, 1916–
Let me entertain you.

1. Brown, David, 1916– . 2. Motion picture producers and directors—United States—Biography.
3. Screenwriters—United States—Biography.
I. Title.
PN1998.3.B76A3 1990 791.43'0232'092 [B] 89-29175
ISBN 0-688-08048-0

Printed in the United States of America

First Edition

1 2 3 4 5 6 7 8 9 10

BOOK DESIGN BY PAUL CHEVANNES

For Helen, Gene, and Bruce

Opening Credits

This is the part of the book in which the author tells who is responsible. I am responsible for most of it because it is about my life. Gene Shalit must share the blame—or credit—because it was his idea that I write it. I was not allowed (by Gene) to mention that in the Prologue.

The book took a long time to write. How long? Earliest records of the beginnings of this book have been found on the walls of caves in the Tigris and Euphrates Valley of Upper Mesopotamia. Some of those whose contributions I am about to acknowledge were not yet born when I started writing this book. (That is true.)

Apart from Gene, I am indebted to Marc Jaffe, an eminent editor, who in his various editorial incarnations at Bantam, Random House, and Houghton Mifflin entreated me to write this book by sending me annually a signed publishing contract until I relented and he brought it to William Morrow and Company, which became my publisher. Marc extrapolated from the more than one million words I had written in longhand what appears here and sculpted it into manageable length and discernible organization. The words are all mine. You can't fault Marc there. Mr. Jaffe, because of his objectivity, was able to tell me what to leave out, and Mr. Shalit, because of his lack of objectivity, what to leave in. The net loss of weight was considerable. Accordingly, they helped me produce a book that you might conceivably be able to put down but you assuredly could pick up.

Mr. Shalit says, "Many people have worked on *Let Me Entertain You* through the years, and many of them (a) don't even remember that's what they were doing—they have gotten married and had kids and moved to Peru and Zimbabwe—while (b) others have slipped my mind. However, every important person who has worked on the book is listed." Relying on Mr. Shalit's memory and my own, which is risky business, the important ones are the following:

Deb Woodin was a powerhouse. She worked like crazy for three years transcribing, organizing, computing, and arranging, and supplied some very sound ideas. I do believe she knows more about me than my wife.

Jeffry Culbreth labored for five years on the book. She was the engine that kept us all going. Today Jeffry is the exalted talent coordinator of the *Today* show.

Among those sadly missing is the late Sabrina Grigorian, a meticulous worker who was always encouraging about the book. She worked valiantly on it for three years, in fact until the day she died.

I don't know what we would have done without Joannie Kaplan, who was so diligent in the pre-computer period when organizing and annotating the material was a laborious task bordering on drudgery. She did it skillfully and with panache.

Another important contributor was Kathleen Murphy, who wrote summaries of various sections and contributed to the organization of the material, taking the immense number of words I had written and putting them into an early configuration.

Karen Stirgwolt must also be mentioned as a willing and wonderful helper.

Samantha Cooper is one of those who was not born when I started work on this book. She is now in college. Samantha has done everything that was asked of her—filing, hole-punching (including some that are in the book), arranging, even typing, all with enthusiasm and high spirits.

I am also indebted to the gifted Ruth Mullen, who typed five drafts of the manuscript and amazingly made sense of the illegible additions, excisions, transpositions, and corrections I made in my abominable handwriting. She produced corrected manuscripts of more than five hundred pages in forty-eight sleepless hours. A great deal of this book was originally in the form of voice tapes that were transcribed. Each typed page was completely rewritten by me in longhand, typed by Ruth Mullen, and then edited by me until each manuscript page resembled a road map of Sicily. Kit Golden worked valiantly as liaison and sometimes interpreter of my instructions to Ruth Mullen. Robbie Capp copy edited this manuscript with extraordinary skill, taste, and sensitivity.

I am grateful to those who cannot read these words but are part of this book. I have written of them as I would if they were alive—with affection and respect.

Finally, I must acknowledge the work of my editor, Lisa Drew, whose encouragement and editorial skills kept me from straying into unassigned territory, and to the chieftains of William Morrow, Larry Hughes and Howard Kaminsky, as well as their colleagues who greeted this book in the bud with such enthusiasm that I was compelled to get on with it, if only for their sakes. Bob Shuman calmly and creatively put up with my demands until he was compelled to say, "Stop him before he writes again."

My greatest debt, of course, is to those readers who have found their way into these pages.

—David Brown
New York

Subject Matters

Prologue *13*
Fade In *15*
Flashback *17*
Cut to Hollywood *34*
The Love Interest *38*
No People Like Show People *40*
Now You See It *46*
Why I Love San Francisco *46*
Some Special Friends *48*
Fade to Blacklist *52*
Hooray for Hollywood *53*
The Great One *58*
Jolie *59*
Life with Father *59*
Back Story *64*
A Couple of Originals *71*
The Movie That Built Century City *73*
Love's Magic Spell *77*
Movieland Malice and Mischief *80*
Zanuck and Other Geniuses *84*
Short Takes *100*
Birth of a Legend: Helen Gurley Brown *102*
The Robert Evans Story *113*
Big Shots *116*
Power Failure *122*
Pick Yourself Up (and Start All Over Again) *132*
Back to Show Business *136*
Popcorn *138*
Making Movies *143*
The Scariest Movie Ever Made *145*
More *Jaws* *150*
Set Pieces *153*

Potpourri *156*
Funny Business *180*
California: The 1930s *182*
The King of Columnists *184*
Outtakes *189*
The Triumph (and Tragedy) of George Stevens *193*
The Way It Was, as It Now Seems *197*
Slow Fades *200*
What Does a Producer Do? *205*
Shop Talk *220*
Musings *227*
Fear of Flying *229*
The Verdict: A Very Special Movie *232*
On *Target* *236*
Selected Short Subjects *238*
Intermission *241*
Mean Stories *242*
Quick Cuts *244*
Fade to Black *249*
Appendix: Herb Mayes's 100 Best Novels List *261*
Index *265*

PROLOGUE

The idea for this book came from a friend* who may have been listening to my stories for too long. No doubt in an effort to deflect me, he suggested that I write this book. Actually, I had written much of it already, some of it at the time the events occurred. It wasn't to be a formal autobiography, but instead a crazy-quilt memoir, containing what might drift through my consciousness if I were going down on the *Titanic,* recollections and musings not necessarily in chronological order but in the haphazard pattern of life itself, as scattered as a dream. Judging by the book's length, the *Titanic* would have had to remain afloat for several weeks.

As in most reminiscences, exactly what was said years ago is recalled with alacrity, if not complete accuracy. I beg you to indulge me in this feat of re-creation. As John Gregory Dunne once observed in *The New York Review,* most stories about Hollywood are not true and certainly not original. My stories about Hollywood and other worlds are as I remember them, and conversations I was able to tape are, of course, indisputable. I confess there is in this

*See "Opening Credits."

kind of work a tendency to revise early personal history because there is no one alive to refute it. I have tried to resist, but if there are any survivors around I can only hope their memory is as bad as mine, except that mine may be artfully bad. On the other hand, memories of the distant past tend to be more accurate than most.

That I have written with some affection and, I trust, good humor about many celebrated people should not lead the reader to believe I am unaware of their darker side. I believe the truth about them is gentler than what can be deduced from revelations of sad and destructive events that tormented a few of them but are far from the sum of their lives.

My purpose in writing this book is to entertain and occasionally touch you, as well as to relive my own life. Why not? As Kander and Ebb observed in *Cabaret,* "Life is a cabaret, old chum." Mine is. On with the show.

Fade In

There was something different about the first preview of *Jaws.* At 5:30 P.M. on March 26, 1975, a line at a suburban Dallas theater seemed to stretch to the horizon. The horizon in Texas is mighty far.

We had scheduled the first preview in Dallas to get a reaction far from shark-filled waters. The theater was packed with people who had sat through a performance of *The Towering Inferno* to be sure of a seat for the first screening anywhere of *Jaws.* Richard Zanuck and I, who had produced the film, were sweating with anxiety. Would the shark, now known worldwide as a fake, scare people, or would it (disaster!) bring laughs? If the latter, the game was over and we could quit the business.

They were scared all right. When the movie shark lunged from a tranquil, sunlit sea, one woman rose in horror from her seat and spilled her Coca-Cola on the woman in front of her, who paid no attention whatever because she thought *she* had wet her pants in fright. The audience screamed and screamed. The cards they filled out to rate the picture made *us* scream—with pleasure: 95 percent rated the film "excellent." So great was the pressure to see the film—and so long the line—that an additional performance was scheduled for 11 P.M. The result was identical: a 95 percent "excellent" card count.

Most postpreview sessions for producers are gloomy, but obviously not this one. Champagne flowed in Penthouse 3 of the Registry Hotel until four o'clock in the morning as Sidney J. Sheinberg, president of MCA/Universal; Steven Spielberg, our twenty-seven-year-old director; Richard Zanuck; film editor Verna Fields; composer John Williams; production executive William Gilmore; Clark Ramsey, head of advertising, publicity, and exploitation for Universal; and I celebrated our good fortune—and good judgment, of course.

News of the preview of a costly film moves rapidly. In a telephone call from my broker at Loeb Rhoades at 42 Wall Street the morning after the Dallas preview, *he* told *me* that we had had two previews, the exact card count at both, and gave me the comments of leading exhibitors who were in the audience. The stock of MCA/Universal went up several points. I was not one of the buyers.

However, two successful previews do not a blockbuster make. So two nights later, on March 28, 1975, we showed *Jaws* in Long Beach, California, at the Lakewood Shopping Center, where we had previewed *The Sting,* to a standing ovation. The Long Beach preview proved that Dallas's reaction was no fluke. Again, it was a sensation, a harbinger, as it turned out, of things to come, things that would change our lives. As *Time* reported in its cover story on *Jaws,* Zanuck and Brown would never have to work again.

How sweet it was, following that event, to sit up all night counting and recounting the cards, reading the comments, mostly extravagant, adoring, great, wonderful. Which scenes did you dislike? None. Which scenes did you like? All. On one card someone wrote, "This is a great film. Now don't fuck it up by trying to make it better."

We did try and we did make it better. Following that preview a shock cut of a fisherman's decapitated head floating into frame was filmed by Spielberg in editor Verna Fields's San Fernando Valley swimming pool and produced a scream of such magnitude that I could hear it outside a theater every time the scene was playing.

When *Jaws* became the biggest movie of all time, my old friend literary agent H. N. Swanson said, "Now all you have to do is stay alive."

Flashback

Being a late sleeper as a young man, I needed a job that didn't require me to go to work until afternoon. I found one on *Women's Wear Daily,* where I became second-string drama critic and night editor. Those were palmy days in the spring of 1937. The newsroom was at 8 East Thirteenth Street in New York's Greenwich Village. I lived at 36 Gramercy Park South with three other men and a girl named Anna. She was mine, although of a communal inclination, as she was a member of the Communist Party. We were quarrelsome lovers, wrangling at breakfast over the Spanish Civil War. I cared little for politics. My beat was Broadway. For *WWD* and later for *Pic,* a picture magazine published by the venerable Street and Smith publications, I wrote about theater, nightclub acts, cabaret performers, and orchestras. New York then was idyllic, almost bucolic. In summer, streetcars rattled down Broadway, their sides removed so passengers could ride in the soft, open air.

Forty-second Street contained a row of legitimate theaters and two burlesque houses, the Eltinge and the Apollo. Burlesque was considered naughty because it featured women who stripped to their G-strings, teasing an audience that kept shouting, "Take it off!" while an orchestra played slowtime, and baggy-pants comedians dared to say, "What the hey." Some of the strippers became famous, among them Margie Hart and Gypsy Rose Lee. Gypsy was an intellectual whose thoughts while musing and disrobing, according to a Rodgers and Hart lyric from *Pal Joey,* included:

> Zip! Walter Lippmann wasn't brilliant today.
> Zip! Will Saroyan ever write a great play?
> Zip! I was reading Schopenhauer last night.
> Zip! And I think that Schopenhauer was right.

Red Buttons was only one of the many comedians who graduated from burlesque to the big time.

While it was considered family entertainment of a sort, burlesque died an unnatural death when it was decreed by the city fathers that nudity and risqué language ("What the hey") were not for the poor people. Those prurient pursuits moved to the higher-priced clubs on Fifty-second Street and to the Broadway theater.

The Broadway theater itself was dead in the summer—down to two or three shows—because there was no air conditioning. Only movie houses featured air conditioning and consequently thrived.

In season, almost everyone wore formal attire—including top hat—to Broadway openings. The highest-priced tickets for a play were $3.30—$4.40 for a musical. Admission price for movies was fifteen cents before 1 P.M. Lindy's on Fiftieth Street, and the original Lindy's across the street and down a block, were open all night, serving cheesecake to die for, great legs of turkey, gooey pastrami, and spicy salami from an enormous menu. The waiters bullied the customers, dictating their food choices and ridiculing them when they protested. Song writers, song pluggers, columnists, gamblers, showpeople, and gangsters hung out at Lindy's, usually at the smaller one on the east side of Broadway. Damon Runyon immortalized the place in his Guys and Dolls stories, many of which took place at "Mindy's."

Sardi's on West Forty-fourth Street was for first nighters and Ralph's for less affluent actors; others went to Dave's Blue Room on West Fifty-eighth Street and the Blue Ribbon, a German restaurant on West Forty-fourth Street just east of Broadway. Dinty Moore's offered the best corned beef and cabbage in an establishment with white tiled walls and blinding illumination, while uptown on East Fifty-eighth Street, Reubens, also open all night, had the best sandwiches in town, named for the stars. They included the Helen Hayes hamburger, the Milton Berle egg-and-pastrami, and the J. Edgar Hoover roast-beef-and-onion. (The Reuben sandwich survives to this day, named after Arnold Reuben, founder of Reubens.)

There was nothing quite like Broadway in the thirties and forties; the girls were sexy in their summer dresses and foxy in their winter furs. Mugging existed only on stage. (The word meant overacting and applied to vaudeville comedians.) The Great White Way was wonderfully glamorous. As an entertainment reporter, I covered Broadway opening nights and shows at the Beachcomber ("only two zombies to a customer") and Monte Proser's Copacabana, where, years later, Dean Martin and Jerry Lewis would break in as summer replacements for Frank Sinatra and Joe E. Lewis. The Copa girls were dazzling, among them June Allyson, who was to become a movie star. By 1937, the Cotton Club had moved downtown from its Harlem roost; Duke Ellington and Cab Calloway alternated as bandleader. El Morocco lured the swells on the East Side as did the Stork Club, the "21" Club, and Latin clubs where we danced the Conga and the Tango. Eddie Condon's in the Village corralled the jazz crowd. Major hotels featured orchestras. Guy Lombardo and his Royal Canadians were fixtures at the Roosevelt Grill, especially on New Year's Eve; Paul Whiteman could be found at the Starlight Roof of the Waldorf-Astoria; Hal Kemp at the Mad-Hattan Room of the Pennsylvania; Eddie Duchin at the Central Park Casino; Vincent Lopez for decades at the Taft (his signature: "This is Lopez speaking"); Leon Belasco at the St. Moritz Roof; Glen Gray at the Glenn Island Casino; Ben Bernie and all the lads were across the river in Brooklyn at the Hotel Bossert roof; and Les Brown and his Band of Renown played upstate with a girl vocalist named Doris Day.

It was exciting to be in New York and get out of strange beds before going to work. As the song from the movie *42nd Street* put it, Manhattan babies don't sleep tight until the dawn. In summer, a Tom Collins at the Sidewalk Café of Longchamps, Twelfth Street and Fifth Avenue, was just the thing and cost twenty-five cents. Other restaurants in the Village included Charles, a grand-luxe establishment at Ninth Street and Sixth Avenue; the Lafayette; the Breevoort; Chumley's; and the Jumble Shop on Eighth Street, a favorite of writers and artists. In those days, gay meant merry, lively, even wanton, as in *The Gay Divorcée,* a hit musical of the period. Men with an eye for the ladies were gay rogues. Everybody drank, smoked, and made love with no fear of cancer, cholesterol, or AIDS. All we knew was that life was for living. In a few years, we would find life was also for dying, as war closed in and some of us went away, never to return.

The Depression was on but the cost of living was negligible. *WWD* paid me twenty-five dollars a week in cash. No deductions. Eleven dollars went for rent and the remaining fourteen dollars easily saw me through an active social and sexual life. Who cared if banks failed in Yonkers?

Ernest Lehman is one of Hollywood's most accomplished screenwriters, as well as a novelist and author of short stories. The films he's written include *West Side Story, The Sound of Music, The King and I, Sabrina, Executive Suite, Somebody Up There Likes Me, North by Northwest, The Sweet Smell of Success,* and *Who's Afraid of Virginia Woolf?* We have known each other for over sixty years, having grown up within a few blocks of each other in Woodmere, on the south shore of Long Island. We began writing in college, on separate coasts, but were paid for our work when we moved to jobs in New York in the summer of 1937. When I became second-string drama critic and night editor for *Women's Wear Daily,* Ernest was a financial writer for a doomed publication called *Dealer's Commentator.* Its death was slow. At first Ernest had a secretary. Then he answered his own phone. Later he was at the switchboard. Finally the magazine and he were gone.

After a vacation visit to Provincetown, Massachusetts, we became enamored of the idea of becoming freelance writers. I quit my *Women's Wear Daily* job and leased an expensive, for me, apartment to ensure that I would have to work hard to pay the rent. We wrote an article on one of vaudeville's most durable stars, Ted Lewis, and—amazingly—sold it at once to *Collier's,* the nation's second-largest weekly, for an incredible four hundred dollars. As our writing style improved, we sold to a better class of, but financially poorer, magazines. Before long we were writing for the distinguished *American Mercury* for the undistinguished fee of fifty dollars an article. That fee was for both of us. When our agent's 10 percent commission was deducted, we were left with $22.50 each. One *American Mercury* assignment was to write a piece on Moe Berg, the catcher of the Boston Red Sox, who spoke ten languages and later was reported to be a spy for our side in World War II. His story required a trip to the team's spring training quarters in Florida and a one-week stay at a hotel—all at our expense.

About this time I formed a company called David Brown Associates. The idea of the company was to find men and women with stories to tell but without writing ability to tell them. We would do the writing. Ernest Lehman asked, "Who are the associates?" I replied, "You."

As Hitler's assault on the Jews intensified, hundreds of talented writers came to America. One of them was Martin Proskauer, a name he Americanized to Proctor. Martin was an important journalist in Germany, but had difficulty writing English. He had information about how Jews and others, forced to flee the Nazis, smuggled their wealth out of Germany. Diamonds and other precious gems were tossed in snowball fights over the Swiss border to carefully designated catchers. We wrote an article about that titled "Black Money," and sold it to *Harper's* for $125 with Martin Proctor's name on it. The $125 was cut three ways after our agent, Maxim Lieber, deducted his 10 percent commission. (*Another* alleged spy, except he was accused of working for the Soviet Union.)

Horoscopes were our main source of income in those Depression days of the late thirties. The Peerless Weighing and Vending Company of Long Island City was our most valued client. It needed whole sets of horoscopes for its subway scales and vending machines. When you inserted a penny and dialed your birthdate, you not only learned your weight, but also received a small piece of cardboard on which your fortune was printed. A cartoon of the period showed a passenger reading his card which said, "Idiot! You just missed your train." We were paid an astronomical six hundred dollars a set, although we knew nothing about astrology except what we cribbed from astrology magazines, as good as astrology source material gets—short of interviews with Zoroaster. Our star gazing was harmless for the reader and helpful for the writers.

We also wrote radio scripts. That happened because of an article Lehman and I had written about Eddie Cantor's five daughters. Cantor, a pop-eyed former Ziegfeld star on Broadway, was now a star of radio and films and had his own comedy show on CBS. He thought our article was funny enough to employ us secretly to provide material he could pretend was his own in his effort to keep his regular writers' salary demands down. He paid us by check from his personal Bank of America account. The amount was determined by the number of jokes actually used on the broadcast. There were two dress rehearsals for the show. By air time, audience response during rehearsals usually reduced the number of our jokes to perhaps two hundred dollars' worth. We wrote for a continuing character known as Mr. Guffy, who took umbrage at anything that was said. If someone said, "Happy Birthday," Mr. Guffy would reply, "What's happy about it?" or something equally grumpy. Our meetings with Cantor took place in his Sherry Netherland apartment. George Jessel, who was Cantor's costar in vaudeville days, would occasionally visit him. George was not doing well. We could tell because Eddie hid his good scotch and cigars before George arrived.

Lehman and I thought that we were Hollywood bound when Cantor bought the film rights to Eric Knight's classic novel, *The Flying Yorkshireman* (a pre-Superman story of a man who discovered he could fly), and asked us to write the screenplay. But Eddie couldn't put the deal together and Hollywood had to wait a while longer for us.

Meanwhile, Ernest and I became intrigued with the idea of writing an article about a lady named Jacqueline Cochran. Jackie Cochran was an aviatrix who won the Bendix cross-country race and flew magnificently through all sorts of weather. She was a speed demon in those early, unfriendly skies of the thirties. This same lady, who started as a manicurist in the once-famed Roney Plaza Hotel in

Miami Beach, buffed the nails of a very wealthy man named Floyd B. Odlum, chairman of the Atlas Corporation. She buffed them so well that he married her. Ultimately she became president of Bonwit Teller in New York. Her life was a full and worthy one.

We interviewed her in the River House on the East Side of Manhattan, a stately tower that still houses the rich, famous, and sometimes infamous. Odlum, who later became my boss at *Liberty* magazine, was not present. But when we delivered our article and it was accepted by *Glamour* magazine, then as now a Condé Nast publication, Harry Bruno, one of Manhattan's corporate public relations men, came around to take a few sentences out of the article that he believed might give offense to the wealthy and influential Floyd B. Odlum. Nothing serious. An example of corporate power in the early years of magazine publishing. I felt that power again when Odlum owned the magazine I edited, even though he was so afflicted with arthritis that I had to take my begging cup to his desert home in Indio, California, to ask for money for the foundering publication.

Pic was one of the early picture magazines that sprang up in the thirties. There were also *Life* (transformed from a humor magazine of that title), *Click,* and *Look,* among others. *Pic* was published every two weeks by Street and Smith, the oldest magazine publishing house in America and long since acquired by Samuel Newhouse for his Condé Nast Publications. When I joined the staff in 1939, *Pic,* like Caesar's Gaul, was divided into several parts. They were Broadway, Hollywood, and Sports. I wrote the Broadway section.

In addition to stories about Broadway, every two weeks I wrote up a famous old murder case as though it had just happened. Old newspaper clippings were my data base. This was not without risk. The judge was mistakenly identified as the murderer in a photo layout. One night my wife woke up screaming to find my hands around her throat as I reenacted one of the crimes in my dreams.

The editorial offices were directly above the presses in an old building at 79 Seventh Avenue in Manhattan. When a sentence wasn't clear, a compositor in a printer's apron would come up and ask, "Whadda ya mean by this?" After the word or sentence was corrected, the presses would roll and the floor would tremble.

During those Street and Smith days in the early forties, a squad of FBI men took over the venerable Seventh Avenue and Fifteenth Street building and secured all the exits. John Campbell, editor of the prescient science fiction magazine *Astounding Stories,* had published a story in which one of the characters discovered how to make an atomic bomb. The G-men wanted to know how come. The atomic bomb project was still a secret to the rest of the world.

Early in 1942 I left *Pic* to become nonfiction editor of *Liberty,* one of the most famous weeklies of the period. Our offices were at 205 East Forty-second Street, where Bernarr MacFadden, the previous owner of *Liberty* and a health nut, ordered his staff to exercise twice a day standing up on their desks and then dropping to the floor to do push-ups. He was succeeded as owner by financier Floyd B. Odlum (Jacqueline Cochran's great and good friend). The new editor-in-chief, E. Jerome Ellison, was fresh from *Reader's Digest,* where he had been a rising star. He succeeded the theatrical Fulton Oursler, an editor of considerable renown, a magician of no little skill, and later a best-selling author and major editor of *Reader's Digest.*

Liberty had been founded by Captain "Joe" Patterson and Colonel "Bertie" McCormick of the *Chicago Daily News/New York Daily News* dynasties and was designed as a blue-collar weekly filling the niche upscale *Collier's* and *The Saturday Evening Post* could not occupy.

It published fast-moving fiction, such as James M. Cain's *Double Indemnity* and Thomas Heggen's *Mister Roberts.* Articles and short stories were timed to tell the reader exactly how long he would spend to read them. "Reading time: seven minutes, twenty-three seconds," for example. Ted Shane's Cockeyed Crossword Puzzle was another innovation. Other authors included Rupert Hughes (Howard's uncle), Thyra Samter Winslow, John P. Marquand, George Harmon Coxe, and, until the war, the Nazi propagandist George Sylvester Viereck. Nonfiction could barely be distinguished from fiction. A feature, "I Was Hitler's Housemaid," entirely fictional but represented as solemn truth, was so popular that the installments were extended by making them shorter and shorter until barely a few hundred words appeared in each issue.

After only a year at *Liberty,* my number was called and I was inducted into the army. I thought I was doing my bit by serving as an air raid warden at what is now the Plaza Athenée off Park Avenue, but World War II was heating up. My entrance into the armed forces did little to alter the balance of military power. I was washed out of Officer Candidate School because I dismissed my men in front of the wrong barracks following an arduous combat maneuver in rough, wooded terrain. "Does not know where his men are quartered," the inspecting officer hastily noted on his pad. Little wonder I convinced the army, shortly after the end of the war, that a hundred and fifty people on *Liberty* magazine would be better protected if I were honorably discharged than the nation would be if I remained in the military service. My letter to the commanding general petitioning him for a discharge on the grounds of national interest argued that the postwar world was going to be rough economically and I had better get back there and put people to work. (My commanding officer was the first to apply for a job. I put him in charge of a column about veterans.)

Actually, I didn't have to wait for a reply from the commanding general. The army base I was stationed at was under fire not from the enemy but from the powerful Washington columnist Drew Pearson. He had revealed that thousands of men were idle there at taxpayers' expense, doing nothing but picking up cigarette butts. The war was over. Why weren't they being discharged and taken off the taxpayers' backs? he asked. His attack was so telling that our commander was ordered by his Washington superiors to get everybody out of the damn camp by sundown, including the regimental mascots.

When I returned to *Liberty,* my old job of nonfiction editor was filled. Under the GI Bill of Rights, I was entitled to get that job back but perky, gifted Edward Hutchings, Jr., then executive editor, asked, "Would you like to be fiction editor?" I had never been fiction editor. I had, in fact, hardly ever read fiction. But I said, "OK. What the hell!" I was young and resilient. It was lucky I did say yes because it taught me how to evaluate fiction—a skill that later got me a job in Hollywood.

Events were moving swiftly. I would not be fiction editor long. Ed Hutchings moved on to California Institute of Technology to teach scientists how to write so others would understand them (good idea). The new executive editor was Jim Bishop, a writer of best-selling books and soon to become a columnist. Luck was my lady again. While the editor-in-chief was on vacation, Jim made the error of telling the publisher what he would do with the magazine if he were editor-in-chief. The publisher mentioned this to the editor-in-chief, who fired Jim and gave me his job. Jim left his pay voucher in his old (and my new) desk so I would know how much to ask. I got the job because I was the only one who had dealt with both nonfiction and fiction.

Pretty soon the editor-in-chief was fired and silver-haired Paul Hunter, president and publisher of *Liberty,* leaned over his desk and said, "You're just a baby, but do you think you can handle editor-in-chief?" I said yes, and I was a baby and I could handle anything then.

My excitement and delight at having succeeded to the power of editor-in-chief (I was actually able to buy ten stories a week without asking anyone's permission) cooled somewhat when I realized I was editing a magazine that was mandated to lose money. Mr. Odlum had bought *Liberty* as a tax loss to offset his profit when he sold RKO Pictures to Howard Hughes at a huge gain. Whenever I needed cash to pay for the magazine's losses, Odlum's response was, "Lose *more:* That's what my tax accountant says I need."

Ultimately, I did not disappoint him. In fact, I exceeded his tax accountant's need for losses. It was a tough climate for weekly magazines in the economic letdown of the post–World War II years. We finally lost enough money for Odlum to dispose of us and were taken over, in lieu of unpaid printing bills, by Chicago's exceedingly rich printing magnate, John F. Cuneo, who was also responsible for helping the Hearst Corporation survive tough times by carrying its huge printing bills in the Depression of the 1930s.

Cuneo wanted me to remain as editor-in-chief of *Liberty,* but was not impressed by an interview I had with President Harry Truman. "Why are you seeing him?" he asked. "He can't give us any advertising." What he did give us, as did Franklin D. Roosevelt, was circulation. Every time I put FDR on the cover, our circulation went up, even after he had died. "Putting a dead President on the cover—that's a good way to kill a magazine," Cuneo insisted until he saw the circulation figures. A cover reproduction of an unfinished portrait of FDR by an artist who was present when he died at Warm Springs, Georgia, sold more copies than any other issue of *Liberty.* The cover of Truman sold nearly as many.

In the years just after the war had ended, New York was at its best, untouched by the war and physically unchanged because of it. Construction and demolition of buildings had been halted during hostilities and New York in 1945 looked the same as it did in 1941 except older. It was good to be young in New York, a civilian again, with a powerful magazine job, and watch the girls go by from my new front-office window at 37 West Fifty-seventh Street. It seemed we all had permanent erections and hangovers in those first postwar days.

They're only shades now, most of them, but once they were alive and ebullient and vibrant, the men and women who made *Liberty* magazine in the forties. Bill O'Brian, witty, cynical and as good-looking as a movie star, was our editorial cartoonist and always disagreed with the editorials he was asked to illustrate. He later moved on to the freedom of *The New Yorker.* Bearded, scholarly E. M. Pillar was succeeded as book editor by the Desdemona-like Helen Greenwood, a tall, blond, skinny, and patrician woman (also sexy). Virginia Spies, our film critic, threatened to jump out the window when I criticized her copy. Liza Wilson, our Hollywood editor, introduced me to Dorothy Lamour, Irene Dunne, Myrna Loy, and Loretta Young, and to the moguls for whom I would one day work.

Liberty expired with the rest of the general magazines (*The Saturday Evening Post, Collier's, Look,* and the old *Life* among them) when television took the advertisers away. But once, the writers, editors, and owners of those publications were as alive as Clay Felker, Tina Brown, Rupert Murdoch, and all the young turks and turkesses of journalism today. A generation passeth, giving way to the new, but oh, what a generation mine was when I was boy editor of *Liberty.*

In every life a little rain must fall. A cliché, but like most clichés, a truism. For me, a lot of rain consisted of a husband-and-wife publicity team named Whitaker and Baxter. Leone Baxter and Clem Whitaker. Back in 1949, Whitaker and Baxter were one of the most high-powered political PR organizations in the country. They had built a reputation in Sacramento for effective "dirty tricks." Now they had been hired by the American Medical Association to kill off the compulsory health insurance program advocated by President Harry S. Truman. My job at *Liberty* magazine had become shaky because wartime prosperity had faded. The prospect of earning the incredible sum of twenty thousand dollars a year was too tempting to shrug off. I moved to Chicago and became what was euphemistically called editorial director of the National Education Campaign of the American Medical Association. It was a front to assassinate the government on a daily basis, undercutting the health insurance movement.

I rented a townhouse on the North Side and traveled to my office at 1 North La Salle Street on the Michigan Avenue bus. Once a month I was in a posh train compartment en route to Washington, where the AMA maintained a deceptively modest presence. The expense account was good, but I didn't like Mr. Whitaker (Clem) and less did I like the seductive Miss Baxter (Leone). One day I was asked to do something which offended even my Philistine values. I was asked to put out a press release stating that the FBI had been ordered to intimidate doctors who were not in favor of the President's national health insurance program. I refused and quit. The CIO reported in its office journal that "even David Brown, a hard-nosed creature of the establishment, could not stomach the tactics of Whitaker and Baxter."

It was pretty gutsy to quit, as I look back. I had no money. My first marriage was on the critical list. Whitaker and Baxter circulated a little note to the Washington press corps saying that I did not resign, but was fired. Four members of the press corps sent me the Whitaker and Baxter communiqué with their own sarcastic comments scribbled on it. Whitaker and Baxter did not convince them. Being "fired" by Whitaker and Baxter turned out to be an accolade.

Herbert R. Mayes was generous about money, particularly expense accounts, and was a mentor, role model, and sometime hero for most of us who worked for him at *Good Housekeeping* and the old *Cosmopolitan* in the 1940s. I thought he was the best magazine editor of his day, and so did he. He was certainly the most colorful. Magazines were his life. He'd drive in from his Connecticut home on Saturdays and Sundays to stand in the art department and gaze at the stats of pages of future issues, thinking how he could improve or change them. He would sometimes "tear up the book" if he had a flash of inspiration, or an idea for adding pizzazz to an issue. He gloried in flamboyant nonfiction ideas and was a snob about writers. He wanted writers to be elegant as well as good. Tackiness was a sin at Hearst's *Cosmopolitan* under Herbert R. Mayes. He was not technically the editor. His title was supervising editor. His primary job was as editor-in-chief of *Good Housekeeping,* but he had taken responsibility for supervising *Cosmopolitan* during a difficult transitional period.

Herb's first move was to revolutionize the look of the book. He did so with panache and theater. He brought—perhaps "bought" is the applicable word—the art directors of the *Ladies' Home Journal* to *Cosmopolitan* at munificent salaries and vast expense accounts, providing Frank Eltonhead and Robert Atherton with enough money to commute daily from their Philadelphia and Bucks County homes to the Hearst Magazine Building in New York City. Herb operated like a Hollywood mogul in dispensing largesse and providing posh surroundings for his crew. There was no more splendid place to work than for him at Hearst.

Mayes liked flashy ideas and I learned much of what I know

about writing cover lines from him. Mayes's blurbs had a twist on them. They resembled a curve ball at a baseball game: They twisted outward, sometimes inward, but always contained a surprise. He readily dispensed outrageous superlatives like "Best Christmas Issue Ever" or "a story that will change your life."

Using his rules, I wrote cover blurbs for *Cosmopolitan* then, and I write them with the same moxie for *Cosmopolitan* now, forty years later.

Cover blurbs notwithstanding, we had very little luck with *Cosmopolitan* in those days. The magazine industry was going through a sea change. As Mayes wrote in his book *The Magazine Maze,* "I think we represented quite a consortium of editorial brains. Among us we turned out a brilliant magazine. It was so brilliant that it dipped to the lowest circulation in its history. We were editing a magazine for a general magazine/dual audience that no longer existed, and we were not smart enough to be aware of it. Nobody knew what to do with *Cosmopolitan* until Helen Gurley Brown came along." Exactly.

In 1949, magazines of general interest could no longer compete with television for readers and advertisers. Television was beginning to reach vastly larger audiences. It took a special-interest magazine to survive. *Cosmopolitan* did not identify itself as a sharply focused magazine, appealing to young women, until Helen Gurley Brown took it over in 1965. It struggled for circulation with pieces by famous writers but sales were down and even stories by Ernest Hemingway couldn't bail it out. Down, down, down. Mayes tried everything. Once he implored me to come up with a slogan that might identify the magazine. I came up with "The magazine for people who can read." Very inside and very dumb. It lasted a couple of issues before we realized it was too smartass to work.

I had the notion that famous Democrat Eleanor Roosevelt ought to write an article titled, "If I Were a Republican Today." I made my deal with her son and agent, Elliott Roosevelt. Mayes liked that and featured it on the cover, but the article had not arrived by the time two million covers had been printed. In panic, I called Mrs. Roosevelt at Hyde Park and explained the situation. She said, "Mr. Brown, I never heard of this assignment. I would never have undertaken it. But if Elliott told you I would do it, I will do it." And indeed she did. And Mayes took the manuscript and spiced it up by underscoring words in every other sentence.

He was a great editor, an inspiring one, one who demanded the best. In those years, he lived on Den Road in Stamford, Connecticut, came into the office three days a week, but worked seven days a week. On one of those days each week, he invited John J. O'Connell, John P. Marquand, Jr., and me—all *Cosmo* editors—to come up to his house and present article ideas.

We'd travel to Stamford on the New Haven Railroad and arrive in Herb's large study at about eleven in the morning. Mayes always offered us a drink at that hour and we never declined. He rarely drank and had no idea of how much scotch or bourbon to pour into a glass. We were young then, the two Johns and I, and drinking was something we knew how to do. Each of us found himself with a tumbler of gin or scotch or bourbon, guzzling it up and being quite soused within the hour.

During that same hour, the idea was to sell Mayes on as many article ideas as possible; our jobs and standing with him depended on our ability to generate ideas that would sell the issue. We were intensely competitive, although we loved each other. When O'Connell or Marquand would leave the room, which was often because of our liquor consumption, I would present my best ideas so they couldn't shoot them down, and they would do the same when I had to go to the john.

We staggered out of there, generally around two in the afternoon, and barely made it to the New Haven railroad station and home. There was no point in returning to the office.

Absent from the Stamford meetings was the other member of our editorial group, A. E. Hotchner. Hotchner was a loner, an associate editor, and mostly in Europe chasing down Ernest Hemingway, whose first novel in eight years, *Across the River and Into the Trees,* was to appear in *Cosmopolitan.* Hotch speaks poorly of Herb Mayes but Mayes gave him as much freedom as any editor might like.

Herb had quite a group around him on *Good Housekeeping,* including a sexy young lady, quite gorgeous, named Judy Tarcher, later to become rich and famous as Judith Krantz, author of *Scruples, Princess Daisy, I'll Take Manhattan,* and *Till We Meet Again.* Judy was then the shoe editor of *GH,* wrote fashion copy, and learned about the world of fashion which she later put to use in her fiction. She had lived in Paris, was able to write and speak French fluently, and even then moved in the trend-setting world.

Mayes ruled by fear, but respected strength. When the time came for me to move on to Hollywood, he was sorry to see me go and made every effort to dissuade me. He even tried to get me the editorship of the Hearst Sunday supplement, the *American Weekly,* but that didn't work out and his final words were, "Well, you could only be going out there for the money." I said, "No, Herb, the truth is that I wasn't able to get the top job here. For whatever reason, it was denied me. And just as companies fire editors, editors can fire companies, and I'm firing this company because it was unable tó give me the job of editor-in-chief."

Later, Herb said that was his greatest gift to me. Probably true. Neither of us knew that fifteen years later a woman named Helen Gurley Brown would become editor-in-chief of *Cosmopolitan* and that neither he nor I would be there while she commenced a reign which, for publishing, was as long as Queen Victoria's.

Herbert Mayes remained my friend during the long years I was in Hollywood; he once tried to bring me back to magazines as editor-in-chief of *McCall's,* the magazine to which he went when he was fired by Hearst because of a dispute over his authority as editor, a firing which rankled him to his last day on earth. I did meet Norton Simon, who owned the McCall Corporation, and took the psychological tests which he thought were necessary for evaluation of a candidate for editor. I scored spectacularly well but didn't get the job because I wanted too much money, being accustomed to Hollywood salaries.

Following the closing of the Fox studio because of the huge costs being incurred by the production of *Cleopatra,* I returned to New York in 1964 to become a book publisher. Herbert Mayes and his remarkable wife, Grace, were there to welcome my wife, Helen Gurley Brown. His was the first telephone call of congratulations when she was appointed editor of *Cosmopolitan* in 1965. "By God," he said, "Dick Deems (the magazine division head who fired Mayes) has at last done something right."

Herb was a man with as short a fuse as many short men have. He never took an insult from someone without striking back, suffered fools badly, and was willing to walk away from any job if it ceased to please him. That was a pact he had with his wife, Grace, for as long as he lived.

I was so afraid of Mayes when I joined the magazine that I waited three hours in my New York office for him to come to the phone at his Connecticut home. He had asked me to call. What happened was that Mrs. Mayes answered and said she would find Mr. Mayes. I waited: no Mayes. One hour: no Mayes. By then, Herb and Grace were on the Merritt Parkway, driving to New York. I learned later that during the drive, Grace asked, "What did David want?" It turned out Herb had forgotten to come to the telephone, but I was still on the line until well after they arrived in New York. I was too frightened to hang up and too petrified to complain.

I don't believe Herbert R. Mayes ever wrote a mundane letter or uttered a commonplace sentence. One of his missions in life was not to bore or be bored. Helen and I gave Herb a small gift on his eighty-fifth birthday and this is his letter of acknowledgment:

Dear Helen, Dear David, (Notice the precision, no patronizing "Dear Helen *and* David")

No Tiffany lamp, lost my standing have I? At the moment I won't complain because I know Halloween and Thanksgiving are on the way and then the Jewish holidays and Christmas, followed, but just barely, by a wedding anniversary, also January 1, 1986. Please make notes in between, don't forget to send books, also in between you might keep in mind that I own no fur coat, Grace has one but could use another. Rent bills arrive promptly on the first of every month, cash is always acceptable. For St. Patrick's Day, it would be nice to have a copy of the issue of *Cosmo* produced for people who can read. Happy memory. What I think I am trying to say is that Helen and David Brown are plumb crazy. Don't let that give you any notions, we do have 3 jars of plum preserve. A hell of a thank-you note this but you know what I mean which includes I have an abiding love for you.

Affectionately, Herbert

Herb Mayes sent the following communiqué to his fellow members of The Book Table, a group of publishers who met for lunch once a month at New York's "21" Club:

At the March 11th meeting of The Book Table there was some discussion about novels that are regarded as classics. I mentioned a list of 100 titles I had compiled and was asked to send copies to members of our group.*

Some explanations are in order.

First of all, I am not qualified to define what a literary classic is, and it would be reasonable for anybody to question the appearance on my list of *The Last of the Mohicans,* certainly after the way Mark Twain tore Mr. Cooper to shreds. But I liked the book, and have included it. Secondly, it should be remembered that the books on my list are my *favorites.* At least I now *think* so. I am not as young as Nat Wartels, so memory may be faulty. Thirdly, I am not familiar with a definition of "literary classic" that has universal acceptance. Such definitions as "A classic is a permanent best-seller" and "A book becomes a classic when people who haven't read it start pretending they have" are cute but definitely not true. Maybe this is a fairly reasonable definition: "Considered classic is a novel that at some point in time was widely regarded by critics and scholars as 'great,' whose literary qualities will continue to be admired by coming generations."

*For Herb Mayes's 100 Best Novels List, see Appendix.

My list contains *Don Quixote.* I loved it. But the truth is that now I remember affectionately only small bits and pieces—Quixote's attack on the windmills, the island of which Sancho Panza was made governor (or mayor), Sancho's comment about sleep—"God bless the man who invented it." Though I was fascinated by *Ulysses,* I know I found parts of it very hard going. (As for *Finnegans Wake* [not on my list], it stupefied me.)

I think anybody could make up a list of a hundred novels that he considered great and have it confined to novels by perhaps two dozen authors. My list is confined to *one* book by any given author: The one of his that I liked most, or now think I did. Dickens' *David Copperfield,* for example. I have read all but two or three of Dickens' novels, and memory makes me feel I was bowled over by all of them. How could anybody choose the *best* among *A Tale of Two Cities, Great Expectations, A Christmas Carol, Dombey and Son, Pickwick Papers, Oliver Twist?* I think I am familiar with Dickens' shortcomings, but by God he could tell a *story.*

Not on my list are novels whose primary appeal is to children; for example, *Alice's Adventures in Wonderland, Black Beauty, Adventures of Robin Hood.* Included on my list, however, are several books whose appeal, it seems to me, is both to children and adults; for example, *Huckleberry Finn* and *Treasure Island.*

Herbert R. Mayes, age eighty-five on August 11, 1985, born when the century began, with any luck could have made it to the dawn of the twenty-first century. It would have been a nice gift for all of us. It was not to be. He slipped away from us just before his eighty-eighth birthday. Grace joined him six months later. It's hard to stop talking about Mayes, most difficult to say good-bye.

Like other newspapers of record, *The New York Times* prepares obituaries of famous people in advance of their death. These obituaries are frequently updated as their subjects live on. Apart from those who write and edit them, few are privy to what they say although it is reported that some celebrated newsmen and their bosses have on occasion pulled up their obituaries on newsroom computers to read what they otherwise would never see. Alden Whitman was one of the best writers of *Times* obituaries and it was a mark of distinction to have one's death reported by him. In more recent years, a number of journalists have sought sanctuary writing obits, some of them from busy and dangerous foreign posts. One such person on *The New York Times* was Marilyn Berger, former White House correspondent for NBC and diplomatic correspondent for *The Washington Post.* When I telephoned to advise her of Herbert Mayes's imminent demise and to seek for Herb and his family as extensive an obit as I could, her computer showed that no advance story had been written. Glumly, she transferred me to the city desk. Breaking news was not her department. "David," she said sadly, "my people aren't even sick yet."

I enjoy some minor celebrity as the man who writes those provocative *Cosmopolitan* cover lines, an unpaid job I have held for the quarter of a century my wife has edited that seductive publication. I wrote my first headline in 1936 on the copydesk of the *San Francisco News.* It had to do with a red flag that was raised over the U.S. Supreme Court by some Harvard University pranksters. The headline: RED FLAG OVER SUPREME COURT ONLY HARVARD CRIMSON.

In writing cover lines for *Cosmopolitan,* I have found that the important word is *you.* The best cover lines deal with what *you* would like to be or feel or have (be prettier, feel better, or have a man, or money, or both). If you're anxious, a cover line tells you how to be less anxious. If unpopular, it promises popularity if you will follow a few simple rules. If fat, it tells you how to lose weight—and still eat as much as you'd like. If poor, the cover line tells you how to be rich. It's connected with "you" and never with "them."

The legendary William Randolph Hearst was alive during my stay at *Cosmo.* I was hired in 1949 with his personal approval. He died in 1951. No editor of rank was engaged without running the appointment by "the Chief." *Cosmo*'s editorial "dummy" was shipped to Mr. Hearst each month. The dummy consisted of a photostat of the cover and illustrations and a pasteup of the contents in type. Mr. Hearst rarely commented on the content but often scribbled his observations about the art. I remember such comments as "I like this hat" or "This would be better if reversed." He was an instinctive editor, clear and pragmatic in his views and reasonable in his edicts unless crossed or enraged by what he perceived as an affront to the Hearst service, as it was called.

W.R. had many favorites, among them my good friend and Hollywood mentor, Adela Rogers St. Johns. Adela, daughter of the great California trial lawyer Earl Rogers, covered the Lindbergh trial for the Hearst newspapers and was one of the highest-paid women journalists of her time. They were called "sob sisters" because they were supposed to wring out the emotion of a story. Adela became a successful author of books and screenplays, and contributed short stories to *Cosmopolitan* and *Good Housekeeping.* Sometimes she was asked to write a story to fit an illustration the editor fancied and bought without having a story to go with it. Clark Gable and Jack Dempsey were her special friends and she was quite a swinger before she got religion . . . then swung a little more in (would you believe it?) her eighties until she died in her sleep. W.R. thought she was neat except when she was drinking, an affliction of journalists of that era. She swore off drinking but little else.

The movie that influenced me most as a young man was not *Citizen Kane* or *Gone With the Wind,* but a far less renowned film titled *The Scoundrel.* Written by Ben Hecht and Charles MacArthur, who jointly directed it, *The Scoundrel* seemed, to my youthful eyes, the epitome of big-town sophistication and cynicism—traits I cherished in my early years. The stars included Noel Coward, Alexander Woollcott, Lionel Stander, Hecht himself, and the exquisite Julie Haydon, with whom I fell in love instantly. *The Scoundrel* dealt with a rapacious, womanizing New York publisher played by Noel Coward and, I'm told, patterned after the life of Horace Liveright. Had I been Mr. Liveright, I would have sent flowers instead of threatening to sue. Anyone would have liked to have been Noel Coward in that role: brittle, swimming in epigrams, and fiendishly attractive.

Cut to Hollywood

While dumb luck provided me with the credentials for a Hollywood career, a divorce got me there. I would have preferred to remain a journalist and done so had it not been for a broken marriage that made me desperate to leave New York and start a new life with a new wife. The opportunity came late in 1951 when Darryl F. Zanuck sent word to his New York vice-president, Joseph H. Moskowitz, that he wanted "the best editor in New York" to head up his story department. I was then managing editor of Hearst's *Cosmopolitan.* Zanuck planned to organize the Fox studio much like a national magazine and engage an editor to be responsible for acquiring the material that was to be made into films. The studio had under contract twenty-eight producers and as many directors and writers, as well as a large roster of actors.

Moskowitz, in receipt of Zanuck's order, turned the task over to

Bertram Bloch, Fox's New York story chief and a onetime playwright as well as creative aide to Metro's wunderkind, Irving Thalberg. I learned later that I was not the only one who had been considered. Bob Fuoss, editor of *The Saturday Evening Post,* was asked but declined.

Bert Bloch invited me to lunch at the Oak Room of the Plaza. I can remember the very table we occupied. The Plaza has always been lucky for me. I was offered my job at *Cosmopolitan* there by Herb Mayes, not in the Oak Room but on a settee in the corridor leading to it. Bert explained the foibles of Joe Moskowitz, whom he disliked, and the idiosyncracies of his West Coast counterpart, Julian Johnson, whom he respected but distrusted. Ultimately, if I got the job, I was to have the resources of Fox story departments around the world, including the one Bert Bloch headed. Bert was always on the verge of quitting but was in his sixties and had a young wife.

My publishing friends spoke well of me, and I was soon on the *Twentieth Century Limited* and *Santa Fe Chief* headed for Los Angeles. Except for a sumptuous lunch at the Ambassador East's Pump Room in Chicago, the watering hole for westward-bound movie types, I remained in my compartment reading up on movies (I had seen very few) until I got off the train at Pasadena, where I was met by a studio car and brought to Zanuck. We had lunch in the executive dining room. All producers in good standing were in attendance and also Walter Winchell, then America's most powerful and feared gossip columnist, who had an office in a dressing room at Fox and was a friend of Zanuck's, who feared him not. Nothing was said about my job until Zanuck invited me to walk back to his office with him. I never did enter his office. Before we got there, he stopped and said, "Tell Joe Moskowitz to make a deal with you." I had known Darryl as a journalist and had been invited to lunch before, but never as a job candidate.

Back in New York, Richard E. Berlin, president of the Hearst Corporation, owners of *Cosmopolitan,* offered to match the Twentieth Century Fox offer. I thanked Berlin, but my mind was set on California. My new wife was Wayne Clark, a brown-haired, beautiful, and bright Vassar girl I had met at Hearst and was now taking away from *her* magazine, *Good Housekeeping.* Her legs were sensational. I noticed them as once again I walked the red carpet leading to the *Twentieth Century Limited.* Frank Forsberg, then as now a close friend, waited in my compartment, a farewell bottle of scotch nestled on the cushions. Another friend glimpsed Wayne, my nine-year-old son, Bruce, and me from his commuter train, literally riding into the sunset in the observation car of the *Twentieth Century Limited* as it made its way into the gathering darkness of the Hudson River Valley.

It had happened. I was to succeed the venerable Julian Johnson, dean of Hollywood story editors and onetime lover of the speakeasy era's famous Texas ("Hello, sucker") Guinan, a lush lady who ran a famous nightclub. Julian started his movie career in the days of silent films, writing the titles that took the place of spoken dialogue. "Story editor" in that period was an important job title, second creatively to "head of production." It has since gone the way of such titles as "vice" president, "president," and the like. There were then only two vice-presidents in the corporation and one of them was Darryl F. Zanuck. Story editors of the day included the elegant Ken McKenna, a former actor who headed up the vast literary operations of Metro-Goldwyn-Mayer; John Mok at Paramount; William Dozier at RKO; Finlay McDermitt at Warner's. Almost at the story summit were two women: Marge Thorson, who assisted McKenna at Metro, and Eve Ettinger, a feisty lady at Columbia. McKenna, Johnson, and I took to lunching weekly at Romanoff's and hashing over the latest outrageous demands of the agents and the idiocies of our colleagues. It was all very civilized and mannerly. The food was good and we actually had a drink or two, New York style. We also compared reports from the spies we employed at New York publishing houses and book clubs to smuggle proofs of new books in advance of greedy agents.

One of the first men I visited on the Fox lot was Nunnally Johnson, who wrote and produced wonderful movies and had also written stories for *The Saturday Evening Post* and *The New Yorker.* Nunnally said, "They're very forgiving out here. If you don't get anything on the screen for a couple of years, they won't mind." He spoke in a soft Georgia drawl, and was one of the wittiest men anywhere. When he was offered Erskine Caldwell's *Tobacco Road,* about the poor inhabitants of rural America's most pitiful slum which, in its play version, ran forever on Broadway, Nunnally said he'd have no trouble adapting it for the screen. He was uniquely qualified. "Down where I come from," he said, "those folks are the country club set."

During my tenure at Fox in the fifties, Joe Moskowitz was my mentor in New York. Joe was not educated, but had street smarts. He fancied himself in competition with the studio general manager, Lew Schreiber, who was strictly Hollywood and sat at Darryl Zanuck's right hand in the executive dining room. Joe felt that Lew wasn't very smart. I thought that Lew was smart enough. In this case, Lew wasn't smart, and maybe I wasn't either. I demanded a new carpet from Schreiber (at a high point in my career) and one was delivered that had obviously been recycled, for it had thousands of little holes in it. Indignant, I showed this to Joe Moskowitz when he was on a trip to the studio and he shook his head. I said, "I'm really incensed, you know." His response was tepid. "Well, I wouldn't worry about it too much. It's not that important." I said, "It is, Joe."

I called Schreiber, who rarely entered anyone else's office and had direct access to his own office from the studio street, and demanded that he look at my pockmarked carpet. Finally, he did come out to inspect it, and I got a new one. When I reported this triumphantly to Moskowitz, he scoffed, "Dave, you have exchanged a genuine grievance for a new carpet. You could have won something big." Perhaps he was right. I never found out what "big" was. Joe believed in settling grievances at the highest possible rate of exchange.

Living in Hollywood was difficult for me because I didn't drive. My wife drove me from our house in the Hollywood Hills to Santa Monica Boulevard, where I took a streetcar to the studio. At the Fox stop, a jitney transported employees across the lot to their offices. Nunnally gave me a ride once or twice. He found it curious that a movie executive would go to work on a streetcar.

Shortly after I joined the studio, television had begun to have a severe impact on the movie business. Zanuck called us all into the commissary one night and said that times were tough, we were going to make fewer films, they were all going to be blockbusters but in the meantime everybody would have to cut down on costs. The lights on the studio lot were dimmed to save power. The gardeners stopped watering when a New York executive threatened to close down the studio if the lawns weren't brown the next time he came out.

Unused to the boom-and-bust cycle of Hollywood, I was concerned by all this and asked my friend Carl Brandt, a literary agent in New York, to look around for a job for me in publishing. Carl wrote back, "Don't worry. Movies are fortune's favorite child. They'll think of something." They did. Wide-screen movies in CinemaScope. In 1953, Zanuck stopped production on *The Robe,* reshot it in CinemaScope, and saved the company. We had the biggest year in our history. I was asked to find stories with width, instead of depth. Every wide-screen movie made money. *How to Marry a Millionaire, Beneath the Twelve Mile Reef, Prince Valiant,* and *River of No Return* filled the theaters and the coffers. The movies had been saved. Not until the sale of old movies to television were they to be saved again.

The Love Interest

I was saved not by CinemaScope but by a lady in a narrow chic frame topped by pepper-and-salt hair. Her name was Helen Gurley. She was brown-eyed, smart, striking-looking, slight, and nervous. Also very sexy, and knew it. I would have died without her. Helen's description of our courtship will make you wonder what her excuse was.

David and I met because I asked my friend Ruth Schandorf to fix us up. Ruth was a good friend of David's ex-wife, Wayne (his second), who departed to marry another man. I *knew* about Wayne's departure, had met David once briefly at a big party at Ruth's—thought he was dishy—and the minute I heard he was single again, asked to meet him.

Ruth said it was too soon—that he was drowning in starlets—David was, after all, a movie executive—and I should wait until he was *ready* for a "sensible" girl like me, all through with his starlet phase. I waited. When Ruth felt the time was right, she arranged a little dinner party—a *wonderful* way to introduce somebody to somebody, but a lot of work—and we met at her house. June night. *Very* glamorous little party. I wore a short blue shift—waistless dresses had just begun to appear for the first time in *my* lifetime and I felt very chic. David was so impressive, forget chic . . . I don't think I said five words all evening but since David likes to talk I don't *think* he noticed.

He took me out to my car when the evening was over and I think that was the biggest point I ever scored with David: Into a great little cloud-gray Mercedes Benz 190 SL he handed me, a divine little sports car I managed to inform him I had *just* bought and for which I had paid all cash. I've never doubted that I eventually persuaded him to marry me because he had never known a girl who paid all cash for a pair of *stockings,* let alone a sports car.

The courtship was glamorous—for me—if sometimes uphill—also for me. David would, could, and *did* sometimes spend as much as twenty minutes describing his "ideal girl"—the qualities of whom seemed to have *nothing* to do with *me.* He wasn't mad for planning ahead. After our original date I didn't hear from him for about ten days, then he called suddenly on a Sunday afternoon and asked if I'd like to have dinner. After *that* I didn't hear for *another* ten. The first dinner was at "Jack's" at the beach, the second at David's house in Pacific Palisades. I thought it pretty spiffy that the man had an elegant house in Pacific Palisades overlooking the Pacific Ocean with a live-in cook and housekeeper. After I inherited house *and* live-in housekeeper, I didn't think either of them quite so great. The house he *didn't* own—he simply paid rent but the rent applied to eventual ownership—if anybody lived that long. Anyway it needed *everything.* Mrs. Neale, the housekeeper, was British, lumbering, a terrible cook, and utterly devoted to David as well as dedicated, so far as I could tell, to keeping him single. When I "won," she was naturally irritated . . . to put it mildly. She had David to herself for a couple of years and who needed a *wife*? David's sixteen-year-old son also lived there but that was another man, not a rival. Anyhow . . . back to the courting days . . . and a certain unreliability—David suggested I go along with him to San Francisco to see a play tryout—*fantastic!* I assembled my wardrobe. He never mentioned it again. We *did* go to nifty places, however—to Hollywood parties, to movie-industry galas, like the Writers Guild dinner, the Academy Awards—and perhaps the *most* starry party I've ever attended—the one Buddy and Anita Adler gave at the Beverly Hills Hotel to welcome Ingrid Bergman back to Hollywood. Nothing before or since has ever equaled that party for sheer glamour—*every* big star was there. I spent about thirty-five dollars having my hair done and never looked back . . . *twice* that much would have been a bargain because David thought I looked nice.

He was more apt to think you looked nice in a black dress. I remember attending a swimming party at Ernest Lehman's house—*the* top Hollywood screenwriter—in something black-widow-spider (to please David) and everybody else is in shorts and T-shirts. Never mind—I got on fine with the Lehmans—his best friends.

I could go *on.* We "courted"—didn't live together—for about a year when I tendered my ultimatum. I would like to be married. I was nutty about him but at thirty-six, it was time for marriage and I wanted *him.* He said why can't we go on like this, we're so happy! I resisted that reasoning and kept up the pressure. Let me mention that the *worst* night of my life I think from that time to this—well, almost—was the night I was streaking down big Santa Monica Boulevard to my apartment, having just come from group therapy in the Griffith Park area, when I spotted David in his white Chrysler 300, stopped for a light with a blonde smashed up against him in the car. I mean this is long after we were going steady, and *I* wasn't seeing anyone else. He said it was his *accountant*! Maybe it *was* but they surely weren't balancing any budgets or reconciling checks. I didn't speak to him for three days but finally caved in. And the *talk* of marriage continued but nothing happened. Then one night when I went to David's house for dinner, Mrs. Neale brought him some fabric samples after dinner and said this was what she had selected for the den and this for the dining room and these would be the draperies in the bedroom . . . she was a regular little Melanie Kahane. Never mind the stuff was terrible, you didn't have to be Madame Curie to figure out if *she* is decorating the house, he isn't planning on having a *bride* around the place any time soon. That's the night I said OK, you are obviously *not* planning to get married so bye-bye baby. If you change your mind, get in touch. If you don't, don't. You have to *mean* these things or they don't work . . . you can't just threaten and not make good. I was in *tatters.* It took a while for David to come around. He called me when I'd gone to my boss Don Belding's ranch for the weekend. And I nearly totaled the Benz getting there—the closest I've ever come to a car accident, I think—took a curve too fast and the car rocked from side to side, just barely getting right again. At any rate, David called and said something like "I surrender"—only he didn't. There were perhaps three more slithering aways before he could really steel himself for marriage. I couldn't, finally, tell my friends at work about getting married the following afternoon—this was a Thursday—because I was fairly certain he wouldn't go through with it. Then one day he decided not to slither away anymore. The day we were married he didn't tell anyone except his son, Bruce, and his secretary. She was our witness, darling Pamela Hedley. But he didn't tell studio boss Buddy Adler, either. He merely said he would be out of the office that afternoon. I wasn't too insulted about all that. I felt he was worth the bother.

No People Like Show People

I knew Irving Berlin for almost fifty of his more than one hundred years of life—that's twenty years longer than I've known Helen, but she became part of his life, too. I interviewed him when I was a young journalist in New York. He played "God Bless America" for me on his piano with the lever that changed the keys. He could play only in the key of F-sharp. Young, thin, he was around forty then, with shiny black hair.

Decades later, he met Helen and instantly adored her. Even into his nineties, he would say, "If I were ten years younger, David, you'd have to worry about Helen." He seemed to take pleasure in what we did. When Helen or I were on a television show, there'd be a note from Irving saying, "Kid, I'd like to do a show with you. Who's your agent?"

Once we went to dinner with him at Peter Luger's venerable steak house across the bridge in Brooklyn. Helen is from Arkansas and likes her meat well done. That's a sacrilege at Peter Luger's. When the waiter looked at Helen arrogantly, saying, "You'll ruin it," Berlin said, "Take that steak back to the kitchen and cook it exactly how Mrs. Brown wants it cooked." Well, it was done. Well done.

That night we drove around Manhattan's Lower East Side, singing Berlin ballads in the very neighborhood where Irving began his career. Helen recalled lyrics Irving had forgotten. He pointed to an old tenement. "That's where I wrote 'Alexander's Ragtime Band,'" he said.

As years went on, we saw less of Irving but always heard from him—by telephone, note, and gift. On my birthday there was a painting signed I. Berlin. When he could no longer paint, there would be an enormous tin of caviar. His beloved Ellin saw to that. One year he sent a bound volume containing sheet music of his compositions. He wrote special lyrics for my seventieth birthday. Each Christmas we sent each other azalea plants. Our plants were added to the garden of his home in the Catskill Mountains. He loved flowering plants.

He never lost touch with show business. Barbra Streisand or Liza Minnelli were his first choices to play in a revival of *Annie Get Your Gun.* He told me, "I'm still writing songs in my head," and promised some day to put them down. He suggested that I work on a movie based on the fabulous Wilson and Addison Mizner. Wilson was Hollywood's acerbic wit and Addison the mad architect of Palm Beach. Addison's work survives. Irving had worked on a Broadway show about them that never got on.

Money interested Irving. Almost to the end of his career, he negotiated his own deals through his lawyer. Once, years ago, he complained to Joseph Schenck, who was head of Twentieth Century Fox, that Joe had paid more for the movie rights to *Oklahoma!,* by Richard Rodgers and Oscar Hammerstein, than he had for Berlin's *Call Me Madam.* Schenck replied, "Irving, there are two of them."

Nicholas Schenck, Joseph's brother, was the boss of Loew's Inc., which owned MGM. Nick reprimanded Irving for asking too much for his work. "You know, Irving," Schenck said, "ninety-one percent of what you make goes to the government. What difference does it make? You're only going to pay more taxes." Berlin, who's always been proud of America, responded, "I love to pay taxes. I love this country. This country has been very good to me. The more taxes I pay, the happier I am." And he increased the price for his show that Nick desperately wanted to buy.

When my book *Brown's Guide to Growing Gray* was published in 1987, and Irving was nearly one hundred years old, he called to say, "Kid, how would you like to make that into a musical? It's your and Helen's love story. I'll write the score."

Ellin was growing weaker, and we'd hear from Irving ever less frequently. But always there'd be a message, sometimes through his devoted secretary, Hilda, that he was thinking of us. Helen would write letters and so would I. And every now and again he'd call, but the conversations were brief. It was as though he had saved up his energy for that one call, and as soon as it was spent, the conversation had to end. In earlier years, Irving was a compulsive telephoner. He would call three or four times within half an hour, if he had something to add to a previous conversation. When his friend legendary press agent Irving Hoffman died, Berlin wept. He loved Hoffman. Hoffman was the only one he could call all night long—they were both insomniacs. Hoffman did drawings of Irving, some of which Irving sent me in later years.

When Ellin died in 1988, Irving could not attend the funeral. He never dreamed, but always feared, he would outlive her; she was alive on Irving's hundredth birthday. He did not attend his huge celebration at Carnegie Hall. It was not expected that he would. In his later years, he never went out. He was reclusive. I was seated in Carnegie Hall near his secretary, Hilda. During the intermission Hilda rushed out, returning as the lights went down for the second part of the program. I asked Hilda what Irving had said, knowing she had telephoned her boss during the intermission. Ordinarily, wild horses could not drag anything out of Hilda because she respected his privacy so fiercely, but on this occasion she thought it would be all right to tell. Mr. Berlin, said Hilda, wanted to know if it looked like they had put money into the production. It did.

"God Bless America" was a trunk song he had written for his World War I army show *Yip Yip Yaphank* and decided not use. He offered it to Kate Smith in 1938 when she asked him for a patriotic song she could sing on the radio. "Easter Parade" also came from another show with a chorus that went something like, "Smile and show your dimple" instead of "In your Easter bonnet."

During his active years, he was melancholy about his dry spells and went into deep depression when he thought his work was not good. He was very generous to other composers, particularly Cole Porter, to whom he telegraphed after a hit Broadway opening, "Anything I can do, you can do better," a play on Berlin's own lyric from *Annie Get Your Gun.*

Irving Berlin's lyrics would be exceptional even if he had been as highly educated as Alan Jay Lerner. Although he had no formal schooling, his lyrics parsed brilliantly. "I got lost [in his arms] but look what I found" is an example. Little wonder Cole Porter wrote, "You're the top, you're a Berlin ballad."

Mr. Berlin called himself a songwriter instead of a composer/ lyricist. His lyrics were so good that someone said that Ethel Merman was cast in almost every Berlin show because you could hear the lyrics when Merman sang, and Berlin's lyrics were meant to be heard.

His love affair was not with American music, but with America and the girl he found there, Ellin Mackay, whom he wooed and wed when it was unthinkable for a Jewish immigrant from Russia named Izzy Baline to marry an heiress to an old American fortune. Songwriters didn't marry Park Avenue heiresses, but after the 1929 stock market crash, Irving was richer than his father-in-law, Clarence Mackay (a telegraph magnate), and offered to give him a million dollars to tide him over.

On his hundredth birthday, *60 Minutes* wanted to bring Mr. Berlin's voice to the American public. He politely declined, saying he was not up to it.

At 5:30 in the afternoon of Friday, September 22, 1989, the heart that had been beating since May 11, 1888, stopped, but his music never will.

George Abbott, at 102, was still directing theater. As I wrote this, he had directed a musical in Philadelphia intended for Broadway. I recall Abbott's attempt to enlist the services of Irving Berlin, when Irving was a mere ninety-eight. Abbott called him and said, "Irving, why don't we get together and do a musical?" Irving said (at ninety-eight), "I'm too busy, George."

When I humorously reprimanded Irving about not working when Abbott was working, Abbott being older than Irving, Irving's response was, "George lies about his age."

Lew Grade, the ancient British mogul and now a lord of the realm, is a smoker of large cigars and a man of wisdom who had come up from ballroom dancing to a position of eminence in the world of films in Great Britain. One of his executives, Ian Jessel, was offered a job in Hollywood and went to Lord Grade to ask his leave to go to Hollywood. Lord Grade said, "Ian, by all means go to Hollywood, but let me give you a piece of advice that will never fail you in America. Remember this always while you are working over there. Look British, think Yiddish."

After Lord Grade's mother was presented to the Queen Mother of England, the Queen Mother said, "You must be very proud of your son." Lord Grade's mother replied, "And *your* children haven't done so bad either."

Danny Kaye said he'd take us to a Chinese restaurant on Second Avenue up near Sixty-seventh Street in New York. We were ready to have a fairly complex Szechuan dinner since Danny was a world-class Chinese chef himself. Suddenly, following a conversation with the owner, he arose quite angrily and said, "Let's get our coats. We're leaving. We're going to Elaine's." We followed, not understanding, until we heard the exchange between Danny and the proprietor at the door. What happened was that the proprietor mentioned to Danny that his autographed photograph was hanging in the window. Danny Kaye became extremely exercised, saying, "You promised you wanted that photograph purely for personal use. You never told me you'd put it in the window. I've taken people here for years but I never allowed you to take my photograph to put in the window as an advertisement for your restaurant." The proprietor remonstrated and tried to calm Danny down, but Danny would have none of it. He simply said, "You did a dishonorable thing. I gave you my photograph. I thought you were going to use it in a family album but you've used it in a window." Whereupon we all went to Elaine's where Elaine has no such compunction about photographs or anything else, and if Danny Kaye had ever made such a fuss at Elaine's, he would have been promptly thrown out.

Ever since I returned to New York from World War II, I've found coming back to this city a delight, and a relief from wherever it was I was coming from. Walking the streets, seeing the people, going to lunch and dinner in restaurants which have known me for years, are like being in a bouncy musical comedy. I used to think that when the "21" Club went, I would want to go, too. All of us grew old with it, which may be one of its problems. Years ago, when Helen and I took Joan Crawford to dinner at "21," they had long perfected the art of star treatment. Tino, then the captain upstairs (Joan insisted that upstairs was better than downstairs), led us to the preferred table, front and center, although we had not announced in advance that Miss Crawford would be our guest; Tino knew that Joan was a vodka drinker, American and not Russian. She was a star in the royal Hollywood tradition. When she looked at you, there was no one else in the room for her, no furtive glancing over your shoulder to see who else (and more important) might be arriving. Joan Crawford was a friend, the first to give Helen a quote for her book, *Sex and the Single Girl.* When I desperately needed her retroactive permission for a photograph inadvertently put on an Atlantic Records label and duplicated in the millions without being cleared by her lawyer, Joan settled for four dozen roses. She never forgot a name or face, famous or obscure. A friend could lose forty pounds and grow a beard, but Joan would recognize him at once.

She was what being a star is all about.

Maître d' Walter Weiss knows more about "21" than anyone but former proprietors Pete Kriendler and Jerry Burns and more than they do about the tastes of "21" 's patrons, past and present. Walter, who has presided over the downstairs bar for more than forty years, never forgets a customer. When Don Ameche, alone in New York, wandered into the club without a reservation after an absence of twenty years, Walter greeted him as though he had been in yesterday, gave him his usual table, ordered the drink he invariably requested, and told the chef to cook his "Hamburger 21" ever so slightly pink, remembering that was the way Don liked it. Trouble is, in the meantime Don had become a vegetarian.

In my long association with David Merrick, one of Broadway's most successful producers, I found him to be a tough, but admirable, negotiator. Others were intimidated and even terrified by his dour demeanor. One of Merrick's ploys was to take offense quickly at some trivial remark and threaten to end a luncheon at the beginning by saying, "Well, there's nothing more to discuss. As far as I'm concerned, this conversation is over." My tactic with Merrick on such an occasion was to say, "Well, let's finish our lunch, David. We can eat, can't we?" Invariably David returned to the matter at hand. Long before dessert he was pressing for a deal. If he were not interested, chances are he would not have had lunch with you in the first place.

Several years ago, David suffered a stroke which made his speech unintelligible. He was unable to communicate even by hand-written notes. But his mind and business acumen were unaffected, as this little incident will demonstrate. I had occasion to discuss a deal with him concerning Dan Jenkins's novel, *Dead Solid Perfect,* to which he owned the film rights. He listened but showed no sign of comprehension until I proposed a sixty/forty split of profits in favor of the Zanuck/Brown Company. Merrick's voice came alive. "Fifty/fifty," he said loudly, in unslurred, clear tones. I've since wondered if he uses his affliction as a negotiating ploy, coming out of it only when it is to his advantage.

Now You See It

The things filmmakers don't see in a movie are often seen by the public. Back when Fox's movie version of David Merrick's *Hello, Dolly* was playing, Richard Zanuck was on a flight to New York seated next to a man who had noticed he was reading a script. "You in the movie business?" he asked to Dick's discomfiture. Dick nodded yes but encouraged no in-flight conversation. He couldn't escape his companion's next remark, however. "Tell me," the man said, "why was there a wreck of a 1947 Plymouth by the side of the tracks in *Hello, Dolly?* It was supposed to take place in the 1890s." Dick sighed and responded, "There was no 1947 Plymouth in *Hello, Dolly.*" "Yes there was," the man insisted. "Look at it again." Dick and I and legions of editors had viewed every frame of the film hundreds of times. It had been looked at during dailies, in the editing room, during dubbing and scoring, and in the lab. Nobody had noticed what the man on the airplane had . . . a wreck of a 1947 Plymouth by the side of the tracks in an 1890 scene from *Hello, Dolly.* Dick Zanuck saw it when he ordered up the first reel of the movie on his arrival in New York. There it was, like the man said.

Why I Love San Francisco

Famous trial lawyer "Jake" Ehrlich, role model for Melvin Belli and all the other cannoneers who followed, was born in Tennessee. Ultimately he had little difficulty being accepted by San Francisco society, although he cared little for it. San Francisco, more than Boston and Philadelphia, was a city of tight little families on the tip of a tight little peninsula. Jake was well known on that tip, but at first was looked down upon socially. He did receive some invitations but declined most of them because he felt he was being asked to be on display.

One day, while walking down Montgomery Street as was his early morning custom, he met a gentleman who bore a famous San Francisco name. The gentleman said something like this: "Mr. Ehrlich, I know you never attend any of our social functions, but perhaps you'd come to a reception at our club." Jake, more out of politeness than interest, said he'd show up. Among the things Jake hated—and he hated a lot of things—cocktail parties ranked high, particularly among the nabobs of Nob Hill. He kept his word and, when the festivities reached a crescendo, decided to slip out. A matron somewhat under the influence spied him and said, "Mr. Ehrlich, where do you think you are going?" He replied, "Madam, I'm leaving for a dinner engagement." In a loud voice, she said, "How dare you leave this party?" And then, really on the sauce, she shouted, "Mr. Ehrlich, we know who you are, but do you know who we are?" Jake, standing tall for all of his five-feet-six, said evenly, "Yes, I know who you are, madam. I know who everyone in this room is." Ignoring the lady, and as guests gathered around him, he proceeded to give the pedigree of every old San Francisco family. To one member, he said, "You are the grandson of a man who was arrested for selling opium. Your entire family was in the opium trade." Then he swept over to another social arbiter and said, "Your family, sir, was in the white-slave traffic. Your grandfather smuggled white slaves to North Africa, while your grandmother—paternal side—was the most sought-after madam on the Barbary Coast." Jake continued to recite choice bits of history from the city's police blotter. "And if any of you want evidence of these statements I'm making," he said, "we can all go down to the Hall of Justice tomorrow morning and I'll show you the arrest sheets and mug sketches." Now really heated up, he revealed the beginnings of the Bay City's most illustrious old families—many of their fortunes rooted in crime, narcotics, and prostitution. It turned out to be a most entertaining evening and San Franciscans being the sophisticates they are, invited Jake to the best parties from then on and dowagers never thwarted his exit again. He still didn't accept many invitations, which made him even more sought after.

Ehrlich played a role in my first divorce. Liberty was my first wife's name and liberty was what she was seeking in a divorce action which threatened to destroy me financially. Her attorney was powerhouse Louis Nizer, a friend who became a foe and then, as years passed, a friend once more. Jake Ehrlich represented me. When the smoke cleared, as well as the alimony checks, I introduced Jake, two wives later, to my newest bride, Helen Gurley Brown. Making a mental note of the fact that she had just written *Sex and the Single Girl* and sold it for a large sum to Warner Brothers, Jake slapped the big Bible that was always on his desk and exclaimed dryly, "Well, David, I think we'll break even on this one." God knows I did, and then some.

Like Paris, San Francisco was (and is) a city of vistas. Every prospect pleases. When I first glimpsed the city, the tallest structure was the Russ Building. The Ferry Building with its famous clock (the time shown by its hands crucial evidence in the trial of radical bomber Tom Mooney) still dominated Market Street.

In 1933, when Prohibition was repealed, San Francisco's bawdy, gaudy Barbary Coast came back to life for a few boisterous months before city authorities closed down its bordellos, opium dens, and other residue of its infamous past. The little cable cars that went halfway to the stars were, then as now, the city's signature conveyances. San Francisco meant the Coit Tower, the music of Griff Williams at The Mark (the Mark Hopkins), Ted Fiorito and his orchestra at the "Frantic" (the St. Francis Hotel), as well as chic lunches at Ritz Old Poodle Dog. The Blue Fox, one of the city's most elegant restaurants, advertised its location as "across from the morgue." Amelio's was for San Francisco's family trade and Jack's for the financial crowd at lunch. Tea dancing at the Palace to Tom Coakley's band brought out the debutantes. Perhaps the best of all the restaurants was the long-vanished Solari's on Maiden Lane. For fashion there were the City of Paris, the White House, Maison Mendelselle, Gumps, and Magnin's. No true San Francisco lady was seen without her gloves and hat with black veil and gentlemen wore hats and sometimes spats.

It was a city in which to be young and gay, which meant something different then. I first fell in love in San Francisco and to this day I don't know whether I was more in love with her or it.

Some Special Friends

Novelist John O'Hara came to Hollywood in 1956 to write a screenplay titled *The Bravados,* which was produced by Herbert Bayard Swope, Jr. We soon discovered that the great O'Hara dialogue, perfect on the printed page, does not play well for actors. When I mentioned this, John wrote me, "You have made an extremely interesting and valuable point and you are the first ever to name it. I *do* tend to overburden my dialogue with matters that rightly belong in the unspoken part of a script." Actors are more credible with dialogue that falters and breaks off, like conversation in real life.

* * *

John always wanted to be a dramatist, and wrote a play based on his novella, *The Farmer's Hotel.* It was his sorrow that other than *Pal Joey,* no work of his was produced on Broadway.

James Michener once told me that he never knew a novelist who didn't want to be a dramatist but knew no dramatist who wanted to be a novelist.

Back in the fifties, I would have liked to have been head of a Hollywood studio, instead of number-two man. It would be thirty years before I formed my own company to become the boss. O'Hara had an explanation for my not having got the job at Twentieth Century Fox when studio chief Buddy Adler died. It was contained in a letter he wrote me on July 26, 1960, later published by Random House in a collection of his letters. I quote in part:

> Dear Dave:
> As you must have read between the lines of my letter, not a little of the irritation I expressed was traceable to my bafflement over the choice of a successor to Buddy. . . . Since my information is limited, I could only *hope* that you would be chosen, without accurately appraising your chances. I would say, however, that one reason you were not chosen is that you are not enough of a son of a bitch. The son of a bitch in a man appeals to those who are in a position to entrust him with power, who themselves already have power, and as sons of bitches can recognize the quality in other men. I suppose it is possible to have power and not be a son of a bitch, but it is much simpler for the powerful to deal with other sons of bitches, so it is hard to find cases of men who have been given power without qualifying as sons of bitches. I am inclined to regard General Marshall as a non-son of a bitch who was given power by sons of bitches, but he got a screwing before it was over. He got his screwing the day Eisenhower shook hands with McCarthy after McCarthy called Marshall a traitor, and there, of course, politics was the motivating force. So we come full circle there.
>
> In the picture business it is almost desirable to have a qualified son of a bitch as the power figure. The head of a studio is a terribly powerful man by virtue of his position, and since there are so many sons of bitches in the industry—producers, directors, actors, writers, set dressers (who are also bitches as well as sons of bitches)—the man who is elevated to head of a studio is more acceptable if he is a son of a bitch, too. If he isn't a son of a bitch, the other ones are going to take advantage of him until he qualifies. And another thing that militated against you is that you are too much of a gentleman, and they know it. In the picture business a gentleman can't be trusted, not, at least, with supreme power. A gentleman gives his word, and he keeps it. Now how could a man like that deal with Jack Warner, Louis B. Mayer, Harry Cohn, Sam Goldwyn? Part of the

> protocol of the industry is the confident knowledge that the other guy is going to give his word, and break it. Therefore, a man who gives his word and keeps it is undependable. He is unreliable in inter-studio dealings, and he is not playing the game to the advantage of his own studio. I wanted you to have the kudos of head of production, but I did not want it for *you.* I would like to see you head of your own production enterprise, which is a very different matter from being head of TCF production. . . . Until that comes to pass, you probably are just as well off in your present situation. The power you now have is not going to hurt you, and the money you get must be satisfactory. . . . You and I will never have the big money, and it is just as unlikely that we will ever get the big powers. So what is left for us is the satisfaction of accomplishment, achieved in the most comfortable circumstances possible in 1960, and with our personal integrity intact. Not bad; and in one respect you are better off than I am: you can have a Martini if you feel like it.*

John would have been pleased to know that I did finally become "head of my own production enterprise."

Buddy Adler is a missing chapter in the history of American film. Silver-haired, lean, handsome, Buddy started work in the short-subject department of Metro-Goldwyn-Mayer and eventually became a producer at Columbia, where he won an Academy Award for *From Here to Eternity.* He was selected by Darryl Zanuck (over many of Zanuck's personal favorites) to head production at Fox when Zanuck decided to quit Hollywood executive life and move to Europe as an independent producer.

Buddy has somehow been overlooked by film historians, perhaps because he didn't choose to exploit himself, although he did win the Academy's coveted Irving Thalberg Award. His production record was extraordinary. When he came to Fox in 1955, he called me into his third-floor temporary office. I had never met him. He said, "Look, tell me how this man (Zanuck) works. I'm here, I want to make a lot of pictures." He always consulted others, which for Buddy was a wise practice. Buddy never pretended to be a man of learning. He asked for opinions. In less than three years as a Fox producer, his films included *Bus Stop,* perhaps Marilyn Monroe's best film; *Anastasia,* which brought Ingrid Bergman back to Hollywood after she left her husband and daughter to marry Roberto Rossellini; *South Pacific; Love Is a Many Splendored Thing;* and *The Inn of the Sixth Happiness.* After Zanuck appointed him studio

*O'Hara was forbidden to drink following a cerebral hemorrhage.

chief, Adler declined to sit at the head of the executive dining room table, a chair customarily left unoccupied when Zanuck was not in residence. After four months, Adler received a cable from Zanuck, reading, "For Christ's sake, Buddy, sit down! You're the head of the studio."

Buddy was pragmatic in his choice of subject matter for movies. He was apolitical, unlike Zanuck, who was a crusader. Buddy was a compassionate man, but would occasionally explode with rage and then apologize. Like many men in power, he was sensitive to the point of paranoia when he suspected disloyalty among his staff. This applied particularly to those in the New York office, because New York was the center of corporate power and reports from the studio had to be carefully screened lest adverse news—a star on an expensive rampage, a movie out of control—reach the board without adequate explanation. My relationship with Adler was close, almost brotherly. We were peers and comrades-in-arms. We went to Romanoff's on working nights to hash over our problems and confide in each other our occasional love affairs, with confidence that they would remain secret.

Buddy Adler had an extraordinary relationship with his wife, Anita Louise. Early in their marriage, *she* was the star and Buddy was little known, even in Hollywood. Anita was never involved in Buddy's films, nor did she wish to be. She would occasionally come into the office and wait to see him. She was still the fragile, exquisite, elegant star whom the critic and raconteur Alexander Woollcott once described as someone whose beauty shone through the strings of the harp she played. She was a great beauty and a special kind of actress, but more than that, a patrician lady, devoted to Buddy and their children, never suggesting that she ever get a part from him when he was studio boss.

In 1959, Buddy became ill. It was cancer. He didn't think so. He called his staff together and said, "Let's talk about my illness." He was told UCLA Medical Center had misdiagnosed him, but Fox had secret information that it had not. Doctors and hospitals sometimes divulge this information when major corporations need to know about key executives. I don't know if Buddy eventually knew the truth of his prognosis, but if he did, he blocked it out.

The only change in Buddy during this period was that he became uncharacteristically combative and volatile in his moods. There was no suggestion of incoherence in his behavior. It was as though he was fighting back, which indeed he was. What terrible luck for him and for us that he was so cruelly cut down. My last recollections are of him in the office, listening to the baseball games on his transistor radio, a soft tweed hat parked in back of his desk. Buddy was always elegantly attired, British country best. Even as he entered the hospital for the last time, he gave me instructions on how to keep the New York vultures at bay, assuring me he would soon return to work. He didn't. On July 12, 1960, he died at age fifty-one.

Fade to Blacklist

During Hollywood's "Blacklist" period in the early fifties, if a writer, actor, or producer was suspected of communist affiliations, he could not be hired by a Hollywood studio unless he agreed to cooperate with the House Committee on Un-American Activities. Buddy Adler submitted to that system of checking with the "Blacklist" not because he wanted to but because it was required by his New York bosses. One film, based on the Broadway hit *A Hatful of Rain,* was ready for production when it was discovered that the screenwriter had not been cleared by the House Committee on Un-American Activities. Production was postponed until a "cleared" writer could prepare a new screenplay.

I had already had some experience with the "Blacklist" when I left *Cosmopolitan* magazine in 1951. While I was managing editor there, I had commissioned an article to be called "The Farmer's Daughter." The idea of the article was that farm girls were no longer rustic maids but had become sophisticated, well-traveled young ladies who were likely to take off in private planes for shopping tours at Neiman-Marcus in Dallas. It seemed like a harmless, capitalistic idea but when the article came out there was quite a commotion at *Cosmopolitan.* The author of the article turned out to be secretary of the Communist Party of Iowa. Nothing seemed more unlikely than that an Iowa writer in the heartland of America writing on the subject of the farmer's daughter and the filthy rich would be a member of the Communist Party. No action was taken against me. Be more careful next time.

Hollywood was divided on the merits of the "Blacklist." Then as now there was a considerable liberal movement there, not typical of America as a whole. America was profoundly anticommunist and many Americans supported the idea of a blacklist. An infamous book entitled *The Red Network* was used by broadcasting studios to identify writers, directors, and performers who belonged to what were considered communist-front organizations. The American Communist Party was still high profile, as were the communist newspaper, the *Daily Worker,* and communist candidates for the president.

Still, only Hollywood insiders knew of the "Blacklist." The studios denied its existence. When a famous director accused studio owner Jack Warner of not hiring him because of the "Blacklist," Warner retorted, "There is no blacklist and you're not on it."

Hooray for Hollywood

I remember the first time I saw Marilyn Monroe. I can remember the very spot. I was coming up the steps of the Administration Building at the Twentieth Century Fox studios in West Los Angeles. Coming down the same steps was the most beautiful girl I had ever seen. She was smiling, her eyes wild and wonderful. Her companion was James Hennagan, a columnist for the *Hollywood Reporter.* He said, "I want you to meet Marilyn Monroe. She's new on the lot." Monroe and I were never close, although I was the producer of her last movie—*Something's Got to Give*—which she never completed. She used to come into my office and sit on my lap, sometimes tickling me. And we'd talk a bit. Joke a bit. Yes, I got paid for that job. She was under contract to Fox. In *All About Eve,* she made a brief but memorable appearance. In *Don't Bother to Knock,* she played a psychotic babysitter. In addition to *Bus Stop,* directed by Joshua Logan, she was sunny and funny in *Gentlemen Prefer Blondes* and *How to Marry a Millionaire.* The world wept when Marilyn died. Those who never knew her sensed accurately that beneath that astonishing surface was a frightened, insecure child demanding attention, longing to be loved and to love in return. Marilyn Monroe. Flowers still adorn that slab in West Los Angeles where her body rests, at peace at last.

I was fond of George Cukor, the elegant filmmaker who directed almost all the great women stars, including Garbo and Hepburn. He was wittily acerbic and impatient with pretension. Built on several acres off Doheny Road above Sunset Boulevard, his home was an oasis of sophistication in the Hollywood desert. Katharine Hepburn occupied a small house on George's property during her visits to the West Coast. The houses were superbly furnished with all sorts of objets d'art. George's taste was beyond taste; it was religion. When George and I worked on Marilyn Monroe's never-completed film, I came to know him well. *Something's Got to Give* was to have been a remake of the comedy classic *My Favorite Wife,* which starred Cary Grant and Irene Dunne. The story was about a man who had had his wife declared legally dead after she was missing seven years, only to find, when he had remarried, that she was alive and had followed him to the very place he had chosen for his honeymoon. I engaged Arnold Shulman, a very talented screenwriter, to write the screenplay. Shulman wrote one of the best first acts I have ever read. In the Shulman version of *My Favorite Wife,* Marilyn Monroe's husband was up for an important promotion. That was the "gray flannel suit" era when executives' wives were scrutinized by their bosses as closely as were their husbands. In Shulman's script, Marilyn was determined to do everything to help the husband she loved win the promotion. Invited to give a cocktail party for her husband's boss, she spared nothing to please him, even responding affirmatively to his sexual overture. Wrong. Unknown to her, that was part of the "wife test." She had flunked by not rejecting the boss's suggestion that she have a fling with him. She was adjudged as being potentially unfaithful to her husband. Heartbroken when she realized what she had undone, she fled to the airport and boarded a flight to the Orient. In Hawaii, she left the plane while it was being refueled, intending to reboard it. She missed the flight. The plane went down over the Pacific and she was reported lost. She decided to remain "lost" in Hawaii until seven years later when her "husband" arrived on his honeymoon with his new wife. It was a perfect role for Marilyn, who could convincingly miss a plane; she was always late.

Fox was uncomfortable with me as producer of *Something's Got to Give* because I had characterized the appointment of its new studio head, Robert Goldstein, as a "death wish," and I wasn't supposed to emerge from "Siberia" with a film starring Marilyn Monroe and directed by George Cukor.

Shulman never did complete the screenplay to the satisfaction of the studio and there was some subsequent conflict between me and Shulman. I never decry eccentricity, especially in the arts, but I thought we might be in trouble when he asked that all the furniture be removed from his office so that he could sit on the floor in a yoga position while writing.

The reports from the executive building were ominous, not because of Shulman's yoga position but because of my producer position. My friend and soon-to-be-partner, Richard Zanuck, reported that he had seen a producer named Henry Weinstein carrying my script in the administration-building elevator.

The studio was in chaos following Buddy Adler's death. Robert Goldstein, his successor, departed in the middle of the night, later sending a moving van to the villa he occupied on the studio lot when he decided to quit his job and return to London. Next up, in rapid succession, was Peter Levathes, a dark, brooding man who, although a gifted advertising executive, had no knowledge of running a movie studio and little aptitude for it. Unused to the demands and temperaments of talent, he soon experienced blinding headaches and fits of rage. His undoing was his determination to rule by edict. One day Levathes said to Cukor, "I have a scheme to bring Marilyn Monroe in on time." Cukor and I knew there was no way to bring Marilyn Monroe in on time, even if her bed were placed on the stage where her next day's scenes were to be shot. Levathes's plan, it turned out, was to replace me as producer with Henry Weinstein, who knew Marilyn's psychiatrist and may, in fact, have been a former patient of his. Levathes thought that between the two of them, they could get Marilyn to the set on time. Cukor was so enraged that he threw an inkwell at Weinstein. After the ailing Marilyn Monroe (who was thought to be home ill) was filmed singing "Happy Birthday" to John F. Kennedy at Madison Square Garden in New York, she was fired by Levathes. Only a few scraps of film remain from *Something's Got to Give.* It was later remade under the title *Move Over Darling* and starred Doris Day and James Garner. It was a hit.

Even during the short, unhappy life of *Something's Got to Give,* and, as it turned out, Marilyn Monroe, George Cukor was a delightful colleague. He drove to the studio every morning in his Rolls-Royce, his lunch in a hamper containing caviar, paté, whatever finger sandwiches he fancied, and Perrier. On his first day at the studio, he was assigned to a decaying bungalow. He ranted until new draperies were installed and the furniture was reupholstered. By this time the film was in intensive care. I said, "George, why are you worrying about your draperies and furniture with all the trouble we're in?" To add to our production difficulties, the studio was nearly bankrupt. George imparted some Hollywood wisdom. "My dear David," he replied, "if there is one thing I have learned in this business, it is that you ask for everything in the first five minutes. Nobody will answer your telephone calls later." And indeed, George got what he wanted and quite a bit more—from life as well as from the studio.

Dinners at his home were memorable both as to cuisine and conversation. On one evening, Mrs. Samuel Goldwyn, General Frank McCarthy, who produced *Patton,* and I were his guests. One of us asked Frances Goldwyn, "How did you come to marry Sam?" Frances said, "I think George should answer that question. Please, George, tell exactly what happened." George complied. "Many years ago," he said, "Frances was working for me as an actress in stock in Rochester, New York. She had met a rich man in New York who was once a glove maker and now was in the movie business. He seemed exceedingly fond of her and she liked him as well. One day she said, 'George, this man wants to marry me—I need you to tell me honestly whether I have a future as an actress, or should I give it up for this man?' I think, Frances, you will agree that I responded instantly, saying 'My dear Frances, run, do not walk, to Samuel Goldwyn, and marry him; you have no future as an actress but I suspect you have a considerable future as Mrs. Goldwyn.' " And indeed she did. Goldwyn, by that time, had already entered the movie business and was, in fact, the Goldwyn of Metro-Goldwyn-Mayer. Through Sam's long life, Frances exerted a profound influence over his career and a most loving and constructive one.

Another Cukor story. During all the flagwaving and God-bless-America reign of Louis B. Mayer, head of MGM, word came to Mayer, who was somewhat to the right of Attila the Hun, that George Cukor, distinguished director of memorable and earthmoving love scenes with the most glamorous actresses in the world, might himself not like women. In fact, horrors, he was said to be attracted to men! Cukor was summoned to walk the last mile uphill to Mayer's desk in Mayer's gigantic office. Mayer invited him to come close. Almost in a whisper, he said, "George, this is a very important matter. A very serious matter. You must answer me truthfully because I must know." George said, "But of course, L.B., what is it?" "George," whispered Mayer, hardly able to get the words out, "tell me, are you a . . . homosexual?" *"Dedicated,"* Cukor replied unhesitatingly. That was the end of the conversation and the meeting. Mayer simply turned away and began reading his mail. It was not the end of George Cukor, however. Even Louis B. Mayer's homophobia gave way to the higher needs of business, money, and stockholders.

Jerry Wald was a rotund, garrulous, tireless producer of films and memos. His movies included *Peyton Place, Johnny Belinda,* and *Sons and Lovers.* His memos were almost as long as David O.

Selznick's and some of them would contain startling changes of tense and style as uncredited passages from literary magazines would be freely interspersed with Jerry's own turgid prose when they made a point more persuasively than Jerry could. Along with Mark Hellinger, Jerry came from New York's tabloid journalism. His news stories for *The Graphic* were largely fiction, making his transition to Hollywood an easy one. He is credited with having brought the Epstein brothers—Jules and Philip—to Warner Brothers, where they wrote hit after hit. They had previously worked—between unremunerative writing assignments—as window dressers at a Brooklyn department store. He offered them a lucrative Hollywood contract, summoning them magnanimously by telegraph to "Take the next bus."

He could be generous, though. Jerry's secretary was Margo Halprin. Each Friday, at the end of the day's work, Jerry would empty his pockets of the cash he had left from the allowance given him by his business manager and dump the proceeds on Margo's desk for her to take home. Invariably, the amount exceeded her secretarial salary.

In later years, Jerry attempted to take over the studio and end the oppression of producers and directors by the despised post-Adler Fox bosses—Levathes and Goldstein. He gathered us "oppressed"—Leo McCarey, George Stevens, Richard Zanuck, and other "proletariat" of Hollywood—for a solidarity meeting in the Crown room of Romanoff's, which was like holding a demonstration in the Czar's Winter Palace.

Walter Matthau is an amusing and witty man, as you might expect. Walter was appearing on Broadway in a George Axelrod play titled *Will Success Spoil Rock Hunter?* He disagreed with Axelrod's philosophical ending of the play. Failing to persuade the playwright to accept his views, he took an entirely different route, that of forgery. He sent a letter to George Axelrod and signed it Dr. A. Schneider, representing himself as a psychiatrist who had attended a number of previews of *Will Success Spoil Rock Hunter?* He made several points about the last act, stating that all his psychiatric experience, which was considerable, convinced him beyond any reasonable doubt that the motivation was flawed. Axelrod waved the letter before Walter and said, "You know, Walter, I think you're right about that. Look at this letter I've received from a psychiatrist. I'm changing it." Walter allowed himself a small smile of satisfaction. Anything more might have betrayed the source of his pleasure.

The Great One

I was asked to write a eulogy for Jackie Gleason. This is what I wrote:

Jackie Gleason doesn't need a eulogy. He needs a cigarette and a drink and a little traveling music. He's not gone, but offstage somewhere, maybe getting ready for a change of wardrobe or enjoying a few lobsters. You all know what a huge appetite Jackie had for everything . . . life, love, the pursuit of happiness, and all you can eat.

How sweet he was.

He told hospital attendants that if God wanted another joke man, he was ready. Well, Jackie was far more than a joke man. His comic genius came out of situations in everyday life, his early everyday life in Brooklyn among the blue-collar set and the neighborhood bars and streets.

In recent years, Jackie didn't care to go back home to New York. He told Cindy Adams, "Y'know I don't come to this town often anymore. Y'know why? Everyone I knew and loved is gone . . ."

Well, the Great One has also gone to wait in God's good time for the rest of us and to finally reunite with those he missed in Manhattan. I can hear him now. "H'ya, pal," he's saying to Benny, Danny Kaye, Joe E. Lewis, Jessel, Toots Shor, Eddie Cantor, Jimmy Durante. He's sharpening up his act. While he misses you all already, he's in heaven up there, learning the real meaning of "away we go." He's finally found a place where smoking is allowed everywhere and there's no limit on drinks or lobster. After all, where he is, there's nothing hazardous to your health.

Heaven can't be strange to Jackie. He once said, "Everything I've wanted to do, I've had a chance to do." Indeed, heaven can't be strange to Jackie—after all, he married an angel.

What has he left us?—I mean apart from the legacy of brilliant comedy and great performances. The world, through press and television and hundreds of tributes from other great ones, has duly noted his place in show business. He has, in fact, no place in show business . . . he *is* show business. What I . . . privileged for years to be his friend . . . take from Jackie are these qualities:

—a love of life

—a disdain for meanness, cruelty and pretension

—a heart . . . like the proverbial diamond, as big as the Ritz

—a fierce unquestioning loyalty to friends and associates

—total devotion to his beloved wife and children

—courage, never better exemplified than his words and behavior of his last weeks on earth

Jackie, I've tried to keep this light because you said, "Life ain't bad, pal . . . but death is the most natural thing in the world. We all have to face it so it's stupid to be afraid."

You were never afraid, Jackie . . . except maybe when you were offstage. You always knew your lines, but you hated to rehearse, playing your life, like good comedy, spontaneously, effortlessly, naturally, passionately. For a while now we'll have to content ourselves with your reruns. Watch your language up there, Great One. We're going to miss you and love you forever. About your exit, first time your timing was off . . . but God brings down the curtain.

Jolie

At thirty-seven thousand feet over Kansas, my friend Red Buttons told this story about Al Jolson. One night in Denver, Jolson's audience was restless. Jolson had not arrived. It was 9:30 and the show had been scheduled to go on at 8:30. Heavy snow was falling. Finally Jolson burst onto the stage. The audience was hypnotized by him—the greatest entertainer of all time. Al put his dressing table on stage. He had snow on his suit. "Jolie," he said to himself, loud enough for the audience to hear, "will you please get made up." He told stories as he was being made up into blackface. Then he started the performance, which was a revue-type show. At 12:30, he told the audience, "You don't want to hear the rest of that show. I'll summarize it." He went on to say Jolie does this, Jolie does that, and so on. He said to the chorus girls, "Look, all you girls, because I've been so late getting here, I want any of you who have dates to get lost. The rest of you—why don't you just sit around here on the stage. Jolie's going to sing." At that point, Jolson took off his tie, opened his shirt, and sang for two and a half hours. He then sent out for candy which was passed out through the audience. At three o'clock in the morning, he invited the audience to have breakfast in Denver's best hotel. All on Al Jolson. Jolson always involved his audience, never took advantage of them, and gave and gave and gave. Red said that Al Jolson *was* unquestionably the greatest entertainer of our time despite being limited by his vocal equipment ("I didn't think Al could sing worth a damn"). His jokes weren't that good, either. In many respects, he was an American Maurice Chevalier, who worked on chutzpah, charm, and love of audience—and above all, supreme confidence on stage, although he quaked in the wings.

Life with Father

Many men and women I know who have failed in life, or were at best ineffectual, have had powerful fathers. It's been the conceit of classic Freudian psychiatry to assume we identify with a strong father. It may be true that we identify, but do we emulate him? For all the Rockefellers and Kennedys and Fords, there are legions of men and women crippled by strong father figures. I know several women who have never married because they cannot find the equal of their fathers. One young editor, the daughter of a powerful and famous father, recently retorted, when her father disapproved of a man she was seeing as unworthy of her, "Daddy, I worship you but I don't want to marry you."

Incidentally, powerful fathers are not particularly thrilled by dependent children. One man told me the best birthday gift he could ever get from his children was a birthday card. A letter usually meant trouble—a request for funds, a plea to bail them out of legal troubles, some untidy need. Not that he wasn't always happy to fulfill those needs, but a simple birthday card was the most welcome gift.

Another powerful man I know, revered by his peers, suffered the disappointment of having a grown indigent daughter angrily demand that he provide a luxurious life-style for her so that she could support her drug habit. Perhaps the best legacy he could have given her was to say no, and let her remain poor.

A friend, Peter Elebush, Yale class of '59, wryly presented another point of view to his classmates on their thirtieth reunion. "One of the good things about having money," he said, "is that it keeps you in touch with your children."

My father had not seen me since I was an infant. When my mother divorced him, she did not seek alimony, but decided during the Depression that she would put the arm on the old boy to send me through college. Had he declined, she would have scrubbed floors to do it herself. She was that kind of woman. She had married again, a man of wealth, thirty years older than she, but his fortune had been swept away by the 1929 Wall Street crash. We were still living on Long Island, but our house was about to be sold for delinquent taxes.

It was arranged for me to see my father for the first time in seventeen years. The intermediary was an uncle named George Wolf. His background was quite different from the Southampton and Fifth Avenue social set in which my father traveled. George, married to my mother's sister, was an attorney for the infamous Frank Costello, then a Mafia chieftain. George called my father and asked him to see me.

I arrived at my father's office on the fortieth floor of 22 East Fortieth Street. I was impressed by a view that could only be surpassed from an airplane. He was a public relations man for the milk industry and had originally worked for Wall Street's J. P. Morgan, later for the Association for the Improvement of the Condition of the Poor, and still later for Averell Harriman's Palisades Interstate Park in New Jersey. He was married to a well-known violinist named Nathalie Boshko and managed her concert tours through Japan, Siberia, Malaysia, Russia, and the United States. Now back in this country, he was propagandizing for the milk industry. At that time, it was believed milk had to be delivered daily in order to be safe. Horse-drawn milk trucks were on the city streets at dawn, leaving milk at doorsteps. Nobody stole the milk, although there were hungry men and women on the streets. Values were different then.

My father took me across Fortieth Street to have lunch at the old Murray Hill Hotel, where birds in gilded cages sang in an atmosphere of splendor. He also took me to the New York Athletic Club, another citadel of good living. We went often to the Divan Parisien, which served splendid Chicken Divan, a Moroccan dish. My father and I saw each other one evening a week. Sometimes he would provide a date for both of us and sometimes I would provide a girl for him. We went to places where he was unlikely to be seen by anyone he knew. The Russian Bear on Second Avenue and Fourteenth Street was a favorite place to get drunk. My father seemed more like a brother to me, and we got into all sorts of mischief. When I was engaged to a young blonde from San Francisco, my father suggested that perhaps she and I ought to live together before we married. The girl's parents were horrified by the suggestion, but not the girl. (Alas, a doctor took her away from me after he glimpsed her walking across a hotel lobby in Washington, D.C.) My father always put on a show in restaurants to impress my girls. He would tell the captain that he was expecting a call from the president and order wines with undecipherable labels.

Girls adored him, and never asked for anything, unusual in affairs with older men. So far as I knew, he never gave anything of material value to any young lady. They brought him flowers. They thought he enriched their lives. His wife, I learned after his death, was aware of his peccadilloes. She was unconcerned because she believed he was impotent. (Apparently, only with her.) "I didn't want to spoil his pleasure in deceiving me," she told me years later. "I rather liked seeing pretty young ladies surround him." Not knowing this, he played what would otherwise have been a deceptive, dangerous game. One night Nathalie returned unexpectedly from the Hamptons on a summer weekend. Father was with a woman.

Nathalie entered the apartment but my father stopped her before she could discover a girl in her bed. Apparently without the slightest show of concern, he said, "Darling, I'm so glad to see you. I wonder if you could do me a favor? I have a terrible headache, and there's no aspirin left in the house. Could you go down to the drugstore right now and get me some?" She didn't mind. Perhaps she even knew. She went to the drugstore and gave him time to get the girl out and straighten the bed.

My father's brother, Al, occasionally provided my father with the company of women not seen at cotillion balls. Al was a musician, and as different from my father as Herbert Hoover was from Louis "Satchmo" Armstrong. Al was show biz. He managed Cab Calloway and his orchestra, then appearing at the Cotton Club. He once invited fifty beautiful, copper-colored girls from the Cotton Club show to my father's apartment when the rest of the family was trustfully summering in the Hamptons. My father loved that razzle-dazzle evening. That was his light side.

He sent me through Stanford. I don't think he realized how much money he spent. He had no interest in money and little knowledge or ability to manage it. It took me five years to earn as much money as my father gave me as an allowance during my college days.

While this new relationship with my father was going on, I knew nothing about his other life with his wife and my half brother and sister. Not until 1951 did they know about me. I was driving my second wife, Wayne, down to the Hamptons for a summer weekend when I realized that my father was probably down there, too. Years before, I had come down to his house in Southampton when his other family wasn't there. We were a secret. My father never listed me as his son in his *Who's Who in America* sketch until I was listed in *Who's Who in America* and included him in mine. He was the worst kind of snob. That summer weekend I impulsively decided to telephone him and to hell with his secret. Unflapped, he said, "Come on over." I learned in a later conversation with my stepmother, that in the fifteen minutes it took me to reach his house, my father had coolly filled her in on his having a son in his thirties, that son having been married twice, and that son having a son, thereby giving him a grandson named Bruce. I found his wife, Nathalie, enchanting and as down-to-earth, sophisticated, and uninhibited as my father was not. We became great friends. I met my half sister, a dark, exquisite girl, who wore white ermine one wintry night when she and my half brother were introduced to me at New York's Metropolitan Club. It was Father's idea to introduce us all there. We later reconvened for a far less formal evening at my Greenwich Village apartment. Edward, my half brother, was straight out of John O'Hara, handsome, preppy, and more on the make for women than money, while my half sister, Natasha, was out of Scott Fitzgerald, dark and glamorous and as doomed as Fitzgerald's Zelda.

Unknown to my father, my stepmother had actually seen me before and, as a result, had decided to commit suicide. In 1919, while she was being courted by my father, she noticed that he never mentioned where he lived. She decided to follow him home one night, trailing him by streetcar to the farthest precincts of Brooklyn, until he reached the then-affluent community of Sheepshead Bay. There she watched him enter a small house. She peered from behind a hedge to witness his embracing a woman (my mother) and picking up a three-year-old boy (me). Her first impulse was to leap into the Atlantic but she settled for a demand that my father obtain an immediate divorce and marry her. She lived to share this story with me.

One afternoon, many years later, in 1973, my stepmother, half sister, half brother, and I condemned my father to death. I had an appointment with the chief of staff at the Veterans Hospital where my father was being kept alive artificially and against his will. We agreed I would consent to the removal of his life-support system. We decided this over fine fresh salmon and a superior 1970 Meursault at the Carlyle. In WASP fashion, we concealed our emotions, as he always did. The way his life ended was not too different from the way it began eighty-seven years before—with helplessness and lack of dignity—but unlike birth, he died alone.

I thought of the good times my father and I had had. He was a stalwart man with almost no fear, surely not of death. I've envied him that. He arranged and paid for his funeral many years before his death, leaving instructions that there were to be no services, no one in attendance, and that his remains be sent in a plain pine box (also prepaid) to a National Cemetery at Pine Lawn, Long Island, where a space was reserved for him as a retired colonel of the United States Army. I never loved my father but I admired his cool and his courage. His only fear was the disapproval of his peers. He was somewhat unctuous toward authority, a trait I unfortunately inherited. Until two years before his death, a fabulous-looking Chinese girl sent him love notes at the Metropolitan Club in New York. My father need not have died at eighty-seven, but he was stubborn and left a minor ailment unattended. He never liked the work he did as a milk-company executive. His best years were during World

War II when he was stationed in Teheran and assigned by the Army's General Staff Corps as liaison officer with the Soviet Army. Hunting boar in the Caucasus with high-ranking Russian officers was not tough duty. For his popularity with his Russian peers, he was awarded a lifetime pass in the Moscow subway and an Order of Lenin medal. The army gave him his own plane and rented a villa for him from some affluent bandits. He did not want to come home when the war ended.

Back Story

My earliest memory is of the Hudson River Night Line, which in the first decades of this century provided service between New York and Albany. These were sidewheelers and the New York Central Railroad sold tickets, via the river voyage up the Hudson, to Albany, where trains would take passengers to Chicago and the west.

Travel by water was part of my early life. My mother and stepfather sailed to Europe each summer. I would see them off in cascading confetti as their ship sailed away from a North River pier en route to Cherbourg. My aunt, a silky blond divorcée who smoked Turkish cigarettes in a long holder, traveled three times a year to Europe, usually on the French Line. She bought hats for Henri Bendel's swank establishment in New York, whose bonnets were noted in a Cole Porter lyric.

Travel by ship was drop-dead elegant, black tie every night except for the first night out. Our family traveled first class. The Depression was years ahead.

When my mother and stepfather returned from Europe one year, I noticed several long crates near their baggage. Labeling indicated they were grandfather clocks, but they contained cases of fine wine and spirits, which were illegal then, as Prohibition was the law. Customs officials were tolerant and corrupt, although no more so than the passengers. It was not unknown for loose currency to be placed next to expensive goods in the drawers of steamer trunks. The currency usually disappeared and duty on the goods was never collected. Inasmuch as Americans were already defying the Volstead Act (Prohibition), why not, they reasoned, defy the customs rules? Genteel lawlessness was in vogue.

After clearing customs (easy), we would drive through New York City to the Rockaway Turnpike, a road that still exists, to our home on the south shore of Long Island. Along the turnpike, we'd pass a vast swampy area to the west that many decades later would become John F. Kennedy International Airport. Aircraft that swooped in and out of this area would replace the trains and ships that transported a nation for a hundred years and move rights-of-way and shipping lanes for passenger travel seven to twelve miles above the earth.

We could not imagine then, back in the twenties, that in three decades our Romanesque train terminals would become shelters for the homeless, and once-stately ocean piers would crumble into nasty, dangerous, rusty ruins. I pondered this years later while traveling by sea aboard the *QE2,* where for some reason time seems to go faster than on a thirteen-hour flight to Tokyo.

(Voyage by sea today *is* a time warp. Class distinctions are unchanged from the grand age of travel. In the upper-deck staterooms of the *QE2,* hangers can be removed from closets. In lesser accommodations, there are what our steward calls "captive hangers." He means they cannot be removed and, heavens, taken off the ship. Grand-luxe passengers do not steal hangers. Another sensible assumption of the British class system.)

I moved to Long Island in 1922. I was six at the time. My family had bought a house in Woodmere, then more commonly known by its original name of Woodsburgh. Our address was 4 Pine Street. Years later it was to become 132 Pine Street, enlarged along with our telephone number by two digits. The house was and is an unassuming affair of stucco and shingles but I remember each room as though it were the only house in which I had ever lived.

The smell of hot fresh tar still instantly evokes that Long Island of the twenties when in early summer our dusty dirt roads were quieted by tar which remained sticky to the feet for perhaps a week. The smell of tar meant school was out and the countryside was ours to roam and camp and build fires and tree houses. A friend named Warren was under my window before dawn to awaken me with the trill of a bobwhite so we could be in the woods at sunup. The Island, as we called it then, was young and dewy and we were Robinson Crusoes venturing to every brook and forest.

The red cars of the Long Island Rail Road, electrified as far east as Babylon, were new and the straw seats were fresh and clean. A round-trip fare to Pennsylvania Station was $1.13 and a thirty-day commutation ticket cost about $10.

There was then on Long Island, as in more recent years, the sawdust-and-timber smell of new houses. The Great War, as World

War I was known, had ended and we were in the path of the first suburban migration. The original settlers inhabited the older section of Hewlett, Cedarhurst, and East Rockaway. Their families were descendants of those who came to Long Island in Colonial times. My scoutmaster (Troop 1, Hewlett) was Charles Hewlett, for whose family the town was named when it was founded more than a hundred years before the American Revolution.

Then came the prosperous New York merchants, many of them immigrants from Eastern Europe, who were leaving Manhattan as their fortunes and families grew. Not that the city was dangerous or undesirable—schools were uncrowded, *anyone* could go to Harlem, and Central Park after dark was as safe as a nursery. The furriers, dress manufacturers, and assorted bourgeoisie came to the near south shore of Long Island because they believed they were graduating to even greater social status than having addresses on West End Avenue, Riverside Drive, or the Bronx's still Grand Concourse.

Although houses were rising all around us, there was still much of the past to be found on Long Island in 1922. I uncovered more than one flint Indian arrowhead in our garden. Not far from Broadway, in Lawrence, a group of us came upon a long-forgotten, overgrown graveyard, its headstones marking the resting places of men and women who died in the seventeenth century. The Lord Estate (as it was called) was a vast wooded area where we boys went in early March to see the first skunk cabbage peek through the crusty old snow of a dying winter.

We were not strangers to the waters around us. Woodmere Bay, veined with inlets, creeks, and channels, provided a treasure of exploration by rowboat (three dollars for a day's rental). We would row clear to the channel separating Long Beach from the mainland and turn back just before the swift tidal waters could carry us out to sea. Other waterways took us deep within the fairways of Woodmere Country Club (where I caddied for William Fox, the motion-picture mogul of whose company I was to become an officer and director forty years later).

Today I view these waters from jet airliners over Cedarhurst on our final approach to JFK Airport or shortly after takeoff with Lufthansa, Air France, or Alitalia as we make our way up the south shore before turning northeast toward Europe. Only the waters are the same.

I lived on Pine Street until 1933—long enough to see Lindbergh take off for Paris, his *Spirit of St. Louis* barely clearing the trees on the edge of the field. Houses in our neighborhood were never painted white because of the dust raised by fleets of Curtis biplanes taking off from nearby Mitchell and Roosevelt fields. In 1928 I viewed the total eclipse of the sun through smoked glasses while standing in the middle of Pine Street (tar sticking to my shoes).

Science dominated young imaginations then, fueled by issues of Hugo Gernsback's brilliant and prophetic magazine, *Amazing Stories,* which foretold the marvels of television, space travel, and nuclear power. My bedroom radio receiver magically extracted music and voices when a "cat's whisker" made of tungsten was placed on a fragment of carborundum crystal. The crystal set was soon replaced by RCA's Model 1, featuring a single, silver-coated vacuum tube. Our first family radio was a Stromberg Carlson, a monstrously complicated machine, requiring the almost simultaneous manipulation of seven dials. Through howls and static one could hear faintly (louder in winter) the programs of WMAQ in Chicago, WIOD in Miami, KDKA in Pittsburgh, and, more plainly, WPG in Atlantic City. What is now New York's WNBC was then WEAF. WABC was the first flagship station of the Columbia Broadcasting System, its call letters later to be ceded for logical reasons to the American Broadcasting Company. There was also WJZ, New York, later to become the Blue Network affiliate of NBC. An SOS distress signal off the Long Island coast would occasionally silence these and all other stations.

I didn't remain a mere listener long. It had been discovered that shortwave signals could travel great distances with low power. On a home-built shortwave radio receiver, I was able to hear dance bands halfway around the world in Australia, squealing through the winter night from VK2ME, Sydney, and VK3ME, Melbourne. I remember the cry of the kookaburra bird which preceded the announcement of the call letters of Australian stations. My friend Ernest Lehman and I decided to build our own shortwave transmitters. We used bread boards on which we mounted naked copper coils. Flashlight bulbs on other coils were used to check the radio frequency output of our primitive equipment. The bulbs mysteriously lighted up when held some distance from our transmitters. That is how we knew our sets were functioning and we were on the air. Our signals from Pine Street were heard throughout the world—first by radio telegraphy and later by voice transmission (all duly licensed by the FCC), although for a brief prelicense period we "bootlegged" signals using fake Australian call letters, causing a flurry of excitement among neighboring "hams" who thought they were chatting with someone down under. Long Island was the heart of backyard invention and discovery, not only of radio but also of aviation. Our cellars and attics were alive with the sound of tinkering. Hadn't Edison and Ford started that way?

We could scarcely wait for school to be out so we could be at our workbenches building radio equipment. Often we remained up until four in the morning listening through earphones for distant signals, the lights in our rooms illuminating the snows that lay deep on a sleeping village.

It was not all nuts and bolts and hobbies. We were living in the John Held, Jr., Flapper Era, after all, and Long Island—Scott Fitzgerald country—was "where it was at." Our parents were awash in the hedonism of the period. They were at the country club breaking the Eighteenth Amendment and one or more of the Ten Commandments, no doubt. We Long Island adolescents (we were not called teenagers then) seemed less inclined toward drinking than smoking. Spud cigarettes, the first of the mentholated brands, were particularly popular because they disguised the breath. Wings were also popular because they were only ten cents the pack. Some of us did have hip flasks filled with White Horse (Long Island's favorite scotch). Liquor could be obtained from drugstores on a doctor's prescription. It was remarkable how many ailments could be cured by whiskey. However, bootleggers were the chief source. On one moonless night, the lights of the city of Long Beach were suddenly extinguished so that a large shipment of whiskey could be put ashore under cover of total darkness.

Sex on Long Island was not rationed but far from free. Occasionally virginity was lost in a rumble seat but one had to be agile to accomplish this. The preferred brands of condoms were Trojans and, for the rich, the slimmer Ramses, but it took courage for a fourteen-year-old to ask for them at the neighborhood drugstore. Mostly, we young Long Islanders were unabashed romantics. Music of Berlin, Porter, and Kern filled us with extravagant dreams of everlasting love. We saw our movies at the Central and Strand Theaters and sometimes at the Valencia in Jamaica. We went with girls named Ruth and Peggy and Margie. "Margie" was our theme song. We danced at Roadside Rest and Pavillion Royal to "Ho Hum," "On the Beach with You," "Little Girl," "Sweetheart of Sigma Chi," "Can't We Talk It Over?" and "Ramona." The social history of our time could be gleaned from the sheet-music covers—replete with moons over Miami and the like, as evocative of our era as record-cover art is of today's.

Long Island was where it started—the good life of the suburbs, the blend of rural and urban, the Hoover ideal of two cars in every garage and a chicken in every pot, the *No No Nanette* dream of "Tea for Two." Westbrook Pegler had dubbed it the "Era of Wonderful Nonsense." Then came, like a coronary on New Year's Eve, the stock market crash of 1929. WALL ST. LAYS AN EGG, proclaimed *Variety.* "Tomatoes are cheaper, potatoes are cheaper, now's the time to fall in love," sang Eddie Cantor, himself caught short in the market. At thirteen, I knew the daily quotations of every stock we owned. As General Motors went, so did we—down, down, down. En route by train from Woodmere to New York, I learned at Jamaica station that the banks had closed. Servants financed their employers' households with the only ready cash there was. It was FDR time and our Long Island childhood, idyllic and innocent, was gone for us and all time. As bad as things were, they were to grow far worse. We could not yet hear the distant thunder of World War II, Vietnam, assassinations, ghetto warfare, and the rest of it. We were down but still far from out. The country was united, wasn't it? "Marching Along Together" was on *Your Hit Parade.*

In 1933, we moved to Manhattan, unable to bear the cost of country living. The house we sold at distress value is worth perhaps sixty times what it brought then. Decades later, I returned to Woodmere on a rainy afternoon with Ernest Lehman to gaze once more at the houses in which we grew up. We did not go inside. Everything seemed smaller except for the trees. Our friends were gone—some killed in the war and others, like ourselves, long removed to other lives and places. We drove off convinced it was better to remember than to revisit.

My house in the Art Village of Southampton preserved the peace of the early years, but my wife and I have long since sold it. In my memory, the twenties and thirties on Long Island were special and enchanting, but possibly any place of growing up is unforgettable. Childhood is bewitched. Indeed, if those seventeenth-century headstones could speak, they would probably reveal that Island childhoods were always rapturous.

I remember a snowy Christmas Eve, probably in 1924, when my mother assured me that Santa Claus was five houses down the street and on his way. I believed her. What other explanation could there be for my new blue Ivor Johnson bicycle, and a Christmas stocking filled with nuts and tangerines? I remember clearly her tucking me in and telling me about him. And through my window I could see the snow on the pine trees glistening in the moonlight and Mama's bright and shining face.

* * *

No woman was as much attuned to my welfare, comfort, and immediate needs as was my mother. She died literally in my arms, concerned to her last with everything I did. Her final letters were filled with admonitions, advice, worry. Fade out, fade in. I'm married—my third marriage—to Helen Gurley Brown, who seems in all respects save carnal desire to be the reincarnation of my mother. Stick a pin in me and she jumps. If someone appears to hurt me she cries out. If I'm overweight or overwrought, she hustles me to a doctor or shrink. She is in all ways as totally attuned to me as my mother was. *Is* she my mother? Is she somehow linked to that aura that escaped my mother's body when it ceased to live? Has she been ordered into my life by the power of a mother's will? How could I be so important in the cosmic order of things? I often wonder.

My father, who had some influence with New York's Health Department, arranged for me to spend the summer of 1933 as a laboratory technician at Bellevue Hospital. The experience not only changed my mind about medicine as a career but also engendered in me a fear of doctors so acute that it took a psychiatrist to rid me of it fifty years later. At Bellevue, I conducted postmortems on white mice which had been inoculated with various strains of pneumonia. I also assisted in sawing the tops of heads off human corpses so a pathologist could obtain brain tissue. I once invited my two-hundred-pound cousin, who played fullback on his high school football team, to watch me at work. Upon entering the morgue, he fainted at my feet.

There was no air conditioning in 1933. The general sultriness and presence of death around us made us feel very horny. I remember a nurse named Jo who was refreshingly uninhibited (you get that way working around a city hospital). My little lab was across the way from a ward for insane women. Hideous-looking former prostitutes beckoned to me with obscene gestures. While the work had its moments, it persuaded me not to pursue medicine. Years later, at New York Hospital, I reflected on that decision and discussed it with a neighboring patient who was a renowned architect. "Medicine does have its advantages," he observed. "Doctors bury their mistakes. Architects grow ivy."

Noel Coward once wrote, "Extraordinary how potent cheap music is." So are the books of one's youth, cheap or otherwise. As an eight-year-old I remember Robert Louis Stevenson's *A Child's Gar-*

den of Verses, Nobody's Girl, and *Nobody's Boy* (whose author I don't remember). Later, Sinclair Lewis's *Arrowsmith* and *Babbitt* were on my reading list as were Paul de Kruif's *Microbe Hunters,* Warwick Deeping's *Sorrell and Son,* Harry Kemp's *Tramping on Life,* and Tiffany Thayer's naughty novel *Thirteen Women*. Julius Haldeman's Little Blue Books contained explicit instruction about sex, to be read by flashlight under bed covers. The *Boy Scout Handbook* cautioned against spilling one's seed on the ground, for which read masturbation. In college years, Thomas Wolfe's *Look Homeward Angel* and *Of Time and the River* were works I most admired. So was Walter Duranty's *I Write as I Please,* a fascinating account of covering the USSR for *The New York Times* in the 1920s. I can still quote many of the jaunty verses from Samuel Hoffenstein's *Poems in Praise of Practically Nothing* and Dorothy Parker's couplets about lost love. The magazines I liked were *Vanity Fair, American Spectator, Time,* and *Film Fun!.*

A Couple of Originals

Mae West told me that she took two almonds a day as a preventive against cancer. That was on the evening Helen and I took Mae to dinner at a now-gone Manhattan restaurant called La Seine. Mae was enchanting. Most of the patrons of that restaurant were well-heeled New Yorkers. During the dinner, a handwritten note was delivered from an old swain of Mae's, one of New York's bluest of blue bloods. It was a well-behaved crowd. Nobody came over to the table but as we left, everyone in the restaurant rose to applaud Mae.

The first time I saw Mae West was not in a fashionable New York restaurant, but in a banana republic on the west coast of Central America. It was September of 1933. I was on my way to Stanford University from New York by ship. When we docked briefly at a Costa Rican port, I rode up into the mountains on a single-gauge railway. There, in a jungle village, was a café with a motion picture screen. And there, while drinking Cuba Libres, I watched Mae West ask a very young Cary Grant, "Why don't you come up sometime and see me?" The movie was *She Done Him Wrong.*

Generations later Mae West was filming *Myra Breckinridge* on the Fox lot. The movie was almost the undoing of my career. Mae was in the film with Raquel Welch and John Huston, about which more later. She had a scene in which she portrayed a talent agent. Mae wrote her own material for that scene. As she swept through the anteroom of her agency, she glimpsed a very tall, rugged twenty-two-year-old. Pausing briefly to look him up and down, she said, "Tell me, how tall are you?" "I'm six feet, ten inches, ma'am," the young man replied. "Oh," said Mae, "well, never mind about the six feet, cowboy. Come on inside and we'll talk about the ten inches."

They call them PR men now, but they used to be known as press agents. Their job in show business was to get their bosses mentioned in the papers and on rare and sensitive issues to keep them out. Twentieth Century Fox's legendary publicity chief, Harry Brand, was the best of them. Harry was no unctuous, ass-kissing flack. He was respected by titans of the press like Bill and Randy Hearst, Roy Howard, Louella Parsons, Hedda Hopper, Walter Winchell, and the like. They delighted in his irreverence, as much directed at them as at his employers. On one occasion, when Harry told off Frank Sinatra in a dispute involving Frank's billing, I suggested that Harry engage a public relations counsel to smooth his way with those he was supposed to represent.

Harry came to Fox with its founders, Joe Schenck and Darryl Zanuck. He had been a good newspaperman on the *Los Angeles Examiner.* Inevitably he fell out of favor with Zanuck when Zanuck fell out of favor and could no longer call on Harry's services on a twenty-four-hour basis. There were successors to be served. Once, when there was a threat that Harry's contract would not be renewed, I planted an item in one of the Hollywood gossip columns that Harry was writing his memoirs. Harry's contract was immediately renewed. What Harry knew could definitely wreck careers and dissolve marriages. In the days when studios were walled principalities with their own police forces and special connections to law enforcement agencies outside, Harry was asked by Tyrone Power to engage a detective to spy on his then wife. As proof of her misconduct, Harry offered to give Ty photographs of her passionate encounters, but Ty couldn't bear to look at them. Too much pain.

On one occasion Harry needed five thousand dollars in cash quickly to pay for an abortion (illegal then) for a young ladyfriend of a top studio executive very much married to a socially prominent and vengeful woman. The studio treasurer at first insisted that the money be properly accounted for when Harry refused to disclose why he needed the money. "If I tell you what it is for," Harry warned the treasurer, "you may have to face a grand jury." The treasurer quickly withdrew his demand. He didn't want to know, and hastily handed over the five thousand dollars, unaccounted for to this day.

A special member of Harry's staff was "Doc" Bishop. Doc could fix anything short of murder. Assigned to rid me of a psychotic young woman who followed me everywhere shouting vile and obscene messages, Doc gleefully informed me that she had been escorted by sheriff's deputies over the county line and would trouble me no more. At that moment, she appeared in my outer office. A more serious matter was at hand. Doc had "shanghaied" the wrong girl. He now needed to "fix" a possible kidnapping charge.

Harry Brand was as funny as Groucho Marx, George Burns, Jack Benny, and the other stellar comics with whom he frequently lunched at the comedians' round table at Hillcrest Country Club. He had a nasty limp which prevented him from acting as a pallbearer and would act up whenever he needed an excuse not to attend a fund-raising event or boring dinner party. Once, while I was a guest at his Palm Springs home, I awoke at dawn and glimpsed him running with the agility of an antelope around his pool, a secret I have kept until now. No man with a game leg could have loped as gracefully as Harry did.

The Movie That Built Century City

When I gaze upon that gargantuan complex of hotels, office buildings, and shopping centers known as Century City, on the border of Beverly Hills, California, I think of how I may somehow have been responsible for starting it all. It didn't begin with an excavator's shovel or a bulldozer but with a memorandum in 1957 from Spyros P. Skouras, president of Twentieth Century Fox. I was then a Fox studio executive and Skouras, the ebullient immigrant who rose to the head of that company, wrote me, "Dave, we need a big picture. We don't have one. Find me a big subject." Movie attendance had declined drastically and recent Fox films had performed dismally. Television was beginning to threaten the domination of motion pictures as a mass entertainment medium. The coaxial cable had made it a coast-to-coast purveyor of free entertainment and the novelty of television was killing the movie box office. Hollywood was in trouble again. I went through a book titled *The Produced Properties of 20th Century Fox Film Corporation* and discovered that in 1916, the year of my birth, Twentieth's predecessor company, Fox Film Corporation, had produced *Cleopatra.* The title role was played by Theda Bara, a star of the silent screen. I ordered up the yellowed synopsis of the *Cleopatra* movie. It was faithful to the classic story of the Egyptian queen who nearly caused the fall of Rome. Spyros and Buddy Adler, head of production, agreed that *Cleopatra* was worth considering. Buddy said, "You know, Fox loaned that title years ago to Paramount and Cecil B. De Mille remade the picture, starring Claudette Colbert. Let's get it over here and run it." Indeed we did. We sat in a small projection room in the basement of the administration building of Twentieth Century Fox and watched Claudette Colbert play Cleopatra, as directed by De Mille. It was shot in black-and-white. I remember Buddy saying that the barge scene could be expensive. How expensive we could not then imagine. Although the actual cost of production in 1963 was thirty-one and one half million dollars, some industry experts calculate the Fox movie eventually cost one hundred and fifty million in today's dollars. I believe it is more than three hundred million, taking into account the cost of money. The best parts of the film, according to Melvyn Bragg's recent book on Richard Burton, are in the Twentieth Century Fox vaults, unseen by the public. It was originally intended by its director, Joseph Mankiewicz, to be shown as two separate three-hour films, one dealing with Caesar and Cleopatra and the other with Mark Antony and Cleopatra.

The making of the film was more dramatic than the movie itself. Rome's paparazzi have never recovered from what writer Brenda Maddox (again from Melvyn Bragg's book) called "the most public adultery in the world." It was also the most public extravagance. Never was so much money given to so few for so little. Actors and crew alike spent months at high salaries and prodigal expense accounts, doing nothing. Only Mankiewicz labored day and night to bring forth a mouse (instead of the lion he would have brought forth, I feel certain, if he had been allowed to make the film he intended). Had Mankiewicz prevailed, Burton, whose best scenes are buried in that vault, would have won an Academy Award. That is the word from those who have seen what was never shown the public.

The story was an epic tale of obsessive love and, made in color with new stars, it could be exactly the big picture we needed. Big was to become a weasel word in describing its future size. It took, however, a long time to find anyone who wanted to produce it. Darryl F. Zanuck said, "No, thanks." George Stevens wasn't interested. Neither was anyone else until one day Walter Wanger, a producer of considerable fame with a long list of films to his credit, was in the outer office waiting to see Buddy Adler. When he said, "You know, Buddy, I have been thinking about making a movie about Cleopatra," we fell on him. Wanger would produce it.

Some of the earliest candidates for the title role included a young actress named Joan Collins, who had appeared in fairly undistinguished films such as *The Virgin Queen.* There was no suggestion of the sexy, flamboyant star of television she was to become a quarter of a century later. Joanne Woodward was also considered. She was then quite a spitfire of an actress who had won an Academy Award for her performance in *The Three Faces of Eve.* It was Rouben Mamoulian, Wanger's first choice of director, who wanted Elizabeth Taylor. However, casting was secondary to getting a script written. For some reason, Walter wanted an unknown actress to write the first draft of the script. Her name was Ludi Claire. Ludi had not written much and we were able to engage her at the Screen Writers Guild minimum, which might then have been as much as twenty-seven hundred dollars. We were also able to acquire the outstanding rights to a novel about Cleopatra for eight thousand dollars. With an expenditure of little more than ten thousand dollars, preparation of the most expensive American movie in history was begun. Forests must have been cut down to make paper for the scripts that followed. Other writers included Sidney Buchman, Ranald MacDougall, Lawrence Durrell, and Ivan Moffett. Uncredited were William Shakespeare and George Bernard Shaw, whose *Antony and Cleopatra* and *Caesar and Cleopatra* were the real source material for the film. No one could imagine that the project would burn out four heads of production, one of whom died (Buddy Adler), bring down the president of the parent corporation (Spyros Skouras), close the studio and, important to my way of thinking, fire me. Moreover, the cash drain of the picture would leave no alternative for Twentieth Century Fox but to sell its entire 262-acre studio lot, one of the richest parcels of urban real estate in the world, for a piddling fifty-five million dollars (most of it to be paid over a period of ten years), perhaps 2 percent of what it is worth today. Nobody could imagine that the picture ultimately would make money even though when the picture was completed the studio would be missing, sold to pay for the movie! All Fox retained was seventy-three acres, at first only leased but later fortuitously reacquired. The rest became Century City. New York real estate developer William Zeckendorf had optioned the property but, pressed for cash, could not afford the one thousand dollars a day required to hang on. It was the Aluminum Company of America that bought the land and had the staying power to build and own largely unoccupied massive buildings until the Los Angeles real estate market recovered. A Fox-owned Century City had been the dream of Spyros P. Skouras, who named most of the streets—Avenue of the Stars, Constellation Boulevard, Century Boulevard, Galaxy, and so on. A mock-up of Century City stood for years in his office. *Cleopatra,* the big picture he also wanted, thwarted the other dream and so the richest prize of the land was lost, even though eventually the remaining seventy-three acres—made far more valuable by what surrounded them—became an enduring and growing asset of the corporation.

As for *Cleopatra,* the production wandered all over the world until it set down in Italy. Sets were built in England, Los Angeles, and finally in Rome. Only the Romans left more ruins in Europe. Not since D. W. Griffith's incredible *Intolerance* had there been such a waste of corporate assets. Rouben Mamoulian wisely quit as director and Joseph Mankiewicz took his place after a year of production yielded no usable film. Stephen Boyd gave way to Richard Burton for the role of Mark Antony and Rex Harrison replaced Peter Finch as Julius Caesar. When Leon Shamroy, the cinematographer of *Cleopatra,* saw the forum set in Rome, his first words were, "There are not enough lights in Europe to light this." At one point, it was necessary to defer photography from autumn until spring when the days grew longer. Everyone remained on salary that winter and the winter that followed. In the course of the production that would give birth to Century City, Elizabeth Taylor and Richard Burton abandoned their respective mates to engage in an incendiary love affair that would result in their marriage. Rex Harrison, receiving little attention on this troubled film, demanded and received equal treatment in advertising to Taylor and Burton. Rex Harrison's picture had to be painted onto the background of the giant outdoor ad in New York's Times Square so that he received exactly the same visual prominence as his costars. Although Joseph Mankiewicz was supposed to be given carte blanche in directing this film, he was allowed appallingly insufficient time to prepare it. He rewrote the script by night and shot it by day. Amazingly, *Cleopatra* returned a bookkeeping profit of about five and a half million dollars, which was exactly what was received for licensing it to television.

There was no way of separating the corporate drama from the on-screen drama. The money was running out so fast that directors and lawyers went daily to the boardroom of Twentieth Century Fox at 444 West Fifty-sixth Street in Manhattan to find out what could be done. Bankers flew to Rome to visit their loans. The film very nearly forced the company into bankruptcy and brought Darryl F. Zanuck back to the company he helped found. So concerned was he about the future of the company of which he was the largest individual shareholder, and for his own production, *The Longest Day* (already downgraded to be filmed in black and white), that he engaged my old friend Louis Nizer (by then a legal superstar) to threaten a proxy fight to dislodge the management. Only the threat was necessary. Zanuck won his war without a shot being fired. He was elected president of Twentieth Century Fox Film Corporation, ending the long reign of Spyros Skouras, and was coincidentally now in a position to see that his own film, *The Longest Day,* received the full attention of the company's distribution and marketing arm. His blood and guts were in *The Longest Day,* which was to restore his reputation as a premier-class producer.

As for *Cleopatra,* he would look at the film and see what could be done, and undoubtedly lock horns with the director with whom he had worked on many previous films, and see if he could bring order out of the chaos of both *Cleopatra* and Fox. He did so in his grand, military style, canceling all productions, closing down the studio, discharging everyone, including me, and beginning to rebuild brick by brick. Had he not done so, future owners of Fox such as Marvin Davis and Rupert Murdoch would have had nothing to buy.

Love's Magic Spell

My eyes may fail, my hearing fade, but I hope I will always be able to fall in love. I hold the same hope for my wife. This doesn't at all mean the breakup of a marriage although it could. In the course of an active life, you see someone. Your eyes take her in. She gazes boldly at you. There is that moment of inexpressible intimacy with a stranger. You know and she knows. The course of your lives may be determined by whether or not you take the next step. It's up to you, generally up to a man. And then, sadly, you turn away, realizing you are no longer up to a convulsive life change. That doesn't diminish the experience or the fantasy of what might have been. Many times in the course of a happy marriage I have met women who have made me melt with desire. And I have met women who clearly seemed to be under the same spell. We never spoke of it, but we knew we would move inexorably toward each other if one gave a sign. I've found that sex, the best of it, is not a matter of bedmanship. It begins with a tantalizing glance. The touch of a hand can put you over the edge. The sound of her voice can cause an erection.

Every encounter between reasonably attractive men and women must pass the point of whether or not to become lovers. The best love stories are those of lovers who don't quite make it. Tristan and Isolde, Abelard and Héloïse, George Bernard Shaw and Mrs. Patrick Campbell. The point is, I believe, that men and women ought to continue to respond (discreetly—not overtly) to romantic feelings. It enriches the relationships one already has. I have been fortunate in my life to have been deeply loved. I find the company of women to be the most interesting, pleasing, and sensuous of experiences. I savor the delicious feeling of being around someone who but for my present circumstances I might love . . . the girl across from me on an airplane, train, bus, or subway. I've always found women to be good, special friends, and have been able to overcome the locker-room syndrome of not being at ease and comfortable with them. I prefer women to men. At Hollywood parties, I join the ladies—and certainly those who are not ladies. As I think back on seventy-three years, I sometimes count girls I've loved instead of sheep when I'm falling asleep, being careful not to call out their names.

Joe Schenck, Hollywood patriarch, had a particularly ardent young girl in his bed one night. The octogenarian with a near-juvenile. And the girl said, in an effort no doubt to please her wealthy lover, "Joe, tell me you love me." Joe, ever truthful (he could afford to be), said, "No, darling, I don't love you. I love *it.*"

How can a person you knew intimately now be less than a stranger? How can anyone you loved, who shared your bed, to whom you spoke extravagantly of your affection and endless devotion, whose life was like your own heartbeat, be dead to you although still alive? How can someone whose every contour, whose every square inch of flesh was like your own hand, be alien and distant? How can someone whose smile turned you on, whose disfavor could throw you into a tailspin, make you drink and become suicidal, be no longer of interest? How can someone who did all that to you, for whom you once would have done everything and anything, and would have followed to the ends of the earth, be utterly uninteresting today? That someone who was your world, all your life, and could make you happy or desolate, is uninteresting to you because you've fallen out of love. You try to avoid her but not appear too fearful of her presence because that might give her leverage for emotional blackmail. An ex-wife or ex-lover is less than a stranger because a stranger has a future, but an ex-lover has only a past. It's an example of the whimsical and capricious quality of emotion and the human psyche. One grows. One sheds. There's debris in life, and much is forgotten and gone forever. It's sad to contemplate.

Conversation on a flight to Paris with a man who's lived as long as I have and been married as often. Subject: the absolute rules for winning a man. My friend and I formulated them during the long transatlantic flight. Not every woman will want to play this game, but if she wants to win she will. Worship of a man is the simple formula. It's so simple that it's practiced by the simplest women who in turn win the most complex men. When you see a man utterly infatuated with a girl, the answer generally is that she's convinced him of her unconditional adoration—that he can do no wrong. That he is great. That he is perfect. That he need not change a thing about him. All who have wronged him are mistaken in their judgment. There's no way for him but to succeed. I remember, during a bad time in my life, calling a girl I had known many years and taking her out to dinner and on into the night. I wanted to talk, to be reassured. I was reassured. She convinced me that everything that had happened to me was someone else's fault. I would triumph, I would be a winner. I was magnificent, she said. Formidable. Curiously, she was a lady I had loved for years but never married because I couldn't get it through my head that she was right about my being wonderful. But more men have succumbed to this kind of worship than haven't. Worship by such women is frequently sincere. A woman I know has made her lover's life virtually tensionfree, completely euphoric. She attends his every need as though he were a pasha. I asked her whether she was a masochist, because her friend wasn't treating her too well. Not at all, she said, although she acknowledged that she felt she was giving all the giving and he seemed to be getting all the getting. I suppose, if one goes along with Freud's pleasure principle, she is probably getting what she wants and he assuredly is. Maybe the arrangement will endure, but there's a price tag for everyone and everything. No free lunch. But for the short or intermediate term (as the Wall Street analysts would have it), if a woman wants a man, all she need do is surrender her will to him, capitulate to his every desire and fantasy, convince him of his righteousness, virility, strength, stamina, and of the complete venality of his enemies, and that man will capitulate. Hell, he'll leave his wife for that woman. Some of the world's richest men have been through this game plan, and have found themselves helplessly outmatched. Families and fortunes were the stakes.

Unconditional worship may be the sure way to win a man but it's hard to sustain. If she stops worshiping him, he becomes disenchanted; if she doesn't, all too often, he becomes bored. Perhaps there are women who have some dark, psychological need to give all of themselves to a man and obtain relatively little from him in return. That may well be true and it may also be true that there are many women who prefer to be victims in a relationship.

I think the most satisfying degree of sexuality is attained when one is in love with a peer. The best men (and women) don't need mindless approbation and servicing, although it can be briefly sweet.

Movieland Malice and Mischief

Oft-told or not, these stories belong in every pop history of Hollywood humor.

Herman Mankiewicz, brother of movie writer-director Joseph Mankiewicz, regarded Hollywood as a madhouse whose inmates had taken over the asylum. Herman was also a writer. Among his writing credits was *Citizen Kane.* When not writing, he amused himself by biting the hands that fed him. His jokes were not appreciated in executive dining rooms. He was constantly being warned about this by his friends when he worked for the tyrannical Harry Cohn, founder of Columbia Pictures. At one point he was advised not to come into the executive dining room as long as there was a possibility that he would say something that would end his lucrative Hollywood career. That is exactly what happened.

First, however, a little background. In the forties and fifties, Hollywood was the place where the money was. There was no question about writers wanting to stay there only until they made enough to go home and write that novel or play. One sold out happily in the Depression years. Dorothy Parker sold out and so did Clifford Odets, William Faulkner, John O'Hara, and, after the 1929 stock market crash, even the Right Honorable Winston Churchill, no slouch as a writer, tried to get on the Hollywood money-go-round. Ernest Hemingway almost did it, and Scott Fitzgerald did.

Now back to Mankiewicz. Well warned, he finally returned to the executive dining room, having promised to eat and say nothing. He listened to Cohn pontificate for over an hour on a favorite theory. Cohn's theory was that when his behind itched in a projection-room seat, he knew that the picture he was seeing would be a flop. His behind had never failed him, he told his captive and beholden listeners. After hearing about forty minutes of variations on this theme, Mankiewicz could stand it no longer. "You mean to say, Harry," he exclaimed angrily, "that your ass is wired to every theater seat in America?" Herman received his severance check within two hours and was off the lot by sunset.

Mankiewicz came back to Columbia once. The occasion was the funeral service for Harry Cohn which took place on one of the largest sound stages on the Columbia studio lot. Notables from all over town, including fawning coworkers, were there. Noting the large crowd, Herman turned to an associate and loudly repeated the old Harry Cohn maxim, "See! When you give the people what they want, they'll come out for it."

While I was an executive at Twentieth Century Fox, Darryl Zanuck forwarded to me a note from his New York financial chief who was critical of the price (too high, he thought) I had paid for the film rights to a hit Broadway play. "Tell your boys," he wrote Zanuck, "that we don't own any oil wells." The next week oil was discovered on the studio lot and it is being pumped from a rich underground field to this day.

Producer Brynie Foy (of the legendary theatrical Foys) had a black belt in the extramarital arts. Once, while he thought his wife was safely away, he brought a comely wench into his house and eventually into his wife's bed. Mrs. Foy arrived to find her husband in her bed with another woman. Brynie was so unflapped by this that when his wife started her tirade, he simply said, "Nothing is going on. Do you believe what I tell you or what you see?"

Brynie's misadventures didn't end at home. He was flushed out of a Malibu fire with a very pretty young black woman and found himself pausing at a red light on Sunset Boulevard next to his wife's best friend in a car parallel to his. Without missing a beat, he pointed to the girl and said, "I want you to meet my maid," whereupon she pummeled him with her fists as he sped away.

Foy's luck ran out when he was rustling up some girls for a party aboard his yacht at Balboa. He found companions for his friends but was lacking a girl for himself. With considerable effort and many phone calls he found one. She was fantastic-looking. Just before he arrived with her at his yacht after a long drive, she said, "You know, Brynie, you could do me a great favor." He looked at her. My God, anyone would do this girl a favor. She then whispered, "Brynie, do you think you could find a girl for me?"

Sam Silver was the barber at the Twentieth Century Fox studios during the Zanuck years, father and son. For about fifteen years, Silver suffered indignities from prank-playing producers and executives. He was also the butt of many a sadistic joke by Darryl Zanuck, who ordered him to learn to play polo, which almost killed him. Sam's only previous experience with horses was dodging mounted cossacks as they galloped through the Russian village of his youth. One of Zanuck's cruelest and most elaborate jokes involved Sam as a masseur. He was an excellent one. Zanuck called Sam into his office and, affecting a very confidential manner, told him that an immensely wealthy Arabian prince from Pindur—or some such nonexistent place—was arriving in Hollywood on a secret mission and would need frequent massages at the studio to relieve the tension brought on by his royal responsibilities. Zanuck then said, in a carefully crafted throwaway line, that the prince was noted for his extravagant gifts to those who served him well. In fact, Zanuck went on, he's given away horses and jewels and even houses. While Sam was pondering that, Zanuck told him he'd be at the studio that following Monday, and remarked, "I want you to give him a good rubdown, Sam."

The prince arrived, as planned, was escorted to Sam's steam room, and helped up onto a massage table. Sam, with visions of lavish gifts dancing around in his head, prepared to give the massage of his life. As he was about to place his hands on the man's body, the prince suddenly asked, "Are you a Mohammedan, Mr. Silver?" Sam said, "No." Whereupon the prince, quite agitated, said, "Oh, this is quite embarrassing (he spoke with a phony English accent), but under the laws of my religion no one but a Mohammedan may touch me." Sam simply muttered, "Oy." In his mind, all hope of lavish loot was gone now. Then, in a small voice, the prince said, "But it is within my power to make you a Mohammedan." (Ten men were crammed in front of a one-way glass panel watching this scene.) He then leaned forward conspiratorially and said, "Mr. Silver, are you willing to abandon your faith for Mohammed?" Sam, not only Jewish but Orthodox Jewish, whispered, "Yes, I'm willing." Those looking through the glass panel saw Sam kneel and submit to a prayer ritual after which he was proclaimed a follower of Mohammed under Islamic law. Finally, Sam was permitted to proceed with the massage and taught to pray an Islamic prayer each time he began. This took place many times over a period of about two weeks. Word came that the prince was leaving town. He wanted one last massage. Sam was ready. Now, if ever, would come the gift. And it did. By this time he called him Sam, and bestowed on him a highly polished giant rock—surely a jewel beyond price. Sam told Zanuck immediately, and Zanuck said, "Oh, my God—very few people get jewels. Probably worth a fortune."

Sam was at the leading jeweler's shop of Beverly Hills when it opened for business at nine the next morning. He asked for an immediate appraisal. The jeweler didn't even put on his glass, but ordered him out of the store, screaming, "What are you trying to pull here? This is no better than a headlight lamp." Disgusted and dismayed, Sam headed back to the studio and waited several hours to see Zanuck. Zanuck said, "I can't believe it. I just can't believe it. There must be a mistake. Have you tried any other jeweler?" A sadder but wiser Sam said, "There is no mistake, Mr. Zanuck. The only mistake is that I'm now a Mohammedan."

Helen is not one to trifle with on matters of marital infidelity. My ex-partner, Richard Zanuck, inherited, among other things, his father's rather cruel joke-playing penchant. While I was in Paris with Helen, I received an amorous note in my suite at the Hotel George V, from a lady who said she was down in the bar and remembered me from my last trip. Could she come up or call? Terrified, as my wife had often threatened to kill me if I was unfaithful, I refused to take a nap or to leave the telephone, in case the woman called. I quickly hid the note. Finally, I took Helen out to dinner, not daring to stop at the bar. Richard and his wife asked whether I'd received any odd notes in my room. Before I could reply, they said they'd been getting messages from someone called Monique. Relieved that we were all being bothered by a crank, I confessed that I had received one too, forgetting I had told Helen the note was a business message from an agent. I displayed my note. Helen's reaction was incendiary. "Why," she demanded, "are you carrying this around? Are you proud of this?" My marriage was almost destroyed by a note written in Richard's own schoolboy French but heavily perfumed and filled with graphic details of my alleged lovemaking prowess.

What is missing in the new, young Hollywood is a sense of play. In the old Hollywood, the business was never so grim that elaborate jokes could not be played. Ernest Lehman was working on the Fox lot while Richard Zanuck and I were running the place. We were stressed out from the rigors of making *Hello, Dolly,* fraught with budget and ego problems. When Ernest, who was producing *Hello, Dolly,* was summoned to Richard Zanuck's office one morning, he assumed it was about the picture. Shortly after he arrived, he received a telephone call. Dick waved him to a booth in his office where telephone calls could be made during meetings, and said, "Ernie, why don't you take it in there; it will be private." As Ernest opened the door to the booth, a full-size gorilla leapt out at him and brought him screaming to the floor. The gorilla was extremely lifelike as befitted a member of the cast of the production *Planet of the Apes.* There was a man inside, to be sure, but for a while Ernest wasn't so sure.

There were other pranks. One was designed to test the loyalty of a man named Harry Sokolov who had, on occasion, said that he would give his life for Richard Zanuck. That's how strongly he said he felt about his boss. Kurt Frings, the colorful and excitable Hollywood agent, was carefully rehearsed to participate in an assassination attempt on Dick, which would take place following a meeting in which Harry Sokolov would be present. To provoke Frings to such an act, Dick Zanuck would pretend to fire summarily two of Kurt's star clients. The prank was to be in two parts. First the meeting would take place and Frings would leave angry and out of control. The next morning, by arrangement, Frings would return and burst into Zanuck's office where we were assembled for our early meeting and wave a large revolver. As he pointed it at Dick, Sokolov, who had once said that he would get in the way of any bullet intended for Dick, dived under a table, leaving the rest of us, including Frings, convulsed in laughter. Harry was not permitted to forget that.

Zanuck and Other Geniuses

After Darryl F. Zanuck banished his son from his life, I hand-delivered to him at the Plaza Hotel, Room 1125, a note dated December 12, 1970, which read, in part, as follows (I kept no copy but you'll soon understand why I have it back):

Dear Darryl:
This note is entirely personal, even self-typed. It is prompted by a simple thing. I'm just about to compose a birthday wire to Dick. Yes, 36 years ago tomorrow you witnessed the birth of your only son. As I was thinking what to say—hardly "Happy Birthday"—it occurred to me that I might send you a message on Dick's birthday as well. This is the message: Why not get back together with Dick? I know or can imagine what has gone on between you. After all, I used to be the peacemaker and wound up accused of being the warmaker. Never mind about that. You are this fellow's father and I know, perhaps better than you, how he feels about you, how terribly hurt and embittered you both are by this situation. Perhaps your problem with Dick is that he is somewhat like you, Darryl, strong-willed and proud. You are older, Darryl, and have had more experience in life. You have been in, out, up, down, excommunicated, embraced, damned, lauded, loved, hated. If Fox were to fall away tomorrow, your films will take care of your reputation forever. In the long run, I believe you have everything to gain by once again doing the strong thing, the unexpected—a specialty of yours—and taking steps with Dick to make peace. You can do it if you wish. Dick is an even abler and better production chief today than he was before. You know it and the industry knows it. A year ago you were putting him up for the Thalberg Award. There's no better man than Dick Zanuck for the job, Darryl. Bury the hatchet, both of you. Life is so fucking short. Don't spend the rest of it cut off from one of the few persons on whom you can truly count. Work a miracle, Darryl, and make a really big decision for yourself and for the company you founded. Put these differences aside. They can be resolved, and your relationship with Dick will be stronger than ever. . . . Think of your pride 36 years ago tomorrow when you knew you had a son. You still have.

Sincerely,
David

The note was returned in an envelope marked "Personal and Confidential." On the last page of the note, in large handwriting, was the message: "No comment. DFZ." The situation referred to was the final alienation of Dick and Darryl Zanuck from each other on the eve of Dick's and my being fired from Twentieth Century Fox because DFZ believed we were bent on usurping his power and I was the evil Svengali who was influencing Dick to take over from him. Dick and his father did make it up years later. When DFZ died, Dick tucked a note in his burial suit reading, "I always loved you. See you later."

Of all producers I have worked with, the one who believed most in the films he chose to make was Darryl F. Zanuck. When you look at his films, *The Grapes of Wrath, Wilson, Gentleman's Agreement,*

The House of Rothschild, Pinky, All About Eve, How Green Was My Valley, and his last great film, *The Longest Day,* they bear his personal mark more than that of those who directed them.

The pure producers such as Zanuck, David O. Selznick, Samuel Goldwyn, and Sam Spiegel were the closest to today's auteur directors. Zanuck and Selznick were obsessed by the story-telling process. In their view, the major work of the film was accomplished when the right story and script and cast had been assembled, with a good director as their artistic surrogate. Zanuck worked endlessly on scripts. During story conferences, he would pace up and down and dictate his notes and changes, as did Selznick. He would analyze and reanalyze every scene to a far greater degree than would be permitted today, when star directors and actors impose their own script demands. Selznick had no fear of telling George Cukor or Alfred Hitchcock that the first act of his script was all wrong, and suggesting how it should be rewritten. Cukor or Hitchcock might protest, but eventually, if he wanted to stay on the picture, he would agree. If you read the production edicts in the book *Memo from David O. Selznick,* you will see the extraordinary extent to which he involved himself, even in the most minute production details. Zanuck, because he also ran a studio, was less obsessive. He allowed producers who served under him at Twentieth Century Fox to indulge their individual tastes to a degree. Still, he was the creative boss. As for the pictures he personally produced, his artistic commitment was total. There was little need for him to be on the set because his work, like that of MGM's wunderkind Irving Thalberg, was done mostly at night after viewing the day's rushes, and extensive notes were sent to the director each shooting day, often with comments on every "take."

Zanuck would come to the set only if there was a dispute or some challenge to his authority. The penalties for insubordination were severe and the words "You'll never work again in this town" were reinforced by action. On *The Longest Day,* Zanuck, then no longer running a studio, was on location continuously. He directed the directors, and he was certainly directing the writers, of whom there were five—author (of the book on which the film was based) Cornelius Ryan, Romain Gary, novelist James Jones, David Pursall, and Jack Seddon.

Selznick's commitment to *Gone With the Wind* was one of total direction of everybody. Irving Thalberg worked primarily with film; rather than rewriting the script beforehand, he made his changes through reshooting. He might look at a film and decide to reshoot the end or, occasionally, most of the picture (as only

Woody Allen does today). The artists were always available and costs were minimal compared to now. Thalberg thought it better to reshoot than to work on the script because, he said, until you saw it on film you didn't know what you had. Those men enjoyed creative autonomy. Although ultimately they did have to answer to their bosses in New York, they suffered no interference in their day-to-day operations.

But they were harassed and criticized when things went bad. Selznick had difficulty raising money to continue making *Gone With the Wind* because costs kept going up. Although independent, he did have partners, notably the elegant and very rich Jock Whitney, who was responsible for *Gone With the Wind* being made by Selznick. Selznick hesitated to buy the rights to the book until Whitney, persuaded by Selznick's eminent New York story editor Kathryn Brown, sent word that if Selznick did not buy the rights, he personally would buy them. Selznick agreed to go forward.

There were struggles of will and ego in those days because the motion picture companies were based in New York City. The Hollywood studios and New York office were distrustful of each other, if not hostile. When box office receipts went down, New York executives questioned the wisdom of making a picture, any picture. Studio executives would send word that a picture they were sending to New York was sensational. If the New York executives disagreed, the explanation was that some son of a bitch in Albuquerque must have tampered with the print on its way east. Then as now the battle was to get a picture made at all. MGM's studio chieftain Louis B. Mayer would answer to Mr. Nicholas Schenck (pronounced Skaynk), his boss in New York, whom he referred to as Mr. Skunk. Once Schenck said to Mayer, "Those people you've got out there are all idiots." Mayer replied, "I know they are, Nick, but they've made millions for us."

I learned more from Darryl F. Zanuck than from any editor I worked for excepting Herbert R. Mayes. Zanuck's philosophy of filmmaking can be summed up in a sentence, his, of course: "They call them moving pictures because they're supposed to *move*." His philosophy: "All my life I believed in action. Even the wrong action can be better than no action at all." The motion picture industry: "Box office receipts have taken an alarming decline; therefore, the selection of the right story material becomes our number one priority. Of course it should always have been our number one priority. We ought not to buy the rights to any play or book regardless of how popular it is unless we feel that it also contains the ingredients of a popular motion picture." On executives: "There was only one boss I believed in and that was me." From a 1940 memorandum to all producers: "I would rather have a bad script on a great subject than a great script on an ordinary subject. Star power is valueless unless the subject matter in the story stands the test. We pay entirely too much attention to good scripts and not enough attention to good subjects. Audiences do not go to the movies out of habit or to pass the time. They go only when there is something playing that they definitely want to see. The greatest cast in the world can't make them see a subject. They don't like a subject that seems slight, empty, or hackneyed. What do I mean by subject matter? I mean stories that are about something, something more than the usual formula output." All this from a memorandum of fifty years ago.

The only truly creative movie geniuses I've known were Darryl F. Zanuck and David O. Selznick. For Darryl, the story was everything. He disliked reading "full material," as books and plays were called. He preferred to read a synopsis. Inability or lack of time was not the reason. He read books for personal pleasure, mainly military history, political biography, and memoirs. As for judging movie material, he thought a brief synopsis did more to illuminate the merits or demerits than reading an entire novel or play would. At that early stage, he did not want to get caught up in individual scenes and detailed description which might tend to obscure the dramatic flaws or even the strengths of the story. He wanted to see the bones before the flesh. Obviously, the writer, director, and producer had to know the full material intimately in order to find the flesh as well as the bones for the screen version.

Zanuck carried his synopsis theory to an extreme when he asked me to have prepared a one-page synopsis of *War and Peace,* one of the longest novels ever written. Lovers of Tolstoy would have been shocked but Zanuck wasn't by the one-page synopsis delivered the next afternoon. In those halcyon days of full-service movie studios (when a mogul's flick of an intercom could provide anything from a false eyelash to a giant crane), readers, as they were called, were highly skilled literary technicians. They were able to extrapolate a cohesive, sometimes vibrant synopsis from what was too often a turgid, disorganized book or play. One reader named G. Byron Sage was the master of our readers staff, which numbered perhaps twenty in Los Angeles and an equal number in New York. Sage prepared a brilliant one-hundred-page synopsis of Lawrence Durrell's *Alexandria Quartet.* His detailed comments and critiques of scripts as well as his suggestions for changes were far superior to any I have received from studio heads or production executives in the 1980s. He and his men and women colleagues were remarkable workers; they could shlep home a thousand- or fifteen-hundred-page manuscript and in a few days produce a synopsis of from ten to forty pages. Frequently they would also prepare a shorter synopsis and a capsule summary of the story, indicating the period in which it takes place, the author's previous works, publishing details, and even lists of characters and production requirements. The readers were so good that there was a real danger that their synopses might be better than the work itself. More than once, we discovered belatedly that the full manuscript was far duller than the synopsis and the reader had extracted the best portions. Darryl F. Zanuck had an instinct about this and was rarely "suckered" by synopses that exaggerated the material. He worked mainly on screenplays, not as a writer but as a producer who would get right to the nub of any dramatization problem and suggest a solution, frequently more than one. He would call his analyses "analyzations" and I guess they were. Zanuck's skills were those of a master storyteller. He had an extremely low threshold for boredom and believed audiences did, too. For Zanuck, less was more, and he could not abide overlong movies.

The same impatience that made him a script surgeon also made him effective in working with film as well as words. He knew what he could lift and he knew what he could transpose in a movie; he was a skilled cutter, as film editors were called in those days. The process of production itself did not interest him as much as script preparation and post-production, although he never missed seeing a frame of the "dailies" when a picture was shooting and sent detailed comments when he felt something was wrong and enthusiastic notes when something was right. On his personal productions, he would remain on the set and live with the picture as it was shot. This was especially true of *The Longest Day,* which he virtually directed. As for studio-made films, however, he would remain in his office unless called to the set because of a crisis. In his earlier days, the movie, whether the locale was Casablanca or Peking, might be filming no more than a few hundred yards from his office, except for occasional location sequences.

David O. Selznick was different, although he too was a great storyteller. While Darryl was a primitive and self-taught, David was highly educated and could draw upon impressive literary knowledge to decide which films to make. David also relied on synopses and I don't believe read *Gone With the Wind* until after he acquired the film rights. But then, unlike Zanuck, he relentlessly studied the novel page by page, making extensive notes and underlining key passages, to ensure that his screenwriters left nothing out that might improve the story on the screen. Zanuck and Selznick were alike in that they were snobs and preferred stories that had panache, Selznick more than Zanuck.

Sometimes they allowed themselves to be intimidated by the author's literary reputation to the detriment of the film version. That happened to Zanuck in the Fox production of *My Cousin Rachel.* "I wish," Zanuck said, "I had changed the ending." The author, Daphne du Maurier, had ended the novel inconclusively, which did not work for the movie. Selznick, on the other hand, objected to Alfred Hitchcock's changing the same author's *Rebecca,* and ordered him to conform to the book after rejecting what he considered a "vulgarizing version of a provenly successful work." Selznick was very skilled, however, in cutting things out of books when there was no room for them. This was the case in the more than four-hour production of *Gone With the Wind,* which could not possibly have accommodated everything in the book unless the miniseries had been invented in 1939. Even then it would have required ten or more long episodes to begin including all that Margaret Mitchell wrote.

Selznick was involved in every aspect of filmmaking, from the choice of lettering in the titles to the hairstyle of an extra; nothing connected with the making of the film was too small or trivial for David O. Selznick's attention. He had a passion for detail that was the despair of his associates. He was not the producer of *Love Is a Many Splendored Thing,* but his wife, Jennifer Jones, was the star. Accordingly, he dispatched dozens of memos to director Henry King, who halted the barrage by announcing that he would either stop production to read the memos or continue production and not read the memos. He would not deign to read them on his own time.

Zanuck, too, dispatched memos, but with the exception of his detailed script analyses, they were brief and to the point. Both men were dedicated and incredibly gifted, articulate, kind, and courteous, although Zanuck, at times, could be somewhat paranoid and, while not discourteous, stubborn. A writer once mentioned a note from Zanuck contradicting the opinions Zanuck had expressed during a story conference. "Let me go upstairs and get your memo, Darryl," he said. Zanuck thundered, "There is no memo! There is no point in going upstairs!" Zanuck did not keep files except for vital confidential documents. He sent memos back to the sender with a reply typed in red at the bottom, "Go ahead" or "I like this" or "Forget it" or "See me about this" or whatever. Business files were not his style. Your files were his files.

Sneak previews were a curious ritual of Hollywood. A film was tested before an audience, who were asked to express their opinions on cards. Today, the preview is only one measurement of audience interest; there are focus groups, exit polls, and other sophisticated research tools. Previews in the late eighties and nineties are held in widely separated cities with diverse demographics, and they are no longer "sneaks."

In simpler times, Riverside, California, was a favorite preview city because it was on the way to Palm Springs where studio executives spent their winter weekends. Consequently, previews were usually scheduled to take place on Friday evenings. On one such occasion in the early fifties, it was planned to return to the studio after the preview to discuss the film. The director was Gregory Ratoff, who was an actor as well as a director and an extremely voluble man. The film, *Carnival in Costa Rica,* was financed by Twentieth Century Fox. It was a disaster. When the theater lights came up, even the manager had fled. Zanuck's executives had learned never to express an opinion before Zanuck told them what their opinion was. There was silence in the empty theater while Zanuck puffed belligerently on his cigar. Finally the man spoke: "I don't give a fuck what anybody thinks. This is a great picture." There was a nodding of bald heads. No more was said until the limousine swept through the studio gates. Ratoff, beholden to Zanuck for many favors and some significant amounts of money, was a close friend. He suddenly exclaimed, "Darryl, the picture is a catastrophe. I've let you down. It's dreadful. How could I have done this to you?" Alarmed by his convulsive sobbing, Darryl put his arm around Ratoff to calm him down. "Don't think about it," he said. "I can fix it. I've done it before. It's not that bad." By this time Ratoff was threatening suicide. He flung himself out the limousine door, and started running. Zanuck said to his driver, "For Christ's sake, get him," which he did. Zanuck took him to his beach house and urged him to spend the night. Meanwhile, downstairs, Zanuck paced restlessly. An hour later he became acutely nervous. It was ominously quiet upstairs. Concerned that Ratoff might have carried out his suicide threat, he went up to the bedroom occupied by the director. Just outside the open bedroom door, he listened carefully and heard the soft sound of quiet, even breathing. Bursting into the room, he bellowed to the slumbering Ratoff, "You son of a bitch! How the hell can you sleep at a time like this?"

I was closer to Darryl, I think, than most of his associates because I was a story man, and so far as he was concerned, stories were all there were to movies.

Very few people got to see him, and some producers served out their contracts without *ever* meeting him. I could call or see him because he was interested in the stories I recommended. Zanuck was polite; he never abused subordinates, only those bigger than he, which could include almost anybody, because of his short stature. I thought he was a brilliant analyst of scripts and stories, and I loved his enthusiasm. The simplest story, if he liked it, became the Second Coming. He infused his associates with his excitement, mostly by written communication. He rarely used the telephone. He answered memos immediately, dispatching them by an office boy who was correctly attired in coat and jacket, and was stationed outside his office to carry his replies at once. "Make the best deal you can but don't lose it," his executive secretary, Esther Roberts, would type on the bottom of memos I wrote recommending the purchase of a book or play. He never wanted to hear a property was lost to another studio (a rare happening) and Esther Roberts was reluctant to give him that message. She'd say, "Tell the boss yourself," and on those occasions, unfortunately, Zanuck did not mind coming to the phone. He was a remarkable executive, and a very creative one. Also a man of courage and concise eloquence. Not bad for a kid from Wahoo, Nebraska, who once dove for pennies off a Venice, California, pier.

Ever wonder how a movie gets started? This one began with a telegram dated June 24, 1966, to Darryl Zanuck at the Hotel du Cap d'Antibes in the south of France:

> DEAR DARRYL DICK HAS HAD SUBMITTED A VERY HILARIOUS AND UNIQUE BOOK ENTITLED QUOTE MASH UNQUOTE STOP IT MAY SEEM INCREDIBLE THAT A KOREAN WAR BACKGROUND STORY WOULD EXCITE US BUT BOTH DICK AND I HAVE NOW READ THE FULL GALLEYS AND WE FIND THIS BOOK BETTER BY FAR THAN QUOTE NO TIME SERGEANTS UNQUOTE AND DESPITE WAR BACKGROUND IT IS DEFINITELY NOT A WAR STORY STOP IT HAS TO DO WITH THE MOBILE ARMY SURGICAL HOSPITAL UNITS PARENTHESIS HENCE THE TITLE CLOSE PARENTHESIS IN WHICH THE COMMANDING OFFICERS WERE REGULAR ARMY MEDICAL CORPS BUT MOST OF THE SURGEONS WORKING UNDER THEM WERE CIVILIAN DOCTORS DRAFTED FOR JUST 18 MONTHS STOP INTERESTED ONLY IN MEDICINE SOME OF THESE DRAFTEES RESENTED ARMY DISCIPLINE AND THE

STRESSES AND STRAINS OF FIENDISH OVERWORK CAUSED SPECTACULAR REACTIONS WHEN THEY WERE OFF DUTY STOP THIS IS THE STORY OF THREE SUCH SURGEONS AT ONE OF THE MASH UNITS STOP BAWDY AND IRREVERENT THEY BECAME A LEGEND DASH PARTLY BECAUSE OF THEIR EXCELLENT AND FANTASTIC SURGICAL SKILL UNDER UNBELIEVABLE PRESSURE BUT MOSTLY BECAUSE OF THEIR TOTALLY ZANY AND MAD OFF DUTY EXPLOITS STOP THEIR LONG SUFFERING COMMANDING OFFICER WOULD HAVE SHIPPED THEM BACK TO THE STATES IN A FLASH BUT HE HAD NO REPLACEMENTS STOP IN FACT HE WORRIED MOST WHEN THEY WERE QUIET AND WELL BEHAVED FOR THIS INDICATED THEY WERE ON THE VERGE OF BREAKDOWNS FROM OVERWORK AND THE DEPRESSING ODDS AGAINST SOME OF THEIR PATIENTS RECOVERY STOP IN TIME THE THREE SURGEONS ACQUIRE A FOURTH TENTMATE A BIG NEGRO NEUROSURGEON WHO HAD ONCE BEEN A PROFOOTBALL HERO STOP IN ADDITION TO BUILDING A FOOTBALL TEAM AROUND HIM AND MAKING A FORTUNE BETTING ON THEMSELVES THE FOUR DOCTORS GO THROUGH CRAZY AND WONDERFUL EXPLOITS THAT HAVE NEVER BEFORE BEEN SEEN OR READ STOP THE CHARACTERS INCLUDE A CAPTAIN CALLED QUOTE TRAPPER UNQUOTE WHO IS A SENSATIONAL TALL THIN YOUNG MAN CARRYING A COMPLETE BAR IN HIS PARKA ANOTHER DOCTOR NAMED QUOTE HAWKEYE UNQUOTE WHO IS A COMPLETE CHARACTER AND A DENTIST WHO IS KNOWN AS QUOTE THE PAINLESS POLE UNQUOTE AND IS SEXUALLY THE PHENOMENON OF THE SERVICE STOP IT IS IMPOSSIBLE TO GIVE YOU A FULL SYNOPSIS BUT NONE OF THE CHARACTERS IS STOCK AND ALL OF THEM HAVE WIVES BACK HOME AND ARE SIMPLY REACTING TO IMPOSSIBLE STRESS STOP THE RESULT FAR FROM DEPRESSING OR DREARY IS TOTAL ENTERTAINMENT AND IN TODAYS GROOVE BECAUSE THESE ARE ALL ANTI ESTABLISHMENT CHARACTERS BEING THEMSELVES AND DEFYING AUTHORITY WHILE DOING A TERRIFIC AND COURAGEOUS JOB STOP THE STORY FOLLOWS THEM THROUGH THEIR TOUR OF DUTY UNTIL THEY PART IN THE STATES VOWING TO MEET SOMEDAY AGAIN ALTHOUGH WE KNOW THEY PROBABLY WONT STOP THE STORY IS LOADED WITH SEX BUT IT IS THE SORT OF DESPERATE COMICAL SEX OBSESSION OF ISOLATED MEN THRUST INTO UNUSUAL SITUATIONS AND FREED FROM THE USUAL RESTRAINTS OF SOCIETY BACK HOME STOP CASTING POSSIBILITIES ARE GREAT AND ONE HILARIOUS SEQUENCE FOLLOWS ANOTHER WITHOUT APPEARING TO BE CONTRIVED STOP IT IS REALLY THE STORY OF WHAT COMICAL AND FAR OUT THINGS HAPPEN WHEN MEN ARE UNDER IMPOSSIBLE PRESSURE STOP THE WAR BACKGROUND IS INCIDENTAL AND THE NEED TO SHOW ANY SURGERY PRACTICALLY NIL AS THE REAL STORY LIES IN THE OFF DUTY HAPPENINGS STOP PRODUCER WHO BROUGHT US THIS IS INGO PREMINGER STOP DO NOT EXPECT BIG BEST SELLER BUT DO EXPECT BIG AND DIFFERENT FILM WITH SOME OF THE QUALITIES OF QUOTE DIRTY DOZEN UNQUOTE AND ENOUGH VISUAL ACTION WITH WAR ACTION STOP READ BOOK ON ARRIVAL AS DICK IS PUSHED FOR IMMEDIATE ACTION AND MAY EVEN NOW BE TOO LATE BUT WOULD LIKE YOUR EXPRESSION AND GREEN LIGHT TO SEE IF WE CAN MAKE DEAL WHICH WILL NOT BE EXTRAORDINARY FINANCIALLY AND WILL NATURALLY INFORM YOU OF TERMS STOP HOWEVER BELIEVE TERMS WILL BE SUCH THAT YOU WOULD APPROVE IF WE CAN GET THIS PROJECT STOP PLEASE TELEX STOP AFFECTIONATE REGARDS DAVID BROWN

Zanuck's cable was received the next morning: GO AHEAD AND TRY TO MAKE A REASONABLE DEAL FOR M.A.S.H. We did and also made its producer, Ingo Preminger, rich through his share of the profits. He moved to Aspen where he lives to this day.

Jack Schaeffer was a writer of many westerns. In one screenplay, there seemed to be a dull spot. I remember a note from Darryl on the margin of the script: "Put a snake in this scene to give it some life." Zanuck knew with a snake in the scene, the audience wouldn't fall asleep.

Darryl read material that was being considered as the basis for a movie almost as soon as he received it. He read in his office, his beach house in Santa Monica, his desert home in Palm Springs, and flashed back his reactions in terse messages such as, "I like this, buy it," or "Don't buy it." He also gave his reasons, succinctly and brilliantly. If we in the story department liked something well enough to recommend buying it, I'd send DFZ a synopsis for his decision. His decision was always based on a synopsis, often no more than six or seven pages. There were no committees or vice-presidents to prejudge the material. Advertising and sales executives were forbidden to read scripts and stories. Unlike the business affairs specialists of today who have little knowledge of what they are dealing for, our story editors negotiated for the properties and writers Zanuck approved. They knew the value as well as the price of what they were buying. It was a matter of departmental pride not to lose a good property. "Property" is an important word in motion-picture making. "Property" has, of course, a stage-craft meaning, but it also has a literary meaning. A property is a story, and properties are material, which is the generic term for anything from which movies are fashioned. "Story material" is the collective term. When story editors and readers saw something they thought would make a good movie—in one famous case, a book concerning a split personality—we'd recommend it to Zanuck. The book, published by McGraw-Hill and written by Drs. Corbett Thigpen and Hervey Cleckley, became a movie called *The Three Faces of Eve,* for which Joanne Woodward won an Academy Award. An excerpt in the newspaper supplement *The American Weekly* first brought it to our attention.

If a major book such as *My Cousin Rachel* or a stage production like *The Sound of Music* attracted our favorable attention, a synopsis would be sent to our producers and directors, asking for opinions and an expression of interest or uninterest. The comments would be sent with the synopsis to Zanuck. If he liked the property he would ask us to buy the rights and would determine, after studying the producers' comments, who he thought was best qualified to make the picture. He took an active role in all his producers' films, going through scripts night after night with his script supervisor, Molly Mandaville; he dictated memos fifty or sixty pages in length in which he analyzed screenplays scene by scene and dissected dialogue and action. These sessions lasted well past midnight, starting about nine when Rex, who guarded the entrance to the Administration Building, awakened Zanuck from his nap. The memos were mimeographed and on blue paper.

Zanuck was respectful of other opinions, unlike the moguls of stereotyped Hollywood novels; when he found a script that pleased him, he trumpeted his enthusiasm to his sales and financial executives all over the world, making them want to prove him right. He did not hide his emotions, like so many cold-ass authority figures. He rarely saw agents except for those who were his friends. Among them were Charles K. Feldman, DFZ's personal agent, Ray Stark, who was associated with Feldman (both became world-class producers), and Irving Lazar. Zanuck put in his time, was precise, pragmatic, always thrilled by talent, and a snob in the good sense.

Next to talent, enthusiasm is the prime motivation in show business. Zanuck knew that. He always began his criticism of a script by saying what was good about it. However slight the merits, he would dwell on those before explaining what he thought was wrong. He would accompany his criticism by suggesting what could be done to remedy the problems. Few of today's executives have the tact, judgment, and experience to do all that.

DFZ was easily bored. Impatient, he wanted to get on with the story in a film. He was intolerant of any picture or film that went on too long. He thought almost all films were too long. He cut, cut, cut. His film philosophy was much like Ernest Hemingway's writing philosophy. In the best of Hemingway's stories, the reader somehow understands what has been left out, and the stories race along with beautiful simplicity. So it was with Zanuck's better pictures.

Darryl, while loyal by nature, was not surprised by betrayal. It was as though he expected it. If betrayal was not forthcoming, grounds for distrust could be found. Fox was like a sixteenth-century French court: There were the king's favorites and those who had fallen out with him. Off with their heads. As Dick Zanuck recalled, DFZ would sooner or later find a reason to "execute" any close associate whom he perceived as growing too powerful or who was otherwise suspect. The list was long, beginning with the talented William Goetz, who ran Fox during DFZ's war service, and including once-trusted business associates Arnold Grant and Seymour Poe, and ending up with his son, who was fired along with me during Darryl's final frenzy of paranoia.

I saw the genesis of this paranoia while in Cannes in 1968. There to participate in a conference of Fox's international sales organization, I was to speak, ironically as it turned out, on unity. DFZ's point man in matters of suspected betrayal, André Hakim, came to my room in the Carlton Hotel and confided that I was "tinted[*sic*]" because of a telex Dick and I had sent urging Darryl not to bring Frank McCarthy, producer of *Patton,* to the south of France for a meeting. We regarded DFZ's intervention in this studio production as undermining our authority.

When I was summoned to meet Darryl in the lobby of the Carlton, I was presented with a bill of particulars consisting of two dozen or so examples of insubordination by Dick and me. These were written out in DFZ's own bold handwriting. I could scarcely believe the extent of our alleged "disloyalties." "You're in trouble, aren't you?" Helen said when I returned to our room, my face white, more with rage than fear.

When I advised Dick of our transgressions, he told me he was resigning from the company at once. We had a big production program going and I was concerned. In fact, foolish me, I was petrified with anxiety, so seriously did I take my job. I begged him to stay on but to no avail. His then wife, Linda, took subsequent telephone calls and said nobody knew where Dick was (I later learned he was listening on an extension and chortling at my discomfiture). When I reported Dick's decision to quit, DFZ's reaction was to announce that he, too, was quitting forthwith.

None of this was known to anyone else in the corporation as I began my scheduled speech on unity. I have since learned that all Hollywood crises, like its product, are make-believe. Before word of the resignations could get out, the Zanucks had reconciled. In a cheerful exchange of telexes, they comforted each other with the thought, expressed in a DFZ message, that "David exaggerated the situation."

Darryl F. Zanuck died on December 22, 1979. His family requested that Orson Welles deliver the eulogy. It was my task to find Orson, whose whereabouts were known only to his New York attorney, Arnold Weisberger. Arnold gave me Orson's private number at

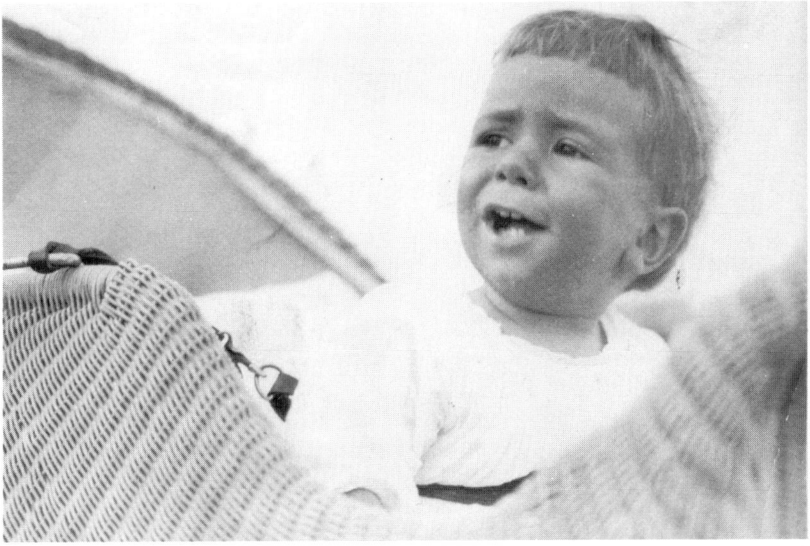

The author at age two contemplating his future

1941. Age twenty-five. Pic *magazine. I was writing one third of the magazine every two weeks as well as a true-life murder case. Hairline the same today but the color is lighter.*

A reception for Alfred Hitchcock in the late 1940s. The lady Hitch is talking to is an editor from Look *magazine. I remember her face and form but, alas, not her name.*

Prenuclear family. My wife (number 1), Liberty LeGacy Brown, and our son, Bruce, referred to on the back of the photograph as "Speaker of the House." Picture was taken in June 1943, when Bruce was less than a year old.

Another family tableau. My second wife, Wayne Clark Brown, and Bruce, nine years old.

General Secretary Nikita Khrushchev comes to lunch at the Twentieth Century Fox commissary in 1959. To Marilyn Monroe's right are producer Jerry Wald and director Joshua Logan. To Marilyn's left is George Cukor. I am in the foreground smoking a cigar. Between Marilyn and Jerry Wald, in the background, is a man who appears to be either KGB or Secret Service (if I have misidentified an old friend, I hope he'll forgive me). He looks on attentively with a sinister glower.

Helen as one of Glamour *magazine's "10 Girls with Taste" on her first trip to New York in 1953. The photograph is by Jon Engstead. The cat's name is Spam.*

At a reception for famed poet Carl Sandburg. I'm trying to charm him into writing the screenplay for The Greatest Story Ever Told. *At Sandburg's left is the golden boy of American theater, Clifford Odets, on Hollywood hiatus as a screenwriter when this picture was taken.*

The first photograph of Helen Gurley Brown at Cosmopolitan. *The photographer is unknown but the subject seems extremely happy. It is March 1965 and she has begun her first twenty-five years as editor.*

In Cannes in 1967 with Darryl F. Zanuck and Helen. Fox's heads of publicity and foreign distribution are taking up the rear. Darryl and production head Richard Zanuck had informed me shortly before this picture was taken that they both were going to quit the company. I was scheduled to give a speech on unity to the sales force.

Ernest Lehman (to my left), Richard Zanuck, and I talk it over on the set of Hello, Dolly.

Being presented to Her Majesty, Queen Elizabeth II, with the Zanucks, père *and* fils, *in background.*

The wedding of agent/producer Charles Feldman and Clotilde Barot in 1968. Charles knew when this photograph was taken he would soon die of cancer. Seated next to Feldman at left is Warren Beatty and standing next to him is Sam Goldwyn. Danny Kaye is at far left. Seated at right next to the bride is Irving (Swifty) Lazar and standing at right behind him are Robert Evans, Billy Wilder, Mike Romanoff, Frank Sinatra, and Richard Zanuck. In back of Feldman and Clotilde are Ray Stark, Louis Jourdan, and me.

Helen and I and Samantha, our Siamese. The year is 1963. The place is our Manhattan apartment.

once. Orson responded to the invitation immediately. In a small room in a West Los Angeles church, he composed these remarks, which he intoned in that somber, sonorous voice that panicked America in 1938 during his *The War of the Worlds* broadcast.

In that grand pageant which was the state funeral of Winston Churchill, there was a moment when the coffin was to be carried out of Westminster Abbey and into a barge and to be taken up for a distance on the river. And for this part of the ceremony there was a special selection of pallbearers from the various military services of Great Britain. One of these was a sailor who broke his ankle on the step coming down, carrying the coffin. There was a fear for a moment that it might have been dropped. Thank God, it safely entered the barge, and afterwards they said, "How did you manage to go on?" And the sailor said, "I would have carried him all over London." That's the way I felt about my friend. Churchill wrote the script for that funeral and designed the whole thing, as did Lord Mountbatten in England. If you're going to have a state funeral they let you do that. They give you what amounts to "the final cut." Well, we don't have state funerals in our movie community but if we did, Darryl would certainly have been given one. And by exercising his rights according to precedent set by the British, he would have produced it. And what a show that would have been. Virginia and Dick, and some of Darryl's closest friends, have reminded me that Darryl himself would not wish this occasion to be too lugubrious. And that's certainly true. I'm pretty sure that if he were the producer in charge of this occasion, Darryl would have wished for us all to leave this gathering with lightened spirits. The trouble is that I'm the wrong man for the job. With the best will in the world, I can't find anything cheerful to say about the loss of my friend. In our Hollywood community we hear on sad occasions such as this, or in various celebrations and salutes and tributes, various leaders referred to and hailed as "Giants of the Industry" or of the motion picture industry. Well, in all that number, only a very few have truly deserved such a description and nobody has deserved it more than Darryl Zanuck. To understand the special nature of his contribution we must understand the full meaning of the word "producer." In Darryl's day there were producers assigned to each movie and then there was the man in charge of all the movies. And in Darryl's day, that was a lot of movies. Forty, fifty, sixty, seventy feature pictures a year. And these men who were in charge of all the movies, these legendary tycoons, presided over that chapter in our history which we look back to with the fondest memories. But the whole point about Darryl is that he did not just preside. He did so very much more than preside. Of all the big-boss producers, Darryl was unquestionably the man with the greatest gifts. True personal, professional, and artistic gifts for the filmmaking process itself. He began as a writer and in a sense he never stopped functioning as a writer. Some few others may have matched him as starmakers, but with all of Darryl's flair for the magic of personalities, I think you'll agree that Darryl's first commitment was always to the story. For Darryl, that was what it meant to make a film. It was to tell a story. And God bless him for that. With half a hundred and more stories to tell every dozen months, this great storyteller was of necessity an editor, and a great editor. And I know we all agree that there never was an editor in our business to touch him. It's impossible not to praise him. And it's even more impossible to do him justice. Every great career of courage is a small roller coaster and Darryl had his disasters. He knew eclipses; he knew comebacks and triumphs. It was a giant roller coaster. And then there's studio politics, which was a more recent historical form of the old dirty business of palace politics. And that's the roughest game there is. But has anybody, anybody ever claimed that Darryl Zanuck advanced himself by dirty tricks or by leaving behind him the usual trail of bloody corpses? Of course there were some aching egos and some bruised temperaments. If you're in charge of a whole regiment of artists, some of your commands are going to hurt and some of your decisions are bound to seem arbitrary. But Darryl didn't sign on to be the recreation director of a summer camp. Of course he was tough. That was his job. But unlike many of the others (I'm almost tempted to say, unlike the others), he was never cruel. Never vindictive. He was—what a rare thing it is to say in this competitive game of ours—a man totally devoid of malice. But he was graced with irony. A great sense of humor, even about himself. Of which of the others can we say that? I'm afraid that the old saw about this town is still the newest word. We're as good as our last picture. But for Darryl you were as good as he had decided you were as a human being because he took you on those terms. He was not the slave of fashion, or the servant of temporary success. If he took you on, you stayed. Of who else could that be said? I always knew, not only in the course of the many films I was privileged to make with him, but also in the many long years of my friendship with Darryl, that if I did something really outrageous, that if I committed some abominable crime (which I believe it is in most of us to do under the right circumstances), that if I were guilty of something unspeakable and all the police in the world were after me, there was one man and only one man I could come to, and that was Darryl. He would not have made me a speech about the good of the industry or the good of his studio. He would not have been mealy-mouthed or put me aside: He would have hid me under his bed. Very simply, he was a friend. I don't mean just my friend. I mean that friendship was something he was very good at. That's just why it's so very hard to say good-bye to him.

Perhaps the most brilliant film executive I've known is, by his own admission, not creative. He is Lew R. Wasserman, chairman and chief executive officer of MCA/Universal, and a former talent agent when MCA was in that business. He is surely one of those few whom F. Scott Fitzgerald characterized in *The Last Tycoon* as being able to hold the whole equation of the film industry in his head. Lew has a steel-trap mind, a hospital-clean desk, and a direct way of dealing with problems and people. With Lew, there is always a right way and a wrong way. He is not pluralistic and assuredly not a concept spinner. He is action- and business-oriented and that's all, folks. His smile is dazzling but dangerous. His anger is terrifying. A long-time secretary he adored (as a secretary) walked out of his office and never returned after receiving a few bursts of his temper. Mostly he is courteous and correct. In his personal life and socially, he is a pussycat. When Richard Zanuck and I formed our company, we joined MCA/Universal after a meeting with Wasserman at his home. There we briefly outlined the pictures we wanted to make and he would say, "Go make the movie" or "I don't think that's going to work." He never asked to read scripts except for *The Sting.* That subject interested him personally. Wasserman rarely sends memos. He deals directly by telephone or emissary. Anyone can get Lew Wasserman on the phone once. If you are a time waster, once will be all.

Zanuck, Selznick, and Wasserman are the three men I consider, in my time, to have been the best of the moguls. Sam Goldwyn, Irving Thalberg, Jack Warner, and Harry Cohn doubtless might have been included, had I worked for them. In the realm of today's master deal-makers and corporate strategists I must also include Time/Warner's Steven J. Ross, for whom I did work and who is without peer as a long-term player and new-age talent magnet. The best judge of show business assets and gutsiest negotiator and risk-taker is, in my book, my friend and Chris-Craft's brilliant chairman, Herbert J. Siegel. The middle initial "J," which Ross and Siegel share, is a lucky letter.

At eighty, Jack Warner was an extraordinary example of longevity without any sign of senility. Humorous, effervescent, life-loving, he demonstrated that health goes with authority. Not authority wrested from others, but authority born of almost instant success and maintained with trust, vigor, and a great deal of nerve. I wonder if he ever suffered a crisis of confidence. Crises of confidence are the bane of most adult men and women of achievement. Ernest Hemingway blew his brains out, possibly because of a crisis of confidence. Scott Fitzgerald may well have drunk himself to death for the same reason. Others who have achieved much wound up doubting themselves and their accomplishments and were unable to savor what they rightly won. With age come crises of confidence. Richard Nixon suffered them and seems to have survived them, but I wonder what it's like for him at four o'clock in the morning. I believe wars are waged by nations that are experiencing a crisis of confidence. For men and women there are personal wars, not only external but also internal, leading to premature death and senility. Success requires a little ignorance to block out that which creates a crisis of confidence. That crisis ironically is sometimes the outward sign of true success. E. L. Doctorow, in commenting on his friend, director and choreographer Robert Fosse, said, "He doubted himself so intensely, wondering whether he had any talent at all, that I knew he was the real thing."

Short Takes

Advice to anyone wishing to be a producer: If you don't have a special relationship with the writer, director, and the actors, you're just a businessman come out to watch the money. You get very little cooperation and no respect.

Jules Stein, founder of the show business goliath MCA, was a wise man about business and life. He said if you want to be a good businessman, hire someone who can do your job better than you can. He did, placing Lew R. Wasserman in charge of his company when he, Jules, was only fifty-one.

Milton Goldman was a New York theatrical agent whose penchant was introducing friends to other friends they usually knew quite well. On three occasions he introduced me to my wife.

It is difficult to comprehend, in these days of faxes, how everyone once sent telegrams and cables. The most extreme example was Florenz Ziegfeld, the Broadway impresario, who regularly sent wires from the back of the theater to his actors and actresses onstage.

Goldwyn is said to have instructed playwright Robert Sherwood in the art of screenwriting with this simple example. A man and a woman are in an elevator. It stops for another woman to enter. The man removes his hat. That means that the man is married to the first woman, for whom he had not removed his hat. Simple visual device requiring no dialogue.

* * *

Jack Warner's memorable definition of a Hollywood writer: "A schmuck with an Underwood."

Joe Mankiewicz once said the lowest form of celebrity in Hollywood is a writer's wife.

Everybody in the movie business speculates as to what weather conditions are best for theater attendance. Marcus Loew, who founded the chain of theaters that still bears his name, was asked the same question years ago. His answer: "It should look like rain, but it shouldn't rain."

George Lucas once said, "If you can tune in to the fantasy life of an eleven-year-old girl, you can make a fortune in this business."

Steven Spielberg and George Lucas are two directors who keep their sets entirely closed to the press. The content of their movies is kept secret. Woody Allen keeps his titles and scripts secret and shows his actors only those scenes in which they work.

Billy Wilder is as famous for his savage wit as for his inspired direction. When I recently offered him a comedy script to direct, he responded, "This can either be the best comedy ever made or the worst catastrophe. I don't like the range."

Early in his career, Steven Spielberg turned down a script given to him by one of the biggest stars in the world because he didn't think the star was right for the role. In explanation, the young director said, "Look, if I ever make a picture again, I'm not going to make those kinds of compromises or I will have a very short career."

The gifted director Otto Preminger was noted for his abusive behavior on the set of his movies. Once, after he was excoriating a member of the crew, another crew member asked, "Why do you take this shit? Couldn't you fight back?" "I couldn't," the victim said, "because I still have relatives in Germany."

It was Orson Welles, creator of *Citizen Kane,* who said while observing the myriad extras, cameramen, assistant directors, and all kinds of technicians milling around a huge set piled high with props, "A movie in production is the greatest train set a boy could ever have."

* * *

I met Goldie Hawn's mother in Las Vegas. Mrs. Hawn, a pleasant, round-faced woman, was talking about Goldie at three trying to play "Happy Birthday" on the family piano. Goldie sat at the piano for hours until her mother came in and said, "Well, have you got it?" "Yes," Goldie said, "I've got it." "Why are you so determined to learn?" her mother asked. "So I can play at parties, Momma." Portrait of a performer as a child.

Hollywood economy wave. When a *Cosmopolitan* story titled "Letter to Five Wives" was made into a movie, it was retitled *A Letter to Three Wives,* thereby eliminating the need for two actresses.

After Ernest Lehman had become one of Hollywood's most successful writers, he was pondering a particularly knotty problem in his office when he overheard his secretary say to a caller, "No, Mr. Lehman is not busy. He is just thinking."

My forever friend and now vice-president/production of my company, Pamela Hedley, says, "When there is an emphatic denial of anything in Hollywood, it always comes to pass. Depend on it." I do.

Birth of a Legend: Helen Gurley Brown

My wife's book *Sex and the Single Girl* was fact, not fiction, being an artful collection of recipes, decorating tips, and foxy advice to the single girl, including how to handle affairs and reasons she should celebrate instead of mope because she is not married. When the book appeared in 1962, it became an immediate sensation, climbing the best-seller lists. It was published in thirty-five countries and in nearly as many languages. Helen almost at once became a world-class celebrity, but I was a struggling producer at Twentieth Century Fox, desperately trying to find something to put on the screen and known, if at all, as Helen's husband. It never occurred to me that *Sex and the Single Girl* could make a *movie.* But Saul David, formerly editorial director of Bantam Books and then a prisoner at Columbia Pictures where he was getting nothing off the ground (as they say in Hollywood), felt otherwise. He claimed to have a way (again, as they say in Hollywood) to "lick" *Sex and the Single Girl.* I was still skeptical about Saul's chances when Walter McKuen, Jack Warner's top aide, telephoned to ask whether Helen would be interested in selling the film rights to her book. Walter McKuen was an old friend and for once I permitted friendship to interfere with business. I said, "Walter, have you or anybody else out there read this book?" Walter said, "No, but Jack seems to think that there's a movie in it." Thinking of Saul, I said, "There is a chap I know who also believes he can make a movie of this." Walter said, "Really?" So Saul David was summoned into the presence of Jack L. Warner, whose name, as he liked to tell those who disputed him, was on the water tower. Saul approached Warner's vast desk, where Warner thumbed through the book. "What do you have to do with this book, Mr. David?" he asked, and then, without giving Saul a chance to reply, he glanced to the dedication page and said, "Oh, I see, it's dedicated to you."

It was indeed dedicated to David.

The film was produced, not by Saul, but by Jack Warner's former son-in-law, William T. Orr. It was a hit. It starred Henry Fonda, Tony Curtis, and Natalie Wood (as Helen Gurley Brown). A third person who thought there was a movie in Helen's book may have been the most persuasive of all. She was a seductive single girl named Jacqueline Parks to whom Mr. Warner listened attentively late at night. The book must have struck a chord in her. She urged Jack to buy it. It is doubtful that he ever read it.

Here's Helen's account of how she came to write *Sex and the Single Girl* and, as a result, later became editor of *Cosmopolitan.*

> I was already a successful career woman before I met David, a quite well-paid copywriter in an advertising agency in Los Angeles, so we couldn't say that he totally discovered me. However, but for him I wouldn't be Helen Gurley Brown—I would simply be Helen Brown (a name I prefer and mostly use) or worse, Helen Gurley. As Helen Gurley, I might have worked a few more years in advertising, married someone else, and retired to become a Beverly Hills matron, if I had not met David and had he not been the odd kind of man he is. I've always accused him of not being able quite to get it off the ground with his talented second wife, because I think he intended to turn *her* into a writer. I think she wanted that, too, but there were other distractions, and although she's probably more brilliant than I could ever be, it didn't quite work for her in terms of David playing Professor Higgins to her Eliza Doolittle.
>
> Anyway, here I was at the advertising agency married to David Brown. He was alimony poor, or I might have quit my job—women in those days got married and gave up working. You weren't supposed to want to work anymore. For me it didn't happen. I kept on trundling to my office at Hollywood and Vine every day. It was a one-hour drive from Pacific Palisades, sixty-six traffic lights each way. I used to count

them when I had a stick-shift Mercedes-Benz. Anyway, there I was at the ad agency but not really having a very good time of it. This agency had lured me and pursued me and pummeled me into coming to work for them. It took almost a year for me to move over from my old shop. Once I was there, I felt undervalued. It's as though once they possessed me, they didn't want me. I consulted David about it. He said, "Just hang in there. They're not firing you, so instead of turning in your ideas half an hour after you've been given your assignment, why don't you just wait a week and then turn them in? They'll think you've been working longer on them and may value them more." I did that. I also turned in lots of unsolicited ideas. It didn't work. I really never heard from anybody about my copy, although I knew it was being seen by the copy supervisor, the account executive, the account supervisor, and sometimes even by the head of the agency. Afterward, I learned it also went to the client, in this case Max Factor, where it was reviewed by the advertising manager, his boss, and sometimes was sent around the office to three or four product managers and their secretaries. Nothing ever got out alive. In addition to which, I was pitted against two other girl copywriters who were given the same assignments. It was demoralizing.

One day David and I were taking our usual Sunday walk in Will Rogers State Park in West Los Angeles. There we were trudging up our mountain in the clean, eucalyptus-scented air. I was deeply depressed because by that time I was thirty-eight and had been a career girl for twenty years. To be working your guts out for that long and not have anybody like what you were doing was the pits. I said to David, "What am I going to do? I don't know of any other jobs. I don't want to leave. They're not firing me but nobody is paying any attention to my work and I'm miserable." I continued, "You've helped lots of other people do some extracurricular writing—how about me? Maybe I could write a book. Do you think so?"

He said, "Well, I don't know. Somebody was in the other day and asked whether I had any book ideas. He was from a New York publishing company." These people frequently called on David because he had come from the publishing world and when they came to California, they went to see him. Sometimes they had books that he could consider for movies. Anyway he had given this man a book outline he had developed having to do with how to have an affair. And he told me a little bit about it. He said there's a chapter on the apartment. There's one on cooking and one on how to clear the decks for action. I said, "David, that sounds like my book. I think I could do something with that." He harrumphed that he had also discussed it with a woman writer he used to know, but she didn't seem interested. Anyway, it was his idea. I said, "You've got to get that outline back from whomever you gave it to." David did get the outline back and I took it and began to work on it. For many weeks I just made notes under the hair dryer, in my little office at Kenyon and Eckhardt where I was undervalued and even underworked. Gradually I began to sit down and do an outline for *Sex and the Single Girl.* David's outline had been a little more frivolous. I guess nobody really believed that a girl could deliberately decide to have an affair and to clear the decks for action. That was a pretty wild idea in 1960. But as I got going, I found that there really was some stuff to be said about the single girl that nobody had ever written before. Here I was full of it. I was single thirty-seven years. Who better than me? I tried one draft after another. And this is where I think I never would have been me now except for David because I had a built-in sleep-in editor. I had somebody who could explain to me at any hour that it wasn't working, that this was not going well, that it was stilted. I probably would have given it up if I hadn't had somebody there who kept egging me on. I guess I tried about four drafts of a first chapter. And one day having torn up the fourth draft I sat down and started the fifth and somehow it just came out quite, quite nicely. I told who I was and what kind of woman I was and that I married late and thought it was OK to be single that long. I also wrote that I couldn't have got the man I wanted if I'd been any younger—he wouldn't have been ready for me if he hadn't been through his two marriages, blah, blah, blah, blah. And so *Sex and the Single Girl* was born. Random House, who distributed the book, insisted it couldn't be titled *Sex for the Single Girl*—too naughty because single girls weren't supposed to have sex. Publisher Bernard Geis changed "for" to "and" and the title was cleared and survives in various versions as part of the language.

David was always into it 4,000 percent. It really does help to have an enthusiastic partner. I know many men marry women who egg them on and keep them encouraged. There apparently aren't many men who encourage their wives to undertake some professional adventure. But David was like a child with twelve pounds of Swiss chocolate. He was just blooming and blossoming throughout the entire writing of *Sex and the Single Girl.* He gave some of it to Oscar Dystel, head of Bantam Books, then solely a paperback publisher. David and I both felt that whoever published my manuscript would make us very grateful, so it really didn't occur to us to go to a hardcover publisher first. Oscar was on the Coast; he was available; he and David were close friends and David gave him the manuscript—I think the first two chapters and a complete outline. (There never was such a complete outline—you could hardly lift it.) Oscar kept the manuscript for several weeks. When he came to California again, he suggested we all have dinner, and during dinner he said he would have to turn down the book. I nearly choked on my lasagna. It was painful. You must never turn anybody down at dinner. Tears were cascading down my face and I was really in pain. But I held out until I got home before I had the real sob scene. A friend of David's and a former associate of Oscar Dystel's named Saul David said there was a new, zany publisher in New York who was promotion-minded and might consider the book. Oscar had actually made the same suggestion at dinner but I was too traumatized to respond. The publisher was Bernard Geis. Saul David called Bernie, who said he'd like to see the outline and the chapters. Ten days later, he wrote to say he'd like to publish the book, and enclosed a check for six thousand dollars. There's no thrill like having your first book published. You just don't realize then how many thousands of books are published every year and some very scruffy writing gets into print. But I was absolutely euphoric and David was euphoric for me and with me. After that, completion of the book was quite simple. It took a year because I kept my job at the ad agency. David edited every chapter. Sometimes it was riddled with editing. However, when he totally crossed out or rewrote whole passages, I realized it wasn't working and I would start over because David's and my styles are totally different. He's formal and stately. I'm less proper and much more casual and conversational. He's a better writer, but I am a more popular writer. The chapter on the affair was written over two or three times before I got it right.

Anyway, fade out, fade in. David left Twentieth Century Fox and came to New York to found a hardcover book division for New American Library. I wrote a sequel to *Sex and the Single Girl* titled *Sex and the Office.* It was somewhat forced. It never came easily, but the book was successful. It sold fifty thousand copies in hardcover, which isn't bad but of course not the phenomenon that *Sex and the Single Girl* had been. I was also writing a newspaper column for the *Los Angeles Times* Syndicate. It was as though my book and newspaper readers had found a friend. I was the sophisticated older sister in whom they could confide. In 1962, most of the advice givers were still pretty puritanical—Abigail Van Buren, Joyce Brothers, churches, teachers. Unless a girl could afford to go to a psychiatrist, which I had done, there wasn't really anybody terribly hip who would be responsive to questions she would not dare ask anyone else. I used to answer every letter. I had no secretary. I laboriously tried to give advice and be that sophisticated older sister-friend. When a new bag of mail arrived one afternoon David said, "You know, there are all these women out there who trust and need you. You ought to have a magazine." That was the nucleus of the idea for the new *Cosmopolitan.*

As I've said before, the difference between David and me and some other people with ideas is that we sit down and do it. Some of our ideas don't seem very spectacular when we're first fooling with them and 98 percent of them never reach fruition. Mostly no one backs our brainstorms. This was just one more that we tried. We sat down to create a format for a magazine that ultimately became *Cosmo.* We each thought up dozens of article ideas and I wrote the advertising prospectus listing the products I believed we could attract to a magazine for women who were not living through their children and husbands and wanted to do something on their own. It was a dear little prospectus. It was all typed. David has written [later in this book] about the publishers who saw the presentation before it went to Dick Deems of Hearst Magazines. The title we selected was *Femme,* unaware there was a successful magazine of that title in France. He said Hearst didn't want to start a new magazine, but might superimpose a new format on its existing *Cosmopolitan* which wasn't doing well at all. They had already begun thinking in terms of making it a magazine for a career woman and I sort of fell into their hands and they fell into mine. It was played very casually. They said, "Please go home and determine who some writers would be for these articles that you've thought up and how much they should cost." David and I went home. He knew some writers and we just sort of used our imagination about how much magazine articles were going for and tried to be as specific as possible. I was so happy to get the bloody thing off my desk and onto Mr. Deems's desk because I hoped he'd keep it a long time. I wasn't absolutely sure that I ought to be a magazine editor. (It's like telling you to go be an astronaut or a brain surgeon—something you simply had never done before. Although it was challenging you weren't sure [a] that you wanted to, or [b] that you could do it.)

But terribly soon he said he'd like to make a deal with me. Then we haggled for a while over money. David was staunch and steadfast throughout, being my agent-advisor with me every step of the way; I never had a meeting without him. The beautiful thing about David is that he doesn't live off me. It would probably be all right if he did, but that's not the way it worked out. What I have loved is that David is stronger than I, has a spectacular career of his own, and a second career in the family is a kind of bonbon for him and for me.

Helen recalls her early days at *Cosmo.* They were crazy, but let her tell what they were like. My version—different—comes later.

The night before I was to report for work at *Cosmo,* be introduced to the staff, etc., David and I were walking down Park Avenue after dinner and I was weeping up a storm—right on the street. Irving Wallace, a giant best-selling author, was with us and I wanted to *be* him. I had had considerable success with *Sex and the Single Girl,* not quite so much with *Sex and the Office,* but I had enjoyed every minute and wished, not secretly at *all,* I could go on being best selling, like our friend Irving, instead of being sent to be an indentured servant at a publishing house—publishing, and my specific assignment, editing, being two things I knew *nothing* about. I had only been *in* a magazine office once, when I was one of the winners of *Glamour*'s "Ten Girls With Taste" contest. The men were sweet and dried my tears—easy for *them*—they weren't being sent off to "slave labor." After all, it had been planned David would be in this *with* me—it was a team effort, our little prospectus for a new women's magazine that went to prospective buyers—we would be in it *together,* but between our creating it and selling it to Hearst to become the new *Cosmo,* David had defected—taken first a job with Paramount and, even as negotiations were going on, defected from *them* to return to Twentieth Century Fox. I was on my own. The night before my arrival at *Cosmo,* David said to think of it as just temporary—I could try it for a while and see how it worked out. I said I would do that but revised the script to think of myself as going off to *prison* for a year—in twelve months I could get sprung. What all this was about was not so much a denigration of publishing—which, as I said, I hadn't the foggiest idea about—but sheer naked *fear.* The next morning as I took off for work, I said, "Okay, David, just what do I *do* when I get there?" "Ask the managing editor to lunch," he said. I did that. The managing editor had a date, so somebody brought me a sandwich. That day I solemnly met the staff—wearing a pretty soft blue wool jersey dress with a ruffle at the hem and at the neck—shook hands, announced I didn't intend to fire a soul—and *didn't*—for a couple of years, though the managing editor—after keeping her lunch date—quit that very week! Several people said to each other—which got back to me—that surely I should have been brought in on a lesser level to *learn* something before being given the top spot. Editor-in-chief. Mercifully, I didn't have to deal with this surmised better way of doing things; to me, everybody was cordial (after all, this strange if unqualified person was their new *boss*) except maybe the lady who quit within two days. I replaced her with an editor who was scheduled to be fired by the man I replaced—are you still with me? He was about the only man in the place, edited articles as well as being the book reviewer, so I figured what the heck. He stayed managing editor for nine years although the mix of him and me wasn't wonderful—he a big political maven, staunch Catholic (I was still considered something of a scarlet woman), family man, not *too* beastly hard a worker, not *just* what I needed but then I had David. That first day I asked to see what was scheduled for future issues. Well, there *was* no formal schedule—nothing written down. April (with a wholesome-looking nurse on the cover) was already on the stands. May and June were pretty well organized, a lot of printing and engraving already done. I brilliantly decided to let "them"—the employees—keep the April and May issues fairly intact and not do anything with them. I couldn't make a real contribution anyway and besides, I needed to figure out how to *do* whatever it was I was supposed to do. I asked for the articles that might be available to go into issues *after* April and May. There weren't any and few were assigned. I went home that night, after dinner at either the Russian Tea Room or Longchamps on Madison Avenue—can't quite remember which—told David about my day; he said I seemed to be doing fine. We went to bed. I went to sleep but it didn't take. About four in the morning, David came and found me under my desk in the den. There was just room enough to get into a fetal position and I don't know exactly how long I had been there. Maybe hours. He brought me back to bed and for the first time, among many times in subsequent years (about three a year), told me this job wasn't the end of the world; that, of course, I could *do* it but if I didn't *want* to, I didn't *have* to—I could leave. (No *wonder* women don't make it to the top as often as we should—we have "options.")

During my first week at *Cosmo,* I made a few article assignments. That was rather heady. Passing out or at least promising big money—a thousand dollars, fifteen hundred for a major piece. Seems to me in retrospect really good writers were easier to *get* then—and the money seemed right to them. Nowadays . . . don't *ask*! I don't assign articles at all. The assigning is quite pleasant but getting fixed what comes *in*—I mean getting the writer to do it—is the pits. So, I assigned "How to Marry a Millionaire" with several case histories of young women who *had* to Doris Lilly (who had written a book of that title). And a piece on Elizabeth Taylor and Richard Burton to Liz Smith, who was already writing for *Cosmo.* Somebody sent me a book by Oscar Levant which was funny so we bought a chapter of that. An article scheduled for the May issue I grabbed for "my" (July) issue. It was the only decent thing in the house and though horribly written the subject was a dilly . . . the new estrogen pill. Several articles had been assigned for *giant* money by the previous editor that I felt could never work out for the "new *Cosmo*" and I had to take back the assignments. I don't remember whether we paid for them. Knowing me, I'll bet I tried *not* to—if the piece was not already begun. About the "pill" article, my reasoning was it couldn't help the "old" *Cosmo* too much, surrounded as it would be by the old format which wasn't working—remember *Cosmo* was about to go toes up which is why they let *me* have a go at it—so I might as well confiscate it for *me.* The three-thousand-dollar articles assigned were to writers the ex-editor liked and they seemed to me monumentally ill suited to a women's magazine.

So. We are clicking along and others are assigning, too. I managed to talk Rona Jaffe into letting us condense her new novel, *Mr. Right Is Dead,* and it was perfect for us—a major message to the reader of what the new magazine would be all about—girls who loved men and sometimes had problems with them. She also loved and loves her job but we have never hit as hard with those articles because they are not as interesting to read about. Rona Jaffe was a star at the time and I was thrilled by my acquisition. David had taken Rona out while he and I were dating, once suggesting I take a nap while he watched her on television—at least he could have asked me to watch *with* him—but I never let David's infatuation—or lack of it—for one of our writers get in the way. Well, that's not quite accurate. And let me get to the reason I'm writing this. Yes, I went to the office every day and gradually fell in love with editing—it seemed very nearly from the first week—after I got out from under the desk—that maybe this was what I was meant to do in life. *But,* I had so much to learn and was frequently *overwhelmed.* David made the commitment to read all our fiction for a while and *he* made the decisions on which short stories and what novels to buy and condense. Big help. He also read manuscripts—by the gross—and helped me determine whether to buy or abandon. A few times he would even meet me in the middle of the day, me clutching manuscripts in my arms; we would get in a taxi and ride around Central Park, while David said buy, or don't buy, get this one edited, abandon hope on this one. Those were the ones that had to be dealt with that *hour*; the rest I brought home. How long did this second-guessing go on? It still goes on but not so much in volume. I learned fairly quickly or maybe it isn't anything you can learn . . . you just *know* . . . what works and what doesn't and whether it maybe can be fixed or is totally hopeless. David put me into this world—this lovely new world I never really knew existed—and watched me flower. He answered 972 questions every day for possibly a year or two—maybe longer. Now the questions have as much to do with personal problems and budgets—not my strong suit—as they do with editing. Early in the game he read something I had edited—and I used to do it *all* myself—hundreds of thousands, it seems to me, of crossed-out words, phrases, sentences, and paragraphs and new ones written in, and David said I must put it back the way it was—that I had crushed the life out of the piece . . . yes, it was scrappy and messy but had a certain joie de vivre until *I* got hold of it. I put it back. David edits my personal column, "Step Into My Parlor," every month. Maybe some people require no editing at all but I don't know who they are. It is *very* handy being married to the editor because you can get him at breakfast.

Those early years at *Cosmo* seem magical because the bloody *sales* went up every month over the year before. I didn't seem even to have to *breathe* hard to make it happen. The world was ready for a magazine for "a woman who loves men," loves children, is traditional in many ways but doesn't want to live *through* her husband and children, wants to achieve on her own. I *do* remember the grief, too—the day we lost the nude photograph Burt Reynolds had personally selected for us to use in his famous centerfold and Burt thought I was lying and only *said* it was lost so I could use another, and one day in Chicago Hugh Hefner uninvited me to go to the mansion because he'd just read something unacceptable we'd said about bunnies and, gracious, the time when Richard Berlin, president of Hearst, read the *Cosmo* cover—my first—and said I'd have to kill my major blurb—"the pill that makes women more responsive to men." I argued until he hung up on me. David said ask if you can take off the last two words and he'll accept it. For some reason he did—the message seems to me the same. The feminists attacked me in 1970—Kate Millett came to the office and I was backed up against the radiator but it wasn't very hot. A new employee wrote a rotten novel with me as the heroine. I didn't read it. Listen, this doesn't describe the daily wash of office squabbles—not with me but two people squared off against each other—and office junk of all types—people *leaving* was a nightmare in the late sixties when jobs were so plentiful—we must have had two assistant (secretarial) jobs open a week, not to mention the editors. That's all over now. And David was there, enjoying it enormously, being totally, unqualifiedly, no-holds-barred, irrevocably and irretrievably helpful. He wrote the first set of cover blurbs and recently his three-hundredth set. I can't believe it *either.* He used to do them without reading the articles—just from the titles—but *occasionally* somebody couldn't figure out *what* article we were publishing that was supposed to correspond to the blurb (which always sounded sensational so that's why they bought the magazine) and in the last few years—on Saturday or Sunday, on airplanes or in hotel rooms or ships or trains, if necessary—he has read synopses and sometimes complete manuscripts of about twenty different subjects. He groans, moans, whines, and procrastinates and never doesn't *not* do it—and actually on time. He is without any question the best cover-blurb writer in the business.

This is my recollection of how *Cosmopolitan* under Helen came about, somewhat different from her version.

Sometime in 1964, I had a notion that a magazine could be created for women who wrote letters to Helen about her books and her newspaper columns, which were distributed by the *Los Angeles Times* Syndicate. It seemed to me that Helen was developing a constituency, if not a cult. The women who read her stuff felt they knew her personally. Why not a magazine for them? I thought.

Helen, her close friend Charlotte Kelly, and I discussed the idea one evening in our apartment. We decided it would have to appeal to single girls, somewhat alienated young married women who were tired of PTA meetings and women's service magazines, and others addicted to Helen's frank, feminist views. I suggested we all put down our ideas and keep a file of them. In our small dining room, Helen and I pasted up a primitive dummy of a magazine to be entitled *Femme,* for the independent woman. This was before the women's liberation movement really got under way.

In 1964, I left my job as executive vice-president of New American Library's hardcover book division. I was offered the editorship of the *Saturday Evening Post,* an executive post at Paramount Pictures, and looming just ahead was an invitation from Darryl and Richard Zanuck to return to Twentieth Century Fox which, owing to *The Sound of Music,* was now resuscitated after the closedown of the studio brought about by the megabudget debacle of *Cleopatra.*

Had the Fox offer not come along, I would have doubtless chosen to be publisher of *Cosmopolitan,* while Helen became editor. I don't think it would have worked. My job was clearly to launch Helen and not hang around.

Launching her meant I would first take our magazine dummy around town to try to sell it. Executives at McFadden-Bartell seemed quite interested but never returned my phone calls. I also called on George T. Delacorte, the venerable and immensely rich founder of the Dell Publishing Company. I had known him thirty years before when I was editor of *Liberty* magazine and George was proprietor of a company which published fan magazines. George then was not yet a revered figure. He outwitted the sheriff many times in the building of his publishing empire.

It was "George" and "David" in those years. We, our wives, and his beautiful daughters used to walk into Schrafft's and have sundaes and sodas after screenings on summer nights in New York. Flash forward to 1964. Mr. Delacorte, who was then worth several hundred million dollars, was taken aback when I addressed him as

George. He remonstrated, "You must never call me by my first name. My secretary may hear you." I was astonished that a man of his wealth and power would care. Ah, anyway, Mr. Delacorte declined to take on *Femme,* saying he could make far more money publishing books.

Jerry Mason of Mayco, a specialized publishing house in New York, also rejected *Femme.* The turning point in our fortunes came at Sardi's East, that very pleasant branch of the original Sardi's which no longer exists in New York. I had lunch there with my old friend Jack O'Connell, himself then between jobs. Jack and I were standing at the bar while waiting for Gino, the genial maître d', to find us a table. I asked what he had heard about the Hearst organization. Both of us had been editors there. Jack said, "They're desperate about *Cosmopolitan.* It looks as though they may fold it. But they're taking one more shot." "What's that?" I asked. Jack replied that they were going to take a kind of single woman, career woman, anti-PTA, anti-child-rearing approach. Make it clearly a women's magazine. I said nothing, but a light went on in my head. After lunch I phoned Bernard Geis, Helen's book publisher, and said, "Don't you know the president of Hearst Magazines, Richard Deems?" I had had a faint notion that Bernie and he were friends. Bernie confirmed my faint notion—resoundingly. "We were on *Esquire* together," he said. I outlined what I had in mind for Bernie to do. I wanted him to send over our dummy of *Femme* to Deems. Bernie put black professional covers on it, negotiated a modest finder's fee, and sent it over. Within hours, Bernie called and said, "You're to telephone Deems. He's very interested in *Femme* as a replacement for *Cosmopolitan.*"

The next night we were in Deems's apartment in the Waldorf Towers, negotiating a deal to make Helen Gurley Brown editor of the faltering *Cosmopolitan.* I think Helen was cowering in a corner somewhere. She had never edited a magazine. I don't think I had ever seen her read one. All we had was this primitive dummy.

They must have been pretty desperate because contracts were drawn, Helen was interviewed by Hearst publicity people for their press release, and the gamble was on.

Helen was ushered into the august presence of Richard Berlin, boss of the Hearst empire, who, upon hearing her name, said, "Well, as long as you're not Elizabeth Gurley Flynn" (alleged communist of the time). (Dick Berlin came to like Helen a lot, invited her to lunch over the years, and ultimately took credit for bringing her into the organization.)

Almost every afternoon after she first reported to work, Helen would call me frantically, saying, "Can you meet me in a taxi outside the Hearst building?" She complained that although she kept telling her staff she'd get back to them on important decisions, as I suggested, they now needed answers. We'd ride around Central Park in a taxi while I went over page proofs, cover blurbs, captions, article ideas, and read manuscripts hurriedly. My advice to Helen on her first day was to bring home as many articles and stories as she could stuff into her briefcase and envelopes, as well as the production schedule. I also suggested that she take the art director to lunch.

That's how Helen Gurley Brown's reign as editor of *Cosmopolitan* began. In the months and years that followed, she presided over one of the most stunning success stories in magazine history. With precious little help from me once she got rolling, I must add. After all, O'Connell and I—and our illustrious colleague Herbert R. Mayes—did much, years before, to put the magazine in the comatose state from which Helen resurrected it.

The Robert Evans Story

In 1964, Robert Evans was in New York after a brief career in Hollywood as an actor, determined to return to California as a producer. I was then based in New York at Twentieth Century Fox, working for Richard and Darryl F. Zanuck. Evans sent me a motion picture treatment titled *The Achilles Force,* which I rather liked and sent on to Dick who also thought it might have possibilities. He asked that I make a deal with Robert Evans to develop it.

Evans obtained the services of a world-class Hollywood agent named Kurt Frings, who also represented Elizabeth Taylor, Richard Burton, and other stars. Kurt was extremely witty, a fine but excitable agent. His first order to Robert Evans was, "Stay away from David Brown: He'll kill you; don't try to negotiate with him." At the same time, Evans was telling me he would do anything to get back to Hollywood. He assured me money was unimportant. When I reported this to Kurt Frings by telephone, he hung up. I engaged Bob directly, without Frings. Dick Zanuck asked, "Do we have to give him an office?" I said, "Of course we have to give him an office. He's not getting anything else." Evans then hired a former *New York Times* Hollywood correspondent to publicize him, and retained an editor of *Publishers Weekly,* who saw all forthcoming books in galley form, to advise him on story selection. He bought the film rights to a novel titled *The Detective* by Roderick Thorp.

Fox had turned the book down but Evans optioned it personally and persuaded Mark Robson to agree to direct. Burt Lancaster, Frank Sinatra, and Paul Newman all expressed interest in playing the title role. We quickly signed Evans to produce *The Detective.* After all this, Evans telephoned me at my office at the old Fox headquarters building on West Fifty-sixth Street in New York, and said, "I want to take a walk with you." We walked across Fifty-seventh Street almost to the East River when he astounded me with the news that he had an offer to become head of European production for Paramount and wanted to get out of his producing obligation to Fox. "I'd rather conduct an orchestra than play an instrument," he explained. "Producing is playing an instrument."

Richard Zanuck couldn't believe the news. "Let me understand you correctly," he exclaimed. "Did you say Robert Evans will be head of European production for Paramount Pictures?" I said, "That is correct, and the odd thing is I don't think Bob has ever been to Europe!" Dick was silent for a moment and then remarked, "He has. Once." Therein lies a tale of chicanery which Richard Zanuck to this day will not admit is true. Evans claims to have documentary evidence. Not quite enough, in Dick's view.

Robert Evans and his brother Charles once owned the successful Seventh Avenue garment firm Evan Picone and sold it to Revlon. Bob was restless and took off for Los Angeles with his share. At the pool of the Beverly Hills Hotel, Norma Shearer was astonished by Bob's resemblance to her late husband, the mythological mogul Irving Thalberg. Bob subsequently was cast in the role of Thalberg in a forgettable movie. Bob was not forgettable, however. His dark, lithe good looks caught the attention of Darryl F. Zanuck on the dance floor of El Morocco and Evans was offered the part of the bullfighter in Ernest Hemingway's *The Sun Also Rises* over everyone's objection, including Hemingway's. Zanuck's response was, "The kid stays." And so, Robert Evans, terrified of bulls, played the brave toreador. Through the artifice of movie magic, the bull and Evans were never in the ring at the same time.

So much for background. Now to the tale of chicanery. About the time Evans was still seeking work as an actor, Sam Spiegel was casting *Lawrence of Arabia,* to be directed by David Lean. Allegedly, Richard Zanuck, in the grand tradition of his father's elaborate hoaxes, arranged to have a cable sent to Evans, signed by Sam Spiegel and saying that he was definitely interested in his playing the title role and would he come to London immediately and bring wardrobe. Evans was overwhelmed, naturally; he and his agent, Kurt Frings, flew to London at their own expense, to find that

Spiegel was in Paris. Evans telephoned him and said, "Sam, I am here." Spiegel replied, "You are where?" Evans said, "I am in Europe, Sam. You told me to come." He then referred to the cable. "I sent no such cable," Spiegel snapped. By now it was dawning on Evans that he was the victim of a terrible prank. He vowed retribution. Somehow, he put things together and they spelled Richard Zanuck, but he could never prove that Dickie, as he called him, was the perpetrator. He called for an FBI investigation. Forging a cable was a federal offense. Bob still angrily displays the tattered "cable" when I visit him. It was typed on a Twentieth Century Fox teletype machine that some say has for many years lain at the bottom of Newport Bay in Newport Beach, California.

There was hardly a marriage more glamorous than that of handsome Bob Evans and smart, beautiful Ali MacGraw. Evans was then head of production for Paramount Studios and his star never shone more brightly than in 1972 at a party on the St. Regis Roof following the triumphant premiere of *The Godfather,* a film which he initiated. Surrounded by New York's most beautiful people, they seemed like a royal couple. But things change. Ali and Bob later divorced; they had produced a son, Joshua, who combines their good looks and smartness. Ali married Steve McQueen, to Bob Evans's distress.

When Bob and Ali broke up, his good friend and then-Secretary of State Henry Kissinger telephoned to offer his help. Bob said, "But she won't even talk to me, Henry." And Dr. Kissinger said, "Will you simply let me get the two of you together? Get you to talk to each other?" Bob said, "It's not possible, Henry." To which Kissinger replied, "It's not possible? I got Sadat to talk to Golda Meir, and you tell me I can't get Ali MacGraw to talk to you?" He couldn't.

McQueen and Ali did not stay married. He married again before he died. Bob married Phyllis George and they too were soon divorced. The years passed. Evans was planning a film titled *Players,* to be shot in England. Ali MacGraw was cast in a starring role and Anthony Harvey was to be the director. Ali and Evans stopped over in New York. Bob called and asked to see Helen and me at our apartment just across Central Park from the Carlyle Hotel, where he and Ali were staying—in separate rooms, he informed us. Bob wanted Helen to persuade Ali to remarry him and provided Helen with every conceivable reason Ali ought to return to him. When Ali arrived, Bob and I walked down Columbus Avenue to an Irish bar. Bob talked only about how vital it was for Ali to come back to him. I listened. I've known Bob a long time. I asked, "Robert, if Helen is successful in convincing Ali to come back to you, can you be faithful to her?" Evans thought only for a moment before replying, "No. Of course not." The occasion for infidelity never arose. Helen's pitch was unavailing. Evans and MacGraw stayed apart, although good friends, as they say in Hollywood.

Evans was a throwback to the moguls of old, conducting meetings in his elegant two-acre Beverly Hills home and rarely venturing beyond its manicured, green borders. Ever since he played Irving Thalberg in a movie, he has played it in real life. No other man I've known, including Selznick and Zanuck, has been so consumed with the legend of Hollywood and insulated from the world outside—until his recent troubles connected with the untidy financing of his *Cotton Club* film. I have never heard Bob answer his own telephone, whatever the hour or state of his finances. He will survive his difficulties if his courage and determination hold out. After all, he is only one hit away from salvation, according to his credo. As I write this, he is working on it, producing *The Two Jakes,* starring Jack Nicholson.

Big Shots

The social life of old Hollywood was an odd mixture of crass and class, and sometimes the underworld. Ben "Bugsy" Siegel was a ranking gangster of his time. He is credited with having created Las Vegas. He was sent out by the Eastern mob to run the Western territory. A good-looking man, he had ambitions to become an actor and at the very least to be part of the Hollywood establishment. On one evening at Romanoff's, he met Mrs. Darryl F. Zanuck. Mrs. Zanuck was, if anything, direct, and said to Mr. Siegel, "I understand you and your cronies kill people." To which Mr. Siegel, by way of defense, replied, "But Mrs. Zanuck, we only kill each other."

Mike Romanoff, old Hollywood's most famous restaurateur and raconteur, is long dead. The last time I saw him was at the Beverly Hills Hotel, where I was having lunch with Bob Evans. Mike and I chatted for a while. We'd been friends for thirty years and planned to meet later on in Europe. He promised to telephone me in New York to give me his itinerary. I did not receive the call because Mike died a few hours later in a bookstore in Beverly Hills while I was en route to New York.

Michael Romanoff was the only American I knew whose citizenship was conferred by an act of Congress. I bought the film rights to his life many years ago, to be based on a *New Yorker* profile by Alva Johnson. The film was never made. One of my favorite stories about Mike is this one. The locale: Romanoff's restaurant in Beverly Hills. The situation: a live, true Romanoff is dining in the restaurant. The crisis: what will "Prince" Michael Romanoff, né Harry Gerguson of Brooklyn, say to the real Romanoff by way of greeting? A real Romanoff, a prince of Imperial Russia, began speaking in Russian when Mike approached his table. There was only a moment's hesitation before Mike disposed of the language barrier. "Please," he remonstrated, "I cannot bear the sound of the mother tongue after all that's happened. That is why I must speak in English always. I beg you to forgive me." The real prince was not amused, but remained polite. Although his Russian was shaky, Mike had an extraordinary command of the English language. His knowledge of literature was remarkable and in his later years he sent all kinds of scholarly books my way. He was, in fact, a literary advisor to my own story department at Twentieth Century Fox studios for many years. He could be depended upon for wise and lively comment on almost any subject. His restaurant ultimately failed because he was too much of a snob. He would seat his amusing chums—even when they could not pay their bills—at better tables than the president of Standard Oil. He turned away prospective guests he did not like, even though the restaurant was half empty. He ran the restaurant as he ran his life—whimsically and to his own idiosyncratic taste. He is said to have been eighty-seven when he died—some say he was older—leaving his beloved Gloria behind and a host of friends who included Frank Sinatra, Richard Zanuck, Irving Lazar, and John O'Hara, any of whom would and did do anything for the love of Mike.

In Romanoff's on any decent evening, you could see Humphrey Bogart, Darryl F. Zanuck, David O. Selznick, Jack Warner, Sam Goldwyn, their glamorous ladies, and scores of other luminaries of the time. The food was good, the service excellent, and Mike was a great host. Kurt Niklas, his maître d', is now the proprietor of Beverly Hills' fashionable Bistro Gardens and Bistro restaurants.

It was in Romanoff's that Darryl F. Zanuck bought the film rights to Cole Porter's *Can Can* from Cole's agent, once again Irving "Swifty" Paul Lazar, and the next day could not recall having purchased them. When Lazar claimed that Zanuck had bought them for $750,000, Darryl asked me to call Mike Romanoff and verify the transaction. Mike reported, "Indeed, Darryl did buy the film rights to *Can Can* and for seven hundred and fifty thousand dollars. I was present at his table when he made the deal." And so, characteristic of Zanuck, the deal was honored and, in fact, the picture was made.

It was also at Romanoff's that another "Swifty"—Swifty Morgan, the legendary gem thief—approached FBI director J. Edgar Hoover and offered to sell him a bracelet for his fiancée. Hoover was thinking of getting married, an event which did not occur. Hoover said, after examining the bracelet which Swifty carried in a handkerchief, "I'll give you five hundred dollars for this." Swifty recoiled in pain, exclaiming, to the nation's chief law-enforcement official, "Five hundred? Why, John, there's a five-*thousand*-dollar reward for this!"

Romanoff's was one of the truly glamorous places of the world, described by its proprietor as "personifying Hollywood." He also said of it, "Here the phony tinsel is stripped away and you can see the real tinsel."

When Helen and I saw Richard Nixon in San Clemente at Casa Pacifica, his Western White House, in 1972, he was relaxed as he entertained Hollywood's high and mighty. Henry Kissinger was there with Jill St. John. Frank Sinatra strolled in. So did John Wayne and the rest of filmdom's conservative clique. There the Nixons were, the helicopters whirring on the lawn, they reveling in the trappings of power. Richard Nixon told the assembled movie moguls, "The real reason I'm running is to have the use of the projection room for another four years," adding, "If I had ever told my old man that someday I'd be shaking Jack Benny's hand, he would have thought me crazy."

On that day Nixon enjoyed his presidency. He was proud of having overcome his crises and become the biggest political success story of his time. In less than ten years, he had gone from the ignominy of being defeated in 1962 by Pat Brown for governor of his native California to his landslide election to the presidency of the United States in 1968. Only six years later, he suffered defeat (and disgrace) as the only president to have resigned from office on threat of impeachment. An incredible roller-coaster career. Neither Wall Street nor labor wanted to see him become president. He was regarded as a loser. He did not go to the best law school and was not part of the Eastern or any other establishment. He did not have the good looks of JFK, the patrician presence of FDR, or the salty, homely look of Harry Truman. Only Jimmy Carter and Jerry Ford were less impressive. But on that day we saw him, the power of the office was clearly with him. He was president of the United States. He could do anything. Or so he thought then.

Doomed statesmen are fascinating in their final days. Columnist Walter Winchell once said, "Dictators look good until their last five minutes." I had met Ferdinand Marcos twice, once on a visit to the Philippines in 1980 and again at the Manila Film Festival in 1983. It was on the latter occasion that I got to know him. Mrs. Marcos had a crush on Helen, or so it seemed. On our arrival in Manila, after a gruesome twenty-four-hour flight, we were rushed through Customs—no declaration necessary—and taken to the Malacanang Palace. There, high above the grand rooms for state occasions, we found ourselves in an elaborate art-deco disco, complete with flashing multicolored lights and a live band. Mrs. Marcos was dancing frenetically with George Hamilton. The president, we were told, never ventured there and was asleep in his room. Mrs. Marcos grasped Helen and swung her around the room. I tried to keep my eyes open. "Why did you report in *Cosmopolitan,"* she asked Helen, "that I was the richest woman in the world next to the queen of England?" "Because it's so," Helen answered, to Imelda's apparent delight.

We became prisoners of the palace, invited every night to dinner and unable to make outside social engagements. One night friends gave a dinner in our honor and we were obliged to break our date at the palace. It was then that the president requested a meeting. Alone except for film distributor Arthur Cohn, we listened while Marcos recounted his exploits in World War II. He was responsive to questions, always insisting that he was America's bulwark against the communist hordes of Asia. Behind the curtains I noticed two men with automatic rifles, on the ready to cut us down if we made an untoward move at Marcos. It reminded me of a tableau of statues I had seen in Japan, the shogun's guards with drawn swords behind a door as he sat entertaining visitors. We were guarded too. A young security man never left our sides from the moment we entered the country until we departed. Not until we boarded our flight for Hong Kong did our guard drop his guard. In bidding us good-bye, he said he was a computer expert and hoped to come to the United States.

Robert Kennedy was a somewhat feared young man before he became a liberal hero. When I was head of the hardcover division of New American Library, I commissioned a book on the Kennedys based on an article by Richard Whalen which originally appeared in *Fortune.* We paid Whalen a substantial advance to write that book, and during its writing, John Kennedy was assassinated. For a while it looked as though the book project might be canceled, but with the help of Victor Weybright, one of the founders of New American Library, there was sufficient support to continue this project.

Bobby Kennedy was known as a hothead. He had awakened steel executives at three o'clock in the morning when they were accused of price-fixing, and threatened to turn the FBI on almost anybody who got in his way. Whalen was worried about reprisals from the Kennedys. While his book was not a hatchet job, Joe Kennedy, the Founding Father (the title of the book), was not a beloved figure. He was accused of having Nazi sympathies when he was ambassador to Great Britain. All in all, the Kennedys were feared more than revered at one time. Therefore, when Whalen called me one night quite agitated, and reported that there had been strange interviews with his neighbors, and men with flashlights were poking around his grounds, we figured, Aha! Bobby has put the FBI on us. The next thing we know, our income tax returns will be audited. Whalen, a man with little fear but with a wife and a small family, did not like the idea that he might be a target for big government. He wasn't. New American Library had given Whalen an advance so substantial that it had taken out a life insurance policy on him. Our insurance agents were the ones who were making these inquiries and scaring the hell out of Dick Whalen. Apologies to the Kennedys.

Frank Costello, mob chieftain of the speakeasy era, lived well into the 1960s. In my early years at *Cosmopolitan,* I wanted to interview Costello, and asked his lawyer (and my uncle), George Wolf, to arrange for me to meet Costello at his home in the Majestic Apartments at Seventy-second Street and Central Park West in New York City. I sat in his dining room with him; his wife, Bobby, attractive, plump, of the Las Vegas school of beauty; and several unidentified cronies. I asked if he'd ever been to Las Vegas. "No," he croaked. "I've never been to Las Vegas." I asked how he felt about being under constant surveillance. "I don't mind," he said. "When I pick up the telephone, I say hello to the FBI because I know they're listening." I was unable to persuade him to be more forthcoming. He did tell me that someone just out of prison had threatened to kidnap him and hold him for ransom. The man was invited to meet

Wolf in his office. "My dear fellow," Wolf said (he was a rather formal man), "do you realize that if you attempt to snatch Mr. Costello [the idea was to take him on his morning stroll through Central Park], you will be seized by agents of the FBI, the Treasury Department, the Narcotics Squad, the New York Police Department, and local representatives of the Interpol? He has more agents of law enforcement organizations tailing him on any given day than the president of the United States." Notwithstanding this, someone took a shot at Costello in the lobby of the Majestic and missed. The bullet hole is still somewhere beneath the glitz of the lobby but all traces of Frank Costello, mobster, are gone.

I might be gone too if Costello or my uncle, at the time he was representing the mobster, had known that I was a close friend of Estes Kefauver, chairman of the Senate committee investigating Costello and organized crime. In fact, I was the senator's "beard" on one occasion when he was dining with a lady who was not his wife. Nothing serious but it might easily have been misunderstood. Senator Kefauver would likewise have been shaken if he knew of my family association with the mob; "the boys," as the Mafia was known, would have liked nothing better than to have something on their inquisitor. Fortunately for them and for me, I "ratted" on neither of them.

I've admired Rupert Murdoch for almost all the years he's resided in the United States. When I first met him, he was proprietor of the *New York Post, New York* magazine, and the *Village Voice,* in addition to his overseas holdings. They were large, but not nearly so vast as they are today. Murdoch is highly educated, an Oxonian. His wife, the beauteous and bright Anna Murdoch, a former journalist, is now a novelist, wife, mother, and citizen of the world. Murdoch has been characterized as an authentic tycoon. There are not many of those around. Lots of game players and arbitrageurs and company buyers and sellers, but not many tycoons. Henry Luce, founder of *Time,* whose publication popularized the word, was one. To the manor born. Murdoch is also a hands-on operator, particularly with the printed word. He can still write a headline or a news story. He is also an instinctive, clever gambler. When he is clearly wrong, he cuts his losses fast. Murdoch does not believe in committees or bureaucratic layers of management. He believes in decision-making. He makes his decision and validates it later. When he decided to buy the three-billion-dollar Triangle Publishing empire of Walter Annenberg, he decided it instinctively and found the means of financing later. I saw him at John Kluge's vast estate in Charlottesville, Virginia, after he had acquired Kluge's television stations. I wondered why Kluge, another brilliant businessman and also a hands-on operator, would sell and Murdoch would buy. Kluge is known to buy wholesale and sell retail. My feeling is that they were both right for their time. Murdoch is seventeen years younger than Kluge.

Murdoch manages his global empire with a show of breathtaking synergy. He once gathered his chief editors, managers, and key personnel in Aspen to talk over the business. He mixed in the editor of *The Times* of London with Twentieth Century Fox chief Barry Diller, and *New York* magazine's Ed Kosner with the chief editorial writer of the *South China Post.*

Notwithstanding the fact that some of Murdoch's newspaper properties are among the most sensational in the world, such as London's *Sun* with its bare-breasted page-three girls and his equally raunchy *News of the World,* Murdoch is Victorian in his personal tastes. He is said by a friend to have been uncomfortable with his acquisition of the *Village Voice,* the carping, somewhat-to-the-left weekly newspaper in New York City. The *Voice* had no hesitation in beating its owner's brains out in print.

Reportedly what upset him was something else. Shortly after he acquired the publication, he was asked to attend an editorial meeting. Murdoch in his conservative English tailored clothes was appalled to see several bare-breasted women staff members nursing their babies during the meeting. The fastidious Murdoch was more offended by that than by the *Voice*'s political views and critical yammering. Bare breasts, Murdoch may have felt, are more appropriately seen on page three of his *London Sun* than in at an editorial meeting.

Power Failure

Siberia is not only part of the Soviet Union, but also of Hollywood. It is that bleak backwater to which disgraced or fallen executives are consigned, there to work out their contracts without duties or telephone calls. Mail, what little there is, is flung at the door outside. In my year (one of my many) of Siberian exile at Twentieth Century Fox in 1963, I was buoyed up by a pretty secretary named Golda who claimed to have a pipeline to the inner councils of the company. "Oh, Mr. Brown," she would tell me, when my fortunes were at their lowest, "I know there's a plan to make you president.

It won't happen for a month or two but it's all set to take place. I can't tell you the source of my information." And on and on. Delightful, dear Golda. I couldn't wait to get in each morning to hear another cheerful bulletin. She kept me going on those grim business days. Golda left the company shortly after I did, but perhaps she is encouraging some other depressed executive.

A high-ranking officer in a corporation can be stripped within hours of his powers and perks. It has happened to me. Being out. A nonperson. You realize you own nothing but your skin. That office and company you ran like a monarch are gone from you. You can no longer press a button and get anything you want. Suddenly even your mail is undelivered. Your files and expense accounts are seized and scrutinized for the least sign of irregularity. You are denied access to the premises that were your office home. The idea is to get you out quickly, if possible on the same day.

Had I decided to go to the men's room on one occasion, my future executioner, Dennis Stanfill, might not have become head of Twentieth Century Fox Film Corporation. He was with the Times Mirror Corporation of Los Angeles when Dick Zanuck and I heard about him in 1968 from Michael Thomas of Lehman Brothers, our investment bankers. Stanfill was said to be a good "no" man. Just the kind of person we needed to keep us from overspending. Things had begun to unravel financially at Fox—we had had some costly flops. Prior to the interview with Stanfill, Dick said, "If you have any doubts about this man, excuse yourself and go to the men's room. That will be my signal not to hire him." I was impressed, held my water, and Stanfill eventually became chairman and CEO of Fox and not only presided over Dick's and my forced departure from that company but also the ouster of Darryl Zanuck not long thereafter. Had I succumbed to an urge to urinate, Stanfill might never have had the chance, and some of us might still be there.

Unfortunately, Stanfill did have the chance. He called it "the ritual of severance," the ceremony by which Dick and I were fired from Twentieth Century Fox, I for the second time. (The first occurred in 1963 when Darryl Zanuck returned to power and closed down the studio.) The ritual began in New York on the afternoon of December 29, 1970. Reporters were waiting in the lobby of the Fox building to photograph our grim faces. Secretaries pressed their ears to the boardroom wall to hear our anguished voices.

Rumors about us had been rampant, to coin a cliché. When I walked into the meeting, my first instinct was to count the number of directors present. Both Dick and I were directors, but many board members had stayed away. There was the barest quorum. I made a quick calculation to see if by absenting ourselves from the board proceedings, we could delay our departure for another month. But no, there was a quorum.

No time was wasted. We were asked to resign forthwith from the board and our positions as president and executive vice-president. Like criminals, we were allowed to place one telephone call—to our lawyer. He said get it over with—resign. Darryl Zanuck wanted us out because he believed we were a threat to his power. We were—because of our concern over his diminishing ability to run the company. Darryl Zanuck got his comeuppance less than a year later. He had put his girlfriend in an expensive failed movie—"a five-million-dollar screen test," an unfriendly columnist called it. DFZ left his office a beaten, unwell man.

In those days, the board met at the old Twentieth Century Fox headquarters at 444 West Fifty-sixth Street, New York—in the heart of a then rapidly deteriorating area known as Hell's Kitchen. It was a dangerous area with a high crime rate. Secretaries didn't want to walk there alone because of the many murders, muggings, and rapes that took place. I never experienced any danger on the street to compare with the treachery, betrayal, and character assassination that took place within that walnut-paneled boardroom. The rapidity with which one can be reduced to corporate nothingness is amazing and frightening.

Since then, I keep nothing in an office that I can't carry out under my arm. No personal files. I have only company-owned property from the "company store." The ritual of severance is identical in broadcasting, government, politics, and every other hierarchical field of endeavor. Those who one day have the power and glory are the next day without title, authority, or identity. It is a harrowing experience. I have learned from it the fallacy of ever assuming that something is yours that you don't clearly own.

The day Zanuck and I were fired had its comic overtones. I thought of another day, years before, when we had entered Fox's New York headquarters building in triumph. We now made our exit through the bowels of the adjoining DeLuxe Laboratory to avoid the waiting press; we quickly entered a hearselike limousine to speed us to the airport for our flight to Los Angeles. We were in a state of mad, inexplicable hilarity during that flight on the evening of December 29, 1970. Our wives met us in Los Angeles. I said to mine, "What would happen if we were a defeated soccer team returning in this condition?" Dick interrupted, "We'd have the shit beaten out of us." We continued in a state of hysterical laughter to the consternation and befuddlement of our mates.

When we reported to our offices the next day, December 30, 1970, Dick and I were still technically in power. Our resignations were to take effect at midnight on December 31, 1970. We were informed by the chief financial officer (whom we had previously hired) that we would have to be out of our offices that night, the night before New Year's Eve. We were told to clean out our personal effects. Our credit cards were taken from us. Only our secretaries were permitted to remain, for thirty days. Our names were erased from our permanent parking spots before our eyes. The cops who had greeted us for so many years were instructed to deny us admittance to the studio lot. "Treat them with courtesy," a memorandum advised, "but they must not be permitted on the lot without an appointment" (to be approved by the same Mr. Stanfill we brought into the company).

That holiday weekend of our corporate execution, Zanuck and I went to Palm Springs with our wives. We made a last-minute reservation to spend New Year's Eve at an "in" restaurant, Don the Beachcomber's. "Look at the table they're giving us," Dick complained. "It's the worst table." I reminded him that we had just called and it was New Year's Eve. "It's chaos here," I pointed out. "The owner of the restaurant is carrying dishes. He can't even get the busboy's attention." Dick was convinced that we were being ignored because we were no longer studio heads. "Wrong," I said, "nothing to do with it." "Oh yes it has," he wailed. "This is Hollywood, and phone calls were made." I now think he may have been right.

We became obsessed with the injustice of the situation. Denied even the savings we had entrusted to the company in the form of salary deferments, we were out of the money, off the payroll, off the perks, excommunicated.

On one dark day, I received an anonymous telephone call from a man who seemed to know everything that was going on behind the closed doors—that is, doors closed to us—of Twentieth Century Fox. He said he had access to the minutes of the board of directors' meetings revealing what they intended to do about our employment contracts. Amazingly, he proved his reliability by sending us copies of the minutes. Dealing with this man was one of the weirdest experiences of my corporate life. Dick Zanuck dubbed him Mr. Minutes. We received calls at various times and places—California,

New York, Paris—from this informer, the Deep Throat of Twentieth Century Fox. His tidbits were actually a welcome diversion. Mr. Minutes revealed who our enemies were, who was standing up for us at board meetings, what was happening to the film projects we left behind, and what arguments the company would put forth in response to our lawsuit charging breach of our contracts. All this came in the form of Xerox copies of confidential memos and reports, which we, of course, forwarded to our lawyers. World War II might have been won in a week if the Allies had had Mr. Minutes in the chancellery in Berlin.

Our curiosity as to Mr. Minutes's identity grew. His voice was not one we recognized. His manner was formal, courtly, even stuffy. We took him to be an older man. When Richard Zanuck's eleven-year-old daughter, Ginny, heard of these shenanigans, she said, "Dad, do you guys really believe all of this stuff?"

Finally came the day when we would meet him—at the Carlyle Hotel in New York in Dick's suite. He was indeed dour, older, nondescript. He was also boastful. He said he was an owner of La Côte Basque restaurant—one of the grand luxe restaurants of New York—and invited us to dine there. "Us" included Dick's then wife, Linda Harrison, and me. My wife declined the invitation. She agreed with Ginny Zanuck that it was crazy to have anything to do with him. We wanted to play the game. On arrival at La Côte Basque, Mr. Minutes was not greeted as a proprietor, but was escorted to a table so remote from the main building area that it appeared to be on East Fifty-sixth Street, although the restaurant is on East Fifty-fifth Street

Mr. Minutes regaled us with more corporate tidbits, but did not pay the bill, believing no doubt that he had sung for his supper. He seemed particularly focused on Richard Zanuck and took a fatherly interest in him. He called him Richard in a sonorous voice. Up to this point, he seemed to be a man determined only to fight corporate injustice and put our world back together with no wish for self-aggrandizement.

Alas, life is not like that. There is no Sanity Claus. Ginny Zanuck and Helen Brown were right. Mr. Minutes wanted to make a movie. He had, in fact, fashioned a script for us to consider and also had an idea for a television series. By God, his means of getting into our good graces was to try to frighten the management of Twentieth Century Fox into making a generous settlement of our contracts in exchange for our approval of his movie and television projects. He also wanted a portion of our settlement. It was not easy to extricate ourselves from Mr. Minutes. We didn't want to offend him, especially when he revealed the .45-caliber automatic he was carrying. A delaying tactic seemed advisable. We told him we would have to think about his proposal and delicately tiptoed out of his life.

His calls ceased as mysteriously as they began after our settlement with Fox. The Securities and Exchange Commission would also like to know who he was and what happened to him, as he had evidently supplied highly confidential documents to dissident shareholders who were threatening a proxy fight. Perhaps he died or found a more generous ex-executive. Neither we nor the SEC ever did find out what he did at Fox to enable him to pry loose confidential corporate documents. In SEC files, he is referred to as "The Fly."

Notice must be taken of a lawyer named Abraham Pomerantz in connection with our Twentieth Century Fox settlement. Abe was a gadfly of large corporations, a distinguished New York lawyer, now sadly gone. When Dick Zanuck and I were about to fly back to New York to face the music in the Twentieth Century Fox boardroom, I picked up a copy of *Fortune* magazine in the American Airlines Admiral's Club. An article related how Abe Pomerantz had won a huge settlement from the giant American Telephone and Telegraph Company, and was usually able to cut large corporations down to size when they tried to inflict injustice on their managers. Obviously, he was our man. I called Abe Pomerantz from the airport. We made a date. There was a bottle of bourbon on the desk of his Manhattan office. His hair was gray and slicked straight back. We told him our story with intonations of rage and self-pity. He listened carefully and, without sentiment or pomposity, said simply, "Let's face it, they kicked you out. They'll claim you did a bum job. You do have contracts, and I'm going to try to get your money for you. It's no use appealing to their sense of justice. They're bastards." He took us to lunch at the Democratic Club. More bourbon. He sympathized with us but not in a mawkish way. He called Otto Koegel, the crusty outside counsel of Twentieth Century Fox and a member of the distinguished law firm of Koegel, Rogers, and Wells. Otto knew Abe Pomerantz. Everybody knew Abe. They respected each other and were veteran street fighters. Abe was a litigator, at best in the courtroom. The threat of his prowess in court won settlements for him. However, in this instance, Abe couldn't scare Twentieth Century Fox into settling our contracts. Fox was adamant. Fox was intransigent. It was run largely by an outside board of directors who wanted to protect their skins against stockholder suits if they gave away too much, and the whole situation took a nasty turn. To complicate matters further, the salary deferments Fox was withholding from us were now also blocked by a Delaware chancery court because of stockholder suits against the directors and former directors of the corporation. We were former directors. Even if Fox agreed to liberate our deferments, Delaware wouldn't let it. Abe spent months on our case, did a lot of hand holding, tried his best to frighten Fox into a settlement. When it became clear that we would have to bring the case to court, he told us that in his judgment, the lawsuit had best be commenced in California, where courts were more sensitive to employees' rights. He said that it would be better to get a hometown boy to try it out there. Furthermore, he was getting old, and he didn't think that several months' trial would be in the best interests of his health. He gave our entire retainer back, refusing to take a penny for the time he spent on the case. And he introduced us to a lawyer named Harold D. Berkowitz, who later became Zanuck/Brown's lawyer during its glory days. Berkowitz was then with the firm of Kaplan, Livingston, Berkowitz and Selwyn. The firm had an unpleasant connotation for me. It had represented my first wife in a bitter property dispute and won. Oh well, I thought, perhaps it was my turn to win. It was. Berkowitz negotiated a substantial settlement of our employment contracts from Twentieth Century Fox and we went on to earn historic amounts of money as producers, with Berkowitz as our lawyer. Had we won an Academy Award for *Jaws* or *The Verdict,* both of which were nominated as Best Picture, we would have thanked the board of directors of Twentieth Century Fox for making the award possible. We would never have made these films had they not fired us.

The three movies that did us in at Fox were *Portnoy's Complaint, Beyond the Valley of the Dolls,* and *Myra Breckinridge.*

Portnoy's Complaint, Philip Roth's homage to self-abuse, was bought but never made by Fox. It was derailed in the boardroom when Darryl F. Zanuck, in his quest for damning evidence of our cupidity, extracted every prurient word from the script and intoned them to his God-fearing, aging fellow board members.

After such unendearing phrases as "motherfucker," "cocksucker," "shithead," "blow job," and others not commonly heard in walnut-paneled rooms, the Fox directors clapped their hands to their ears and wondered how the hell they could get off the board . . . or get us off. Our disgrace was compounded by *Beyond the*

Valley of the Dolls, the raunchy film written by Pulitzer Prize-winner and now television star Roger Ebert, and, finally, Gore Vidal's far-out sex comedy *Myra Breckinridge.*

Portnoy's Complaint followed Zanuck/Brown to Warner Brothers, where it was adapted for the screen and directed by Ernest Lehman. Poor Warner Brothers. The picture failed. *Beyond the Valley of the Dolls* was directed by Russ Meyer, the soft-porn king I found in the pages of the *Wall Street Journal,* which extolled him as a moneymaker. The movie made money but lost most of it later in a lawsuit won by Jacqueline Susann, who claimed it was an unlawful sequel. A jury of Pasadena's elderly church ladies agreed it was not only unlawful but awful.

Myra Breckinridge was amusing in the making but apparently not so on the screen. A discussion of the script at New York's Plaza Hotel turned into a shambles. Attended by writer-director (and pop singer) Michael Sarne, producer Robert Fryer, author Gore Vidal, Zanuck and me, it broke up in disarray when Vidal excoriated us for approving the script. Fryer excused himself while the argument raged around him. Vidal left shortly, shouting, "I am convinced by what I have read that the next thing I will hear is that Fox is in receivership!" As he went out of the room, he stumbled over Fryer, who was lying in the hallway, quietly sobbing. Or was he laughing?

Vidal was not too far wrong. Fox almost did go bankrupt. Critics assailed the movie. The film failed at the box office. Zanuck and I were the only ones to laugh during the preview. Even our wives were silent. I still thought it was funny. Years later, I brought a print of the film down to the West Indian island of Antigua, where we were shooting *The Island.* As entertainment-starved as our crew was, once again I was left alone with the projectionist when the lights came up, just as I had been when we first showed *Myra Breckinridge.*

During production, film critic Rex Reed, who played *Myron* Breckinridge (Myra after the sex-change operation), was required to exclaim, "Where are my tits?" as he woke up after surgery. Reed declined to say these words until I threatened to use someone else's voice to mimic his and have the offending words reverberate throughout the hospital corridors. Rex Reed never gave a Zanuck/Brown picture a decent review again.

Myra Breckinridge was not Robert Fryer's only traumatic experience in Hollywood. He was brought there by Richard Zanuck and me after a successful career as a Broadway producer. Helen Strauss, a wonderful agent and friend, persuaded us to buy the film rights to *The Boston Strangler* for Fryer to produce as a movie. The author of the best-selling book, Gerold Frank, provided a legal clearance from the strangler, giving us the needed permission to portray him on the screen. Trouble was that after the movie was completed at a cost of several million dollars, the courts declared the strangler legally insane and therefore incompetent to give permission to anyone. Another problem was that the strangler had never been convicted. It was worrisome for Fryer and us but fortunately nobody came to the strangler's defense and our right to make the film was not challenged.

The biggest mistake in business is to think you're beloved or should be. Except for a very few friends, you will find no feeling for you when you are shorn of your power. Dead executives are almost instantly forgotten by their corporate families. When Twentieth Century Fox studio head Buddy Adler died and the power passed, I went to his funeral at Forest Lawn in Glendale. I was asked to choose whose car I would ride in. I chose to go with producer Jerry Wald, whose office was near mine. An executive told me, "You know, I don't think it's wise going out there with Jerry because he's a contender and he's not going to get the job."

Part of the separation process of high-ranking persons such as the Zanucks of Twentieth Century Fox has to do with removing all vestiges of their reign until their names are history, and no threat to the present rulers. In the Twentieth Century Fox commissary there is a mural of Darryl F. Zanuck as a young man. Only the possibility of an outcry from film historians prevented the painting-over of this artifact. After the elder Zanuck's death, however, when there was no threat of his return, one of the large projection rooms was named the Zanuck Theater. Fox was never removed from the corporate logo—in fact, the parent company was renamed Fox, Inc.—because founder William Fox has been dead too long to matter. If the name had been Twentieth Century Zanuck, Zanuck's name might have come off. When Louis B. Mayer became persona non grata at the company he founded, the corporate name was eventually contracted from Metro-Goldwyn-Mayer to MGM. It has since been restored to provide some much-needed luster to the current shell of a company. Goldwyn's name was never at issue. He left too early.

Fear is the currency of executive life. The more money and

perks, the more fear of losing them. I've seen executives reduced to pitiful stooges when threatened with the loss of a job. The exceptions are those who have independent means and even they run scared because of their fear of loss of status. In a memorable book on the advertising business, *From Those Wonderful Folks Who Gave You Pearl Harbor,* by Jerry Della Femina, there is an account of an executive who was petrified by the prospect of losing a client, although he was a much-decorated hero who had shot down fifteen German planes during World War II. How can anyone who has been through all that be upset by what happens on Madison Avenue? Crazy priorities, that's how.

Failure is always at your heels. There is no way to avoid it. No life is failure-free. It is unjust, dramatic, and brings out your best and worst. It's terrifying. It unsettles you. It disorients you. It puts you into deep depression. It is a form of death. Whenever I have had a failure, I go into mourning.

That means you wake up mornings and for a second or two everything is serene until—flash, bang!—it hits you: your movie that's a disaster, your book that isn't selling, your job that you are out of. But before you are really awake, you are still in that blissful period of not knowing what has happened to you until you wake up to the dreadful, sour taste of failure.

One of my good friends, who was let go by a television network after thirty years in high positions, had lunch with me the day after he got the dread word. He regarded me as an expert in failure because I had been fired a number of times. He said, "David, I don't know how to look for a job. What do I do? I mean, I've read that suddenly you are in a phone booth with a handful of coins telephoning people to have lunch with you."

I tried to describe what he would soon discover, what it was like to be unemployed, not to have an office or a secretary: He was cushioned temporarily by having been given a secretary and car for a few months, but he would find out that from the moment you are fired, there is a gap between you and your former associates that widens like the one between a departing ship and a pier. You are left on the pier waving good-bye until the ship is out of sight. You are progressively out-of-date. When you are gone as little as two weeks, the information that came across your desk is no longer available to you and the old job indeed is like a ship going out to sea and you aren't on it. Learning to deal with failure is, most of all, experiencing paralyzing loneliness, no matter how supportive your family is. You feel you have failed them, too. You look at the people going to work in the buses, the subways, and the taxis and wonder why you are not one of them. It's hard to imagine you ever will be again.

After losing multiple jobs, I decided never again to be in the position of having someone walk up and down in another office, saying, "What are we going to do about Brown? He's been here twenty years. He can't go on forever and it's too early to retire him." When it happens, you tell yourself that they fired the wrong person and kept the wrong person. You are probably right about that, but soon you will believe the worst about yourself. There are other failures that sear the soul, but job failure is the worst because your office occupies so much of your life. It is a sanctuary during deaths, divorces, and other personal disasters. It is a place that is always clean, where relationships are usually orderly, people are polite, and civility rules. You can depend on an office. I went to my office the way nineteenth-century gentlemen went to their clubs after domestic disputes. To be safe. Take that office away and your support system, whether one secretary or a staff of hundreds, and you are naked to the world. They take away your credit cards, your office extension in your home, your company car, your *identity,* for Christ's sake.

Pick Yourself Up (and Start All Over Again)

So how, I have often been asked, have I dealt with this situation, having experienced it so many times? I have dealt with it by keeping something "in the mail." It may be as crazy as an idea for a magazine, such as what became today's *Cosmopolitan.* Whatever it was, I've always had something out there that was sent to somebody who could do something about it. If you don't have something "in the mail," whether a book proposal, an idea for a column or a product, nothing can happen. Nobody may ever offer you another job. The moment you stop communicating with the outside world, no one is likely to come and get you. Maybe if they have heard of you, somebody will ask what you're doing now, but to make sure it happens, I never waited. I always had something out there that *might* happen.

Cosmopolitan happened and other jobs happened because I was in the marketplace. I let people know I was in the marketplace. If

I didn't have a job I'd have to borrow an empty office if only to sit around reading the newspaper. It would be someplace to go and be seen. It would be near the marketplace.

In the real world, failure is not a matter of shame: Shame is when you act ashamed and hide out. When something dreadful happens to you, go to lunch and let everybody see you. You want them to know that you are not in a cave somewhere crying your eyes out, that you are not catatonic. You are out there and you have survived and there may be a little gallows humor in your attitude. Joke about it if you can, but don't act overly happy. Simply let people know your life hasn't come to an end. Don't act ashamed. There is no shame in having struck out on some venture. If you failed because your judgment has been rejected by your corporate peers, so what? They put out products that don't sell. People who fail today are not considered lepers. They are legion in number because in our hyped-up society companies fail, politicians fail, and the world rocks with failure. Check the six o'clock news. Failure is action that doesn't pay off. Still, it's action, which is better than inaction. Bosses fail more often than their employees, but they have the luxury to replace unproductive subordinates for a time . . . until their failures become visible to *their* bosses. Still, failure is not a disease. It is not contagious unless you act as though you are a carrier. You act as a carrier by carrying your sadness around and making people feel sorry for you, by being self-pitying, by not being positive. Even if you are dissembling, make people feel you are alive and are going to survive, because you will. True failure occurs when you are no longer trying.

Certainly one element of success (in addition to luck and timing) is the ability to get a job done. However modest the job, the will and energy to tackle it at once instead of fiddling around thinking about it, or making excuses, is, in my view, essential. Do the job, make the telephone call, answer the letter. Go across town and pick up what it is that you are supposed to pick up and deliver to someone, but do it now. No screwing around.

Work seems to be the only thing that keeps my wife and me whole. We've tried playing, but it doesn't work. Only work works. I think people have the greatest talent for play when they're young. There was once a movie titled *Holiday,* based on a play by Philip Barry, in which a young Cary Grant shocks his prospective father-in-law by announcing on the eve of his marriage that he is going to retire. When his father-in-law-to-be demands to know why, Grant says, "I thought I would retire now, because this is the time I can enjoy things most. When I'm older, I will go to work." When you've lived a long time, there is hardly anything you can do well except work. Surely you can't drink or eat much of anything. Therefore, for me, work, agreeable work, is obligatory in the later years. Not so for many people who dream of retirement as a reward for years of labor. When, however, they are pensioned off, that dream of retirement often becomes a nightmare. How many holes of golf can they play? Wives and even mistresses are upset by seeing a man around the house. There is that clever Hollywood aphorism, "I married you for better or for worse but not for lunch." In the Zanuck/Brown film *Cocoon,* those little boys of great age found something to do next door and saw their lives taking an exciting new turn.

If you have a bright idea, don't sell too soon. The chief asset of Triangle Publishing, once owned by Walter Annenberg, was *TV Guide,* the number-one newsstand seller in the United States. *TV Guide* is no more than a list of television and cable TV programs with some very good articles filling out the magazine. It is pocket-sized, so that it can be put in a small rack in supermarkets and airport counters. The man who sold *TV Guide* couldn't wait for the sales agreement to be signed lest the buyer change his mind. That man was Burt Garmise, who thought up the idea of the magazine in the late forties when he was a member of the circulation department of *Liberty* magazine and I was its editor. Television was less than ten years old. I don't know whether Garmise sold it directly to Annenberg or to an intermediary, and I believe there was another man at *Liberty* magazine who may have been his partner. His name was Lee Wagner, also of *Liberty*'s circulation department. *TV Guide,* originally sold for one million dollars, was resold, along with smaller properties, to Rupert Murdoch for more than three billion dollars. I guess Lee and Burt should have held on for a while.

Don't worry about growing older or pleasing others. Please yourself. I survived the movie business without losing my sanity by working according to my own standards, and being able and willing to quit at any time. I ignored advancing age. You don't realize you are getting older if you are healthy, and you are healthy if you continue to work. Ask eighty-year-old Don Ameche. In *Cocoon,* we found that actors Hume Cronyn, seventy-four, Jessica Tandy, seventy-six, and Jack Gilford, seventy-seven, had to be "aged" to play their characters' ages. If, like them, you continue to work at something you like, life is good. I don't think about the past. Some other person lived it.

Every communication, even to one's haberdasher, should contain something lively, interesting, and unexpected. A one-line or four-page letter need never be mundane. Letters reflect charm when they are written with forethought, feeling, and daring. Make your letters memorable if only for the fun of expression. Don't be a dullard.

Keep notes of what you think. Put a value on your ideas whether they're sales ideas, ideas for books or businesses, or whatever. Work them out in reasonable detail but don't keep them to yourself. This means work. Work is difficult; that's why it's called work. It requires an expenditure of energy that one does not necessarily feel like expending. But it's that expenditure of energy, more often than not forced, which can result in a successful endeavor and without which there can only be failure to achieve what you *can* achieve, and you *can* achieve more than you think.

Diary entry: It's May 1, 1976. Last night at the desk of the Bel Air Hotel in Los Angeles, I had a brief discussion with Robert Redford about success. I asked whether he was enjoying the success of *All the President's Men,* and before he could reply his wife, Lola, said, "No." Robert allowed he was stunned by it. I observed that success is often accompanied by depression. Redford agreed.

I was once asked whether I could define the specific pleasure success gives, and explain why making more money is necessary if one already has enough money to last the rest of one's life.

As to success, I can't define it, but the pleasure is fleeting. Once you've made enough to live on, you may find that you still have to work and achieve even more. In work-oriented American society, most of us are brought up to value work for its own sake and feel guilty without it. Therefore those dreams of never having to work again when one has gained economic security turn out only to be dreams. Even lottery winners discover that they are as anxious and work-driven as they were before winning. What's confusing is that economic independence deprives you of the need to make money to pay the rent, one of life's strongest motivations. Money does provide choices. One need never look at prices on a menu, or hesitate to buy an automobile, a house, or a ticket on the Concorde. And if a job ceases to be pleasurable, one can quit and try something else. But beyond a certain point, what money can buy becomes meaningless unless you're a consumer of yachts and fine art. Why, then, do some people have to make more millions if they already have millions? The only answers I can think of are ego and the quest for power. Nothing else makes sense, nor does that. Improving *your performance,* in a quest for excellence, however, does. Money has nothing to do with that.

Money does not cure depression; if anything, it can bring it on. While it's idiotic to say money is unimportant, those seeking only to be rich may find that getting it was all the fun. When you take stress and strain and need out of life, there's not much left. One of the most difficult things for people with money to sustain is motivation. "Why do this?" they ask. Or, "What are we doing here?" Well, the reason we do what we do and are where we are is that everybody's got to be somewhere and do something. When wealthy Bob Hope was asked recently why he was doing his show at Westbury, Long Island, he said, "What else would I be doing? I'm working."

Back to Show Business

In this world of supermergers and mega-takeovers, there is, in my opinion, an erroneous notion that these combinations stifle competition. I don't believe they do. When a company becomes too big it often loses the ability to solve its simplest problems, except through the most convoluted procedures. There are any number of big companies that have had to become smaller to survive—because of the gross inefficiency of size . . . and the corporate stupidity it begets. A man who was elected president of CBS admitted that he never watched television. What kind of nonsense is that? Most large companies are inexplicably foolish in the simplest performance of their corporate duties. They'll put a man who doesn't read in charge of a book-publishing division. Men and women who have never made a movie are selected to run a movie production company and evaluate the work of those who have far more experience than they have. It can't work except by luck.

In Hollywood, the pioneers of the business seemed barely literate but they were smart. They respected talent. Before the industry became rich, they used stories that were in the public domain—and therefore did not have to pay for them. That accounts for the great taste of early moguls. They knew that not only were the classics free but they were also the best stories money couldn't buy. Why don't creative companies appoint the knowledgeable to positions of authority? Most media failures result from focusing on administrative, legal, and bureaucratic activities rather than creation of a salable product. The noncreative executives who rule these companies are vastly overpaid to bring nothing to the bottom line except unnecessary losses.

When Twentieth Century Fox was in deep financial trouble in the late 1960s, Stanford Research Institute was asked by our banks to analyze our production performance. Their conclusion was that our success, when we had it, depended solely on what they termed "nonrecurring phenomena." Those clods didn't realize that phenomena rarely recurred because a phenomenon is by definition a rare or unusual occurrence. However, we understood what they meant. They meant that if you took *The Sound of Music, M*A*S*H,* and *Butch Cassidy* out of the mix of pictures we made during a given year, we would not have been successful. Inasmuch as all motion picture studios rely on one or two hits to make them prosper, with other films either breaking even or somehow canceling each other out, all motion picture companies survive and sometimes thrive because of "nonrecurring phenomena." *E.T., Star Wars, Close Encounters,* and *Jaws* are "nonrecurring phenomena." You can wait a lifetime for one to recur, except as a sequel (which is really the same phenomenon).

One of the great motion picture directors was in a slump. In previous years he had been in demand by every studio and star. The pioneer producer Samuel Goldwyn, unaware of his circumstances, waved him over at a cocktail party and said, "Frances and I have been talking about you, wondering where you have been and wanting desperately to have you for dinner. You must come over to the house. How about next Tuesday?" The director said, "That would be wonderful, Mr. Goldwyn." Goldwyn then asked, "By the way, what have you been doing recently?" In a fit of candor, the director replied, "Mr. Goldwyn, the truth is I haven't been doing anything. I haven't been able to get a job since my last picture." Goldwyn, looking around, quickly said, "You know, I've just remembered that next Tuesday Frances and I have to go to Europe so we'll have to make it another time," and he walked away. Cruel, yes. Nowhere is cruelty more openly practiced than in Hollywood.

In my early days in Hollywood, it was thought that the only reason any gifted writer, actor, or director would go there was for money. Movies were not regarded as an art form, including those that are worshiped today by film aficionados, and anyone who signed up for Hollywood was accused of "selling out." There was no more dedicated worker in the theater than Clifford Odets, an angry man who wrote such fiery proletarian dramas as *Waiting for Lefty* and *Awake and Sing* and mainstream hits like *Country Girl* and *Golden Boy.* Odets was lured to Hollywood and told me he never regretted it. When I asked whether he missed the New York theater as much as it missed him, he said that he preferred his paintings, his Beverly Hills mansion, and his high writing fees to anything Broadway could offer. America's premier playwright of the working classes embraced the bosses when they met his price.

When Dick Cavett applied for a writing job on *The Jack Paar Show,* Paar said, "If you really want to make it on my show, there is something you have to do for me. Tonight Jayne Mansfield is going to be on the show for the twelfth time and I don't know how to introduce her. Now, if you have any ideas, that'll be your passport to writing for *The Jack Paar Show.*" Cavett did. He suggested that Paar introduce the exceedingly voluptuous Miss Mansfield by saying, "And now, here they are, Jayne Mansfield."

Popcorn

Rupert Murdoch says it never happened. So does Marvin Traub, chairman of Bloomingdale's. But the story is so good that it ought to have happened. When Mr. Murdoch owned the sensational New York newspaper the *Post,* famous for its headline HEADLESS BODY FOUND IN TOPLESS BAR, he is said to have run into Mr. Traub at a social event and in the course of conversation asked, "Marvin, why don't you have Bloomingdale's advertise in the *New York Post*?" "Because, Rupert," Mr. Traub is alleged to have replied, "your readers are our shoplifters."

At a luncheon on Rupert Murdoch's chartered yacht there was a long line for the buffet table. I was taking a plate for Helen in addition to my own. I noticed Mrs. Walter (Betsy) Cronkite taking only one plate. When I asked Betsy why she wasn't bringing a plate for Walter she replied, "Only second wives do that." She is one funny lady.

A few years ago, in London, I read in *The Observer* a review of Joseph P. Lash's book *Eleanor, The Years Alone,* which included references to Eleanor Roosevelt's romances. Mrs. Roosevelt, the wife of President Franklin D. Roosevelt, seemed particularly disturbed, according to Mr. Lash, by her failure to arouse men sexually. This was true in her relationship with Mr. Lash and others, he claimed. Random thought: Women are more pleased to know they have attracted a man because of mindless sexuality than by wit, brainpower, or personality. Sexual chemistry is never triggered by anything cerebral. Gene Fowler, the American author, journalist, and onetime editor of the *Denver Post,* said, "One strand of pubic hair is stronger than the Atlantic cable."

Ernest Lehman would have been regarded in nineteenth-century England as merely another eccentric. Here, in this waning century, some would call him a wacko. Ernie has so many eccentricities that they are known to his friends as Lehmanisms.

When he lived in a penthouse on West Ninety-sixth Street in New York City, he often noticed dark smoke gushing forth from chimneys visible from his terrace, in violation of city ordinances requiring buildings to use incinerators that spew forth white rather than black smoke to keep ashes and cinders from falling. Ernest acquired a telescope with which he could identify law-breaking smokestacks. He was the biggest pain in the ass on the island. He would regularly report violations at the Plaza Hotel and other buildings whenever he saw the slightest sign of soot.

In the railroad era, he was also known to take apart air conditioning equipment in compartments of the *Twentieth Century Lim-*

ited when he could find no other way to shut off the cooling system. He regularly carried on his travels a small tool chest for this purpose, given to him by my wife.

In the jet age, he complained so vocally about minor infractions of service on a transcontinental airliner that before Lehman relented, the captain threatened to land the plane in Kansas City and put him off.

Back in New York City, he conducted a war against rocking manhole covers when he lived on West Fifty-fifth Street. He claimed to be kept awake by the sound of taxis going over these loose manhole covers. He identified thirty such manhole covers that rocked, reported them to the city, and was so insistent in his complaints that the city repaired most of them.

New York might be better if he still lived there, but is glad he left.

Screen heavies are often different away from the set. Jack Palance, customarily seen in movies grinding a man's hand under his boot or in similar brutal action, was in real life frightened of his diminutive wife. I have seen him cringe when she fired a verbal volley at him during a dinner party. Not that I don't cringe when my wife attacks me, but then I don't grind hands under my heels.

Dick Zanuck and I previewed *Butch Cassidy and the Sundance Kid* for members of the United States Supreme Court. The preview went well. When the lights came up, octogenarian Justice Hugo Black rubbed his chin and said, "You know, I think I had those boys in my court once."

During the usual carping about the outrageous demands of agents in the Twentieth Century Fox executive dining room one day, producer Walter Wanger said, "You chaps just talk about agents. I'm the only one who ever did anything about them." Wanger was referring to the fact that although a producer of occasionally great films, he was perhaps best known for having shot off the testicle of an agent whom he suspected of having made love to his wife, movie star Joan Bennett.

Don't think all the stars in old Hollywood were the slaves of overpowering studio heads. When I interviewed Bette Davis in her dressing room in the early forties, she was known as the fourth Warner Brother. The often tyrannical Jack Warner feared Bette's tantrums as much as his wife's. Almost all the tough studio heads I knew were afraid of women, and Bette was one feisty lady.

Royalty has its privileges but also its precautions. King Hassan of Morocco did not attend the luncheon he gave for Malcolm Forbes's seventieth birthday. His reasoning, so we are told, was persuasive. The luncheon was held at the Tangiers Country Club. On a previous occasion, when the king did attend a party there for friends, fifty-seven of them were assassinated.

In order to baffle a colleague who was flying from Los Angeles to London (in pre-Concorde days), producer Leonard Goldstein said he would get there before him. The colleague said, "That's impossible. I'm leaving tonight." Leonard saw him off and waved him aboard in mid-sentence of a spirited conversation. When the man stepped off the plane in London he was greeted by a gentleman who looked and was dressed exactly like Leonard and completed the sentence that had been interrupted ten hours before. The thoroughly confused traveler was finally introduced to *Robert* Goldstein, Leonard's identical twin brother, who was living in London at the time.

A screenplay consists of dialogue, descriptions of characters and action, but not of camera directions. Those are what the director will add. If a writer puts those in, the first thing a director will generally do is go through the screenplay and simply ignore all the directions unless they are critical in making a story point.

On the set of *Target* in Paris, Gene Hackman told a story that brings forth howls from a show business audience and silence from everyone else. According to this story, Mother Teresa was visited by an old friend who asked what she would like as a personal gift for Christmas. Her reply was, "You know I don't ever want anything for myself. All I want is to see hungry people fed, violence disappear, love banish hatred, and the world at peace." The old friend said, "Yes, Mother Teresa, I know all that, but come on, we know each other too well. I am asking what you would wish for yourself if poverty disappeared, war were a thing of the past, nobody was hungry—in short, if everything you prayed for came to pass. Surely, in those circumstances, you must have some personal desire." Mother Teresa thought for a while and then said, "You know, there *is* something. What I really would like is to direct."

Danny Kaye enjoyed telling this story. When Leo Durocher, the immodest manager of the Brooklyn Dodgers, and Danny were driving together in upstate New York, Leo inexplicably cut in front of a truck. They almost got crushed. Danny yelled at Leo, "You stupid son of a bitch, how can you possibly have done that?" Durocher yelled back that the truck was in the wrong and was supposed to have yielded. Kaye said, "Not true. I saw it, and you were wrong." Durocher exploded, "Listen, you red-headed son of a bitch, I may not always be right, but I'm never wrong."

Of all the sybarites I have known, none quite equaled David O. Selznick. Another showman, Mike Todd, once proclaimed, "I've been broke, but I've never been poor." So had Selznick. He demanded grand-luxe service to the end or nearly the end. One stormy night in the 1950s, I flew with him to Rome aboard one of the early Comets. The aircraft buckled and spun in a sickening series of downdrafts over the Alps. Baggage and trays were flying all over. We were strapped into the first-class section, then located in the aft portion of the aircraft. Selznick had ordered champagne. The terrified steward, on hands and knees, finally arrived. Offended by the sight of plastic glasses, Selznick demanded, "Go back and bring us some proper glasses."

If we were going to go down, we would do so holding tulip-shaped Baccarat. In Selznick's view there were only two classes, "first class and no class."

Both Ray Stark and Irving Lazar claim the rights to this story but I'm inclined to think it was Ray, whose sense of the absurd and daring make him more likely to have survived a gaffe of this magnitude.

In the early 1950s, studio heads were still all-powerful and agents could be barred for life for a single misdeed. It was Ray, I believe, who discovered he had sold the same sought-after novel to two studio heads, MGM's Dore Schary and Twentieth Century Fox's Darryl Zanuck. Any other agent would have fled the country but Ray, apprised of this capital offense, suggested calmly that Dore and Darryl toss a coin to determine which of them should get the property. Incredibly, they did and Schary won. The picture was never made.

Making Movies

When Dick Zanuck and I were fired from Fox (I for the second time), we were invited by Ted Ashley, then head of Warner Brothers, to join his company in jobs comparable to the ones we had lost. Ego got the better of our judgment and we signed on as executives again in order to prove that Fox was wrong in discharging us. This honeymoon did not last long. Warners did nothing wrong and the pay and perks were pretty good. It was simply that we had had the executive suite and its false security.

On July 7, 1972, only a year and a half into the job, we tore up our contracts as executives at Warner Brothers (with more than a million dollars in compensation and other benefits still owed us), and decided to form our own independent movie production company. As supervising executives, we'd made between us more than two hundred movies without having our names on a film. We'd taken the blame for some bad films and made millionaires of those who were credited with some highly successful films which we actually initiated. It was time to get some of that luster and lucre for ourselves. I wrote the press release on American Airlines Flight 1 en route to Los Angeles from New York. It stated that Richard Zanuck and David Brown had requested and been granted a release from their contracts at Warner Brothers. Ted Ashley was reluctant to see us go, and half of Hollywood couldn't believe we didn't have a deal in our hip pockets when we resigned, or that we hadn't been fired. Well, we didn't and we hadn't.

I was on the telephone most of Saturday, July 8, 1972, at the Bel Air Hotel in West Los Angeles, telephoning all my troops in my former life as an executive. My, they were worked up and shocked. They were accustomed to coming to Daddy to have their problems solved. I enjoyed solving them, and holding their hands—actors, directors, writers, producers. Now it was time to be making demands instead of responding to them.

We had a company but no office or money. And then, miraculously, came Mike Medavoy, agent for producers Michael and Julia Phillips and Tony Bill, to offer us a script by David Ward called *The Sting,* which became one of the most successful and beloved movies of its time and won the Academy Award for Best Picture. That was the start of the Zanuck/Brown Company. Perhaps "miraculously" is not the apt word for how *The Sting* came our way. It was in appreciation for Dick's and my steadfastness in supporting a project at Warner Brothers titled *Steelyard Blues,* produced and written by the same team.

When Gregory Peck agreed to play Douglas MacArthur in our film about the general, he was concerned that some of his friends would be critical of him. "I'm a dedicated liberal," he said, "and for me to play MacArthur is to glorify what I abhor in the man, in his actions, and philosophy." Then Peck did a great deal of research, studied newsreels, listened to tapes of MacArthur's speeches, and delved into MacArthur's policy pronouncements. As he became more deeply involved in the role and consequently the man himself, he became increasingly more understanding of MacArthur, even to the point of suggesting that Truman's role in the film be diminished. He felt the script was too kind to Truman and possibly misleading. He particularly objected to the scene showing Truman's plane circling Wake Island so that he would not arrive before MacArthur. His research indicated this was gross dramatic license. Soon we were listening to Gregory Peck, Hollywood liberal, support the philosophy and views of Douglas MacArthur. It was a genuine belief on his part, not merely immersion in the character. Peck is a scholar, and he came to admire some of MacArthur's views, especially his conviction (all too true) that the Pacific rim was the coming arena of world power. When the film was completed, MacArthur the man had convinced the actor who portrayed him of the rightness of his position. Unlike George C. Scott, whom I believe had little use for General Patton although he played him brilliantly, I had the feeling that Peck liked General Douglas MacArthur.

Even Mrs. Douglas MacArthur, who occasionally sees Greg in the elevators of the Waldorf Towers in New York, where they both reside, is warmly cordial toward him although, for deeply personal reasons, she has not seen the film. I have told Mrs. MacArthur, who is a friend, that she would like it if she had and I think she believes me.

The Scariest Movie Ever Made

When Richard Zanuck and I acquired the film rights to Peter Benchley's seminal novel, *Jaws,* we experienced a panic of unpreparedness. If we had read *Jaws* twice, we might never have made the movie. Careful analysis could have convinced us that it was too difficult to make. Imagine. We had bought the book in manuscript, before publication, in 1973. The book was published and became a wild best-seller. Experts had determined, for a host of technical reasons, that the island of Martha's Vineyard, Massachusetts, was the only place in the world we could make this film. We had to shoot in summer. If we lost the summer, we'd lose a year before the movie could be released and the book would be less popular by then. Besides, an actors' strike was threatened, and a studio edict had come down that no picture would be started that couldn't be finished before June 30, 1974, the expiration date of the contract with the Screen Actors Guild. On April 22, 1974, Dick Zanuck and I met in the Bel Air Hotel with director Steven Spielberg and writer/actor Carl Gottlieb, who was called in to revise the script, which had already gone through three rewrites—two by author Peter Benchley and one by Pulitzer Prize playwright (and more important, experienced diver) Howard Sackler. Sackler gave only five weeks to the project and requested no credit.

Spielberg said, "There's no way I can start a picture on Martha's Vineyard in three and a half weeks. I'm unprepared. The script is far from ready." To complicate matters, there were production problems which could not have been anticipated: the effect of saline on the artificial shark, and all sorts of other spooky malfunctions. Even if we could have delayed the start of production, the Eastern winter would be coming on, and the foliage would be gone before we finished shooting. As it was, the water in late spring was so cold at Martha's Vineyard that we had to start shooting on the surface of the water, and wait for greening of the leaves for the land sequences. It was a nightmare and a daymare, especially for our able, unflappable production executive, Bill Gilmore. Filming began on May 2, 1974, without a final script or other evidence of complete preparedness. Richard Zanuck and I later philosophized that we might not have done as well if we were prepared.

Zanuck and I could have engaged a safe, older director for *Jaws,* but our experience with Steven Spielberg on *The Sugarland Express* convinced us that he was the best choice. We wanted more than "safety"; we wanted dramatic and cinematic surprises. There were times early in the picture when we felt we had made a mistake, because Steven was maddeningly perfectionistic. He was out there on the water every morning at five. He had the stamina. He had never worked on water (although his crew thought he walked on it), and it was amazing to see how quickly he adapted. We were all concerned that the film would be technically faulty, that it wouldn't seem true. Our gifted production designer, Joe Alves, was so meticulous in seeking expert counsel that when the finished film was shown to shark specialists and marine biologists, they could find nothing significantly wrong, allowing for some dramatic license. A couple of lines had to be redubbed—there was originally a mispronunciation of the Latin name for great white shark—but the movie was certified as remarkably accurate. Peter Gimbel, a world-class adventurer and creator of the magnificent great white shark documentary *Blue Water, White Death,* was one of our early advisors, and Spielberg himself took a scholarly interest in sharks. We took a chance on Steven because we thought we'd get something different and better, and we won. So did he.

Casting, to some extent, was a group effort. Richard Dreyfuss applied for the role of Hooper. So did Joel Grey. Spielberg liked Dreyfuss. Dreyfuss then read the script and wanted to rework it. He didn't think his character was right. We all liked Roy Scheider, although Spielberg was slow to come around. Robert Shaw was my idea. We had tried to get Sterling Hayden. Spielberg, Zanuck, and I decided early that we didn't want Steve McQueen or Paul Newman or Robert Redford, who might undermine the sense of realism we sought in the film because of their superstar personas. We wanted a film in which the actors would blend in with the locals. Many of those seen in *Jaws* had no acting experience. Our selectmen were the real selectmen. Our doctor in the autopsy scene, Robert Nevin, was a local doctor. Shari Rhodes, our casting director for *The Sugarland Express,* came aboard and proved she was as adept in casting Yankees as she was in casting Texans.

One of the most difficult things about *Jaws* was keeping the actors from developing "island fever." Roy Scheider threw a plate of food that displeased him to make a point about the catering. Richard Dreyfuss was so unhappy that he told people *Jaws* was probably one of the worst-produced movies he had ever been in. Nobody knew what the hell they were doing, he complained. When he saw the picture in a Broadway theater, he was so astounded by how good it was that he telephoned the head of the studio at three in the morning to exclaim, "It's the greatest. If I'd had any idea it would be this good, I'd have had a better time making it." While he was on Martha's Vineyard with Scheider and Shaw, it seemed like Devil's Island to him. We had been on this island for five and a half months. After Spielberg set up the last shot on September 17, 1974, he had a speedboat race him to a waiting car and driver for the ride to Boston, where he boarded an L.A.-bound jet. If it had lasted longer, I believe some of us would have dived off and tried to swim to the mainland. Although a paradise for tourists, it was very boring to work month after month there. *The New York Times* arrived at 10:30 and was brought to the set by speedboat. Everybody was reading about Nixon and Watergate. The set consisted of three men in a boat and a lot of technicians. Robert Shaw said, "If I hear anyone's life story again, I'll shoot him." Only director Steven Spielberg and editor Verna Fields had the pieces of the movie in their heads. For days, we were dealing with isolated shots of barrels. All the camera would do was shoot barrels bobbing up and down. A movie like this was a mosaic of a million pieces, each of which had to be photographed, coded, catalogued, edited, remembered, and ultimately assembled in a cohesive whole.

For the actors, there was nothing to do in the morning but wait for the fog to lift. Richard Dreyfuss knew almost every waitress on the island (pretty college girls working during their vacations)—some of them biblically. We shot any day we could—Sunday, Saturday, holidays. To add to the morale problem, I think unconsciously the actors were jealous of the shark. They hated reading that the shark was the star of the movie. When we were ready for the shark shots the shark wasn't. When the shark was ready we sometimes were not. Our shark handlers spoke a language we could not understand, all about hydraulic systems. Sometimes when the shark would work, his skin would begin to fall off, because of, they told us, a reverse polarity of electricity which would also cause one fin to go one way and another fin to go another way. Often his teeth would be too white and makeup men would have to swim out and blacken them. The salt water would make them pearly white. In a fit of frustration, Spielberg dubbed the special effects department the special defects department.

The shark was created by production designer Joe Alves, who had advice from a host of experts, and built by Bob Mattey, who had created underwater creatures for Disney for seventeen years. Mattey was called out of retirement to create a creature that had never been made before. This twelve-ton monster required fifteen men to operate it and consisted of three separate components. It was operated by means of a hydraulic system which we never understood and you won't understand if I try to explain it because I can't explain it to this day. I don't believe the shark quite understood it either, in view of the trouble we had with the monster.

As our production executive Bill Gilmore remembers it:

The great white shark rewrote the script of *Jaws.* The Dreyfuss character in Peter Benchley's book went down in the cage to fight the shark with his electric prod. The shark attacked the cage, mangled it, and ate the Richard Dreyfuss character. Not so in the movie. The real shark dictated a new ending. Here's how.

From the beginning we believed we could build a mechanical shark that would work in close-ups—i.e., close-angle shots of the shark and victim—but there was no way we could get full-length credible shots of this man-made creature circling the cage. Joe Alves, the production designer, and I considered photographing sixteen-foot white sharks (which we had every reason to believe we could find off the south coast of Australia) and by reducing the scale of the cage and the Dreyfuss double, their relative size would be the same as a twenty-four-foot great white shark attacking a full-size cage and man. The size of the man had to be reduced. I found a midget scuba-diving stuntman in California to double for Dreyfuss in a diving suit (actually Dick Zanuck's idea). One would never know it was not the real actor. Joe Alves set about to miniaturize the cage, costume, equipment, etc.

One day, weeks later, he walked into my office, his face white as snow, and said, "You know, Bill, we are reducing the scale of everything, right?" And I replied, "Right." Joe held up a tiny little air tank and said, "The little guy has twelve minutes of air."

We had no answer but we went ahead with the plan anyway. We sent the equipment and the midget down to Australia. We learned through ship-to-shore radio that they had lured a sixteen-foot white shark around the boat and were commencing to shoot. Two days later I got a telephone call from Ron Taylor, the famous underwater cameraman (*Blue Water, White Death.*) He was excited to a point of incoherence. At first I was worried that something had gone wrong. He assured me everyone was fine and then reported that he had just shot the most incredible footage of a great white shark that he had ever seen. The shark's gills had become entangled with the line to the miniature cage and it couldn't get loose. The shark went crazy and the results on film, apparently, were breathtaking. My first thought was about the twelve minutes of air and I asked if the little guy in the cage was OK. Ron said he was, because the event took place before the midget was lowered. My heart sank because I believed the footage would be unusable without Dreyfuss's double actually in the cage. I told Ron to send up the film he shot and we'd have a look at it.

When we saw the film it was indeed fantastic. It was so good, in fact, that Spielberg and the producers decided we had to use it in the movie to establish credibility. We would be able to say there were real sharks in our film, an important promotional consideration.

The only way to use the Australian footage was to rewrite the script to show the Dreyfuss character leaving the cage to retrieve the prod he had dropped in the rocks (while the shark was going berserk), and thereby survive (to the stand-up cheers of audiences around the world). While some of this action had to be filmed in a tank at the MGM Studios in Culver City, California, Dreyfuss's character was actually saved by the actions of a real live sixteen-foot great white shark off the coast of Australia.

About halfway through the 159-day shooting schedule of *Jaws,* our technical staff advised Richard Zanuck and me to suspend production so they could attempt to solve some of our problems. They thought it would be easier to work out our serious technical difficulties without a lot of expensive, impatient actors around. Robert Shaw had an opportunity to do another movie. It was suggested that we release him for a couple of months. We would be relieved of his considerable salary during that time. We listened and agonized, but finally concluded it was wiser to keep on going, however slow the process. Experience had taught us that the momentum of a film, once interrupted, can rarely be recaptured. Besides, no one knows what may happen to actors once they go away. They may get fat. They may get killed. Or never look quite the same again. There were other considerations. We were supposed to finish shooting at the end of June; now hotel rates for our crew tripled as the vacation season began. We were up against a seasonal deadline. Summer at Martha's Vineyard is short, and the leaves change color in early autumn. Any interruption of shooting might require us to return a year later to complete the film. So we continued shooting, never being certain we could finish the movie. Our budget for the film was about four and a half million dollars, which we exceeded by 100 percent. How could we anticipate costs? We were budgeting a production unlike any previous production. Nobody had ever budgeted a shark.

While Zanuck and I were marooned on Martha's Vineyard for more than five months making *Jaws,* the suggestion was made to the chairman of MCA/Universal, Lew Wasserman, that the production company be brought back to California to complete the film there. He asked his colleague, "Do we know how to make it better than they do?" The answer was a reluctant no. "Then," he said, "let them keep going." The production was never threatened with suspension, contrary to rumor. None of the studio executives ever flew to the location except at our invitation.

* * *

Almost as important to the success of this film as Peter Benchley and Steven Spielberg was the composer, John Williams. It was John Williams who created the frightening BUM BUM BUM BUM shark theme which scared the wits out of millions of people around the world. John is a modest and kind man. His generosity and the lavish gift of his talent will always be remembered by us who were part of *Jaws.*

More *Jaws*

It was inevitable, within a week after *Jaws* opened, that there would be a sequel. MCA/Universal insisted. Spielberg would have none of it—he had made the definitive shark movie and thought a sequel would be a mistake for him. Dick and I, on the other hand, felt if we didn't make it, someone else would, and we wanted to protect our turf . . . at least for one sequel. In many ways *Jaws 2* was more difficult than the first film, not only because of the impossible expectations it set up in audiences, but also because of production problems and costs that far exceeded the first.

There were many suggestions for *Jaws 2* when the decision came down to make a sequel. *Jaws* author Peter Benchley had a couple of ideas. One involved a shark about a hundred feet long that existed only in the mythology of sharklore. Before we could consider this, Peter became involved in the filming of his next novel, *The Deep.* Master science-fiction author Arthur C. Clarke checked in from Sri Lanka with an idea calling for a giant squid disabling an oil refinery in the Indian Ocean. Howard Sackler, who had worked on the original *Jaws,* wanted to reenact the Robert Shaw monologue describing in haunting detail the sinking of the USS *Indianapolis* in shark-filled waters, and using a young actor to play the role of a younger Quint, portrayed in *Jaws* by Mr. Shaw. Sackler was finally engaged to write a screenplay of *Jaws 2,* but not one reenacting the sinking of the USS *Indianapolis.* The MCA moguls decreed (and of necessity we agreed) that what was needed was more *Jaws,* a story in which the vengeful great white would return to Amity and threaten, among other children, the son of Chief of Police Brody, reprising Roy Scheider in the role of Brody, with Lorraine Gary once again as his wife and Murray Hamilton returning as the beleaguered mayor.

Jaws 2 employed a crew of 364 for eight months. It also had a navy of eighteen sailboats which had to be anchored each time they were photographed. Boat-to-boat photography is dangerous and the *Jaws 2* crew was lucky not to have had any serious accidents. One fellow who was supposed to be brought down by a shark as he was swimming was weighted for the scene, and when he couldn't release his weights and rise to the surface, four divers were dispatched to find him.

The logistics involved in a helicopter scene of *Jaws 2* (shark attacks helicopter) were described in perhaps half a page in the script but took about eight weeks to shoot. Everything on the ocean had to be individually anchored to the ocean floor in such a way that it did not interfere with the progression of the shark. The camera boats then had to be positioned so that they would not be in the shots. After eight hours of setting this up (plus three twelve-hour days to anchor the helicopter), we faced the threat that if the wind changed, causing the sails on the sailboats in the background to flip over, we would have to start all over again.

The "island" used in *Jaws 2* was actually a set constructed on a barge, and it weighed one and a half tons. It had to be able to float yet had to be heavy enough so that it wouldn't move much once it was anchored. While filming this second shark movie, the company encountered hurricane alerts and unexpected ocean movements. One Sunday morning the director and I arrived at the location to learn that a storm in the night had broken our island from its anchor and driven it five miles down the coast; that one of the sharks was treacherously perched on its side and held only by one string and a diver; that four sailboats had turned into sausage; and that the police boat (which was the main set) had landed on a real island miles away. These were but a few of the problems to be overcome in order to make credible one of the best advertising lines ever devised for a movie, "Just when you thought it was safe to go back in the water."

Good producers must occasionally dissemble to their masters, the studios, in the interest of the filmmakers. When Steven Spielberg was directing *Jaws,* every scene that was in the movie (and some that weren't) was sketched on a storyboard. The production manager was required to report to the studio the exact number of scenes that had been photographed on a given day. After each scene was completed the sketch of that scene was crossed off on the storyboard. No other scenes were authorized for shooting, but through the connivance of the producers, sketches of a number of unauthorized but essential scenes were kept under the table to be shot, in effect, when the studio wasn't looking. That was the easy part of being a producer on the set.

In the middle of production of *Jaws 2,* a monster of a movie, Murray Hamilton, the actor who played the mayor of Amity, decided to leave the location permanently after several million dollars had been spent establishing his presence on film. His departure would mean having another actor replace him and reshooting that portion of the picture he was in. It would also mean missing a crucial summer release date for the film in prebooked theaters, and the return of millions of dollars of theater advances. The consequences would be terminal. The movie would surely be canceled. We were already millions over budget because of the replacement of the first director and attendant delays.

I hurried over to the Holiday Inn where Murray was staying, and found a good-bye note in my box and his luggage piled up in front of the hotel. Murray was fighting alcoholism and I supposed his decision might have something to do with that. Still, quitting in the middle of a production was unthinkable and Murray was a professional. I caught up with him as he was leaving and begged him to have a cup of coffee with me. He revealed that his wife was about to undergo exploratory surgery for cancer. "I couldn't care less about my career or finishing the movie," he said, "or that you'll have to start over with another actor." The sequence Murray had yet to complete was inside a town hall, and it might be weeks before it was shot as "cover" during inclement weather (during good weather, the company was at sea, where Murray wasn't needed). Any actor in his situation could go crazy waiting while his wife at home was threatened by terminal illness.

My decision was simple but costly. I asked, "What if we shoot your remaining scenes right away and send you home?" Murray replied, "You can't—not while the weather holds." I said, "The hell with the weather. Dick and I will reschedule." We moved the company indoors and finished the actor's remaining work in three days. Naturally, the weather was perfect while we worked inside the Town Hall but the decision saved the film. The actor's wife recovered but, sadly, Murray died a few months later in New York after looping his final lines of the movie in a recording studio.

It was only a movie, but we had to get this shot, or one hundred thousand dollars, the daily cost of production of *Jaws 2,* was gone irretrievably. We had been on the set ten hours, rigging and setting up, and now the light was going. The shot called for the destruction of a man-made shark by explosives offshore near Pensacola, Florida. Michael Butler, the cameraman, was impatient. Director Jeannot Szwarc asked, "Are you ready?" and Butler snapped, "You tell me when you're ready and I'll tell you if I'm ready." The director said he was ready. A cameraman can abort the shooting if he believes there isn't enough light for an exposure. There was, but barely. At the director's command of "action," the device to detonate all this movie magic—the blowing up of the shark—decided not to work. And all because of a twelve-volt battery that had gone dead. A battery that cost ninety-five cents. The light was fading fast. Suddenly, a grip seized a couple of cables that jump a dead car battery and stuck them where the device was, setting off the explosion. Six cameras were rolling. One cameraman was in front of the shark's head, whose jaws were clenched on an electric cable. The cameraman had to be bandaged to keep him from being burned. We got that shot and the others. Later, we set up for our master shot, which would be the same shot except involving all the actors on a nearby island, a huge wide-angle shot. At that time, the explosive powder had become wet because some idiot had dunked the shark when he wasn't supposed to. And the question again was, would the shot work? Would the powder detonate? There was no backup powder in case it didn't. Well, the beauty of it was it did work—with lots of smoke! We never figured on the smoke, but it conveniently obscured some of the defects of the shot. We were on that Florida location so long that we were still shooting at Christmas, having been there since summer. There would have been a mutiny if we'd gone past Christmas. The kids in the picture were growing up. It was freezing cold—under twenty degrees on the water. There was ice on the camera slate. We put ice cubes in our teenage actors' mouths for a few seconds before dialogue scenes in order to prevent their breath from showing on film, as our scenes were supposed to be taking place in the summer. We huddled in our parkas and furs while they stripped down to bathing suits and prepared to shoot.

Set Pieces

Most journalists who write about films have no idea what producers must do to keep actors acting and appreciated during that out-of-body experience known as production. When a movie is shooting, actors are out of their normal skins and those who work with them are similarly disoriented—usually in strange surroundings away from home, and under stringent time and performance pressures. One of the first things good producers do is to comment on the actors' work as they see it in the dailies that are viewed every night. It is also important to observe their birthdays, make certain they are protected from nutcases, and ensure that their work conditions and living environment are good. Stars are not spoiled the way they used to be because stars are not the way they used to be. Elizabeth Taylor expected to receive a ton of caviar and perhaps a diamond necklace from her producers. Robert Redford, Tom Cruise, Paul Newman, Meryl Streep, and Dustin Hoffman would be embarrassed by a show of largesse.

The best gifts you can give today's stars are a good script and director. Some of them do like to be taken to dinner occasionally. Others want no company at all. The main thing is to try to keep them from becoming bored or depressed.

I've always made it a point to go to dinner with each member of the cast and key members of the crew early in the schedule and show up on the set to chat between takes almost every day of shooting.

When the film completes photography, there is a "wrap party," a kind of farewell to a closely knit group. These can be lavish or simple but are always sentimental. The stars like to get close to the crew. They feel a bond to those who operate the cameras, the hair and makeup men and women, the script supervisor, the assistant director, and the auditor who cashes their checks.

Practical jokes can defuse the atmosphere of dangerous tension during the deadly "midstretch" of the shooting schedule. On Roy Scheider's birthday, we decided nobody on the *Jaws 2* set would mention it. Birthdays were usually noted and celebrated and Scheider knew that. As the shooting day wore on, he was at first puzzled and then furious. Nobody, including his closest friends on the picture, had said anything about his birthday.

It finally became clear to him that he was going to be spending the evening alone in his room at the Holiday Inn at Navarre Beach in western Florida. Teddy Grossman, his closest friend (and one of mine), talked with him toward the end of the day, but said nothing about his birthday. Finally Roy said, "Teddy, are you doing anything tonight?" Teddy replied, "Well, Roy, as a matter of fact, I do have a date." Roy snapped, "Jesus, I hoped you were free." Teddy then said, "You know, my girlfriend knows a terrific girl; maybe I can get her to come with you." Roy's expression brightened perceptibly. "Can you?" he pleaded.

Roy was married, but the idea of a dinner date was appealing.

Arrangements were made to meet in a remote café where a married movie star and his date were not likely to be noted by the local paparazzi. Meanwhile, the entire company secretly prepared to dine at the same café. As they entered and spied Roy at a secluded corner table, they roared, "Happy birthday!" The party was on.

On another occasion during the eight-month shooting schedule of *Jaws 2,* Scheider was the star of another event.

The director, Jeannot Szwarc, and Roy had it in for each other almost from the start. Roy's room was next to mine in the Holiday Inn and too often he would slip a message under my door with derisive references to Jeannot. He went off to Martha's Vineyard to film a brief sequence and continued to complain by telegram.

I thought about this war between our star and director and wired Scheider to meet me in my room at the Holiday Inn immediately on his return. Szwarc was also invited. Verna Fields, the Academy Award-winning editor of the original *Jaws,* who was now a Universal executive, was visiting the set that day. I invited her to the meeting. When they were all gathered in my room, I asked Scheider and Szwarc to say everything they had on their minds and settle their differences once and for all. Jeannot remarked to Scheider, "You have quite an ego." Scheider exclaimed, "*I* have an ego? Why, you son of a bitch!" He grabbed Szwarc and flung him against the wall. Szwarc was fifty pounds heavier but Roy was in great shape. They started wrestling. When they fell to the floor, I piled on top of them. Verna screamed, "Don't hurt his face!" She didn't mean mine or Jeannot's—we weren't on camera. As we were wrestling in a ludicrous tableau, Verna decided to enter the fray and get on top of us. Verna was so heavy that we screamed for mercy and started to laugh uncontrollably as we disentangled ourselves. Once freed, I put a bottle of scotch on the table and poured enough in each glass to get us gloriously drunk. We then played the truth game about what was really going on between Roy and the director. The truth was that Scheider wanted more attention, "love," if you please. There were nineteen young children of varying ages in *Jaws 2*—some of them nonprofessionals—and they required intense directorial attention. Roy wanted the same attention. He said, "I need to be directed, too." Stars are sensitive to neglect, whether intended or not. The director had so little time, and the pressures were so extreme on *Jaws 2,* that Roy was thought of as someone who could take care of himself directorially. From that time on Jeannot directed Scheider as carefully as he did the least professional actor in the company, and the war between director and star was over. The movie was a hit.

By the way, Jeannot, director of *Jaws 2,* never set foot on Martha's Vineyard, where the original *Jaws* was filmed. That location was "established" by William G. Gilmore, who directed Scheider and Lorraine Gary for six frantic, frost-filled days in the Vineyard, where even the leaves had to be sprayed summer green. Filmgoers were never aware when Chief Brody's police car crossed the Mason-Dixon line and entered Florida, where most of the film was shot—the dunes of the Gulf Coast masquerading for New England.

Potpourri

There is no sure formula for success in movie-making except to surprise them. Box-office hits are moving pictures that move the emotions. Action, as John Ford once told John Wayne, is not so important as *re*action. Audiences must become *involved* with the characters if a film is to succeed. They must care about the characters. No film has ever succeeded without audience sympathy for one or more characters. In the film trade it's called "rooting interest." That's the key to it, wanting that character to surmount his or her difficulties, survive, and triumph.

Love Affair was one of Hollywood's classic love stories, starring Irene Dunne and Charles Boyer. When I was an executive at Fox, we remade it with Deborah Kerr and Cary Grant and retitled it *An Affair to Remember.* It was directed by Leo McCarey, the same man who made the original version, and it was based on a true story. Delmer Daves, who wrote the original film, had fallen in love aboard a transatlantic liner, although he was involved with someone ashore. So was his shipboard amour, he suspected. McCarey and Daves had a picture commitment but no story. They decided to use Daves's romance as the basis for a movie. The two main characters meet on an ocean liner. They are attracted to each other, but she's being kept by a man in Chicago, and he's involved with someone else somewhere. They suspect each other of being romantically unreliable, but now they're in love. After ten days at sea together, they promise to meet at the observation tower of the Empire State Building in six months, the time presumably it will take them to free themselves from old ties. She is hit by a taxi while looking skyward and rushing across Fifth Avenue to keep her rendezvous. He waits around for hours, then shrugs, thinking, of course, what did he expect? They are finally reunited in a great love story of cheating cheaters who will cheat no more. Where are the love stories like that today? Will someone fall in love who can write! Please.

Margaret Mitchell managed to write one of the greatest love stories of all time and we wanted to continue it, although, had she lived, we would never had had the opportunity (Miss Mitchell opposed the idea of a sequel to the day of her death). Her heirs had no such compunction. Richard Zanuck and I asked James Goldman, who wrote *Lion in Winter* and *Follies,* to write the screenplay of the sequel to *Gone With the Wind.* We had secured the sequel rights from the author's estate. In fact, they had been offered to us by Kay Brown, who represented the estate and, interestingly enough, had bought the rights to the original property back in the thirties when she was David O. Selznick's story editor. In Goldman's version, Scarlett O'Hara became romantically involved with another man after she and Rhett separated. The other man, based on a governor of South Carolina who was said to have killed a bear with his own hands, was formidable opposition for Rhett, who had never got Scarlett out of his blood.

There were many scenes in the Goldman screenplay, and the Anne Edwards screen story which preceded it, that were very good, and we were pleased with it. Our partner, MGM, did not like the script and may never have liked any script because it didn't want a sequel to be made. I think our other partner, Universal Pictures, would have gone along with us but MGM had veto rights. To compound our difficulties, MGM suffered two changes in top management and with all the confusion at the top, the rights we acquired from the estate of Margaret Mitchell were permitted to lapse.

The idea of a sequel to *GWTW* fascinated the world press and we receive inquiries about it to this day. An example of the interest is what occurred one evening when my wife and I were dining with Barbara Walters at her home in New York. It was a small dinner party, but, like all Barbara's gatherings, most interesting because her guests were a mix not only of power figures but also of old friends, regardless of rank. Barbara had just returned from the hospital bedside of the shah of Iran, then in exile in New York, where she had obtained an exclusive interview the world awaited. The flight of the shah, a monarch under sentence of death by his pursuers and with no place to hide, was top news everywhere, an extraordinary true-life drama. Barbara, one of the world's most gracious hostesses, began the after-dinner conversation by saying,

"I'm going to tell you everything I can tell you about my visit to the shah, but what I want to hear first, if David Brown will agree, is the story of the sequel to *Gone With the Wind.*"

Groans from her guests were not forthcoming. After relating the never-before-revealed plot of the proposed sequel in some detail, I concluded by saying I doubted that the picture would ever be made because of disagreements between the studios that were supporting the venture. One of America's rich men called me aside privately after dinner and said, "I'll give you a check for a million dollars tonight if that will help get this picture started." I thanked him but explained that financial support was not the issue. It was creative support that we needed.

I have little doubt that sometime, somehow, this story will be made as a film. The estate has commissioned an author to write a novel of the sequel. Publishers around the world have bid for the rights based on seeing only two chapters and an outline of the rest of the story. Zanuck and I hope someday to reclaim the movie rights, if we like the book.

Dennis Brown of the *Los Angeles Times* asked me these questions. Here are my responses.

Dennis: The telephone rings and somebody from the William Morris Agency says, "You're it! You're going to produce the sequel to *Gone With the Wind.* We're sending you the new novel. You're going to love it." Who are the first three people you will call?

Me: Dick Zanuck, my agent Sam Cohn, and my wife.

Dennis: What do you say to your wife?

Me: "Guess what? Dick Zanuck and I are going to produce the sequel to *Gone With the Wind.*" Helen says, "Oh my God," but with an intonation that is hard to read.

Dennis: Like, oh no, this isn't getting revived *again* is it? She's been through it all before.

Me: She'll love it. She'd be perfectly happy going through it again. However, my fourth call would be to my internist. I'd say, "Look, you've got to keep me going for another ten years."

Those of us who were involved with Old Hollywood rarely read anything that resembles the truth of what it was like. Every now and then, but most infrequently, I read something that's on the money as far as the way it was. Today, most of the new filmmakers practice a kind of Shintoism or ancestor worship in which they revere what was put on the screen in the forties and fifties and even before, as though we were all artists instead of artisans. They seem to believe that the good work of the past came out of a conscious effort to create art as opposed to doing good work or professional work, work that would earn us a living and put bread on the table. I quote from an article that appeared in the June 30, 1988, issue of the *New York Review of Books,* or *New York Review,* as it's now called. The author is James Harvey. Mr. Harvey gets right to the point of what I remember Hollywood to be. He speaks of the great days of Hollywood as the late forties and fifties, saying:

> It is nearly always a surprise to survivors of old Hollywood that people now think so highly of the work they did. They're pleased, of course, but to have other people interpreting, even appropriating, your past can be disturbing. . . . For the actively creative types, the directors and screenwriters, the admiration can be threatening, as if it were depriving them of their pasts, even of their achievements. There is almost always some element in appreciative accounts of their work that strikes them as deeply wrong. They never meant all that, they say, and shouldn't they know what they are talking about?

Latter-day appreciation seems to suggest an intent to their work that was never there for them. That's the point, says Harvey. He goes on to say:

> I doubt that a great movie comedy like Leo McCarey's *The Awful Truth* (1937), for example, or Preston Sturges's *The Lady Eve* (1941), could have had the brilliance and depth they have if they had aimed at such achievements. It is this refusal of importance and ambition that characterized the Hollywood studio movie, the best and the worst of them. When they were magical or inspired, they were also casual, offhand, coming out of the commonest reality and transfiguring it. They may have been fantasies but they were about our everyday life, precisely because they seemed continuous with it. They testified to its possibilities even at their most fantastic. The star of a movie in those days was probably at a greater distance from its effect than most of its other principal contributors. That distance was almost in the nature of stardom.

I've had the luck to be able to observe Hollywood as a participant and also write about it, although my best years, I believe, were those spent as a newspaperman, editor, and writer of books and magazine stories. Perhaps that is because I was young as a journalist and middle-aged-to-old as a movie man. I remain a journalist in spirit. My admiration for stars of the press is greater than for stars of the screen. In fact I am star-struck by news gatherers (whom entertainment stars generally hold in low repute).

The good journalists I know have tremendous enthusiasm, and are rarely jaded. They are relentless in getting a story but have a balanced view of what a story is. Abe Rosenthal, former executive editor of *The New York Times;* Mike Wallace, correspondent for CBS's *60 Minutes;* ABC's Barbara Walters; Don Hewitt, executive producer and creator of *60 Minutes;* and Walter Cronkite come to mind as prime examples of the best. Not one of them is under fifty-five and three of them are over seventy. Energy, curiosity, intelligence, and an ability to write are the main prerequisites for success in journalism. Accuracy helps too.

There's nothing wrong with the magazine, book, record, television, or motion picture businesses that imagination and appealing to basic human interest cannot remedy. There are a lot of people out there willing and able to buy, but you mustn't bore them. If you bore them, they turn away. Top management types in the communications field can be extraordinarily insular. At Twentieth Century Fox, we had a board of directors who knew nothing about motion pictures, understood nothing about motion pictures, and never saw motion pictures—except with their own kind at fund-raising society premieres. These men—there wasn't a woman among them—didn't understand why motion pictures couldn't be manufactured in the same orderly manner as package goods. Box-office phenomena are not the product of committee action or research. Research held that *E.T.* could never succeed. What the Beatles accomplished could never have been programmed on a computer. Someday, shareholders will demand that chief executive officers take personal responsibility for failures instead of blaming their committees and middle management.

Years ago, when *Look* magazine folded, everyone mourned the demise of a great magazine and indeed the decline of the magazine industry in general. What they really were observing was the decline of the general-magazine industry: Special-interest magazines flourished as never before and magazines are now richer than ever. Proof is the fact that, as noted earlier, press lord Rupert Murdoch paid over three billion dollars for Walter Annenberg's magazine empire, more than he paid for his movie company and television stations combined. Hachette paid close to a billion dollars for the onetime CBS magazine properties.

Look ceased to be interesting before its demise. I well remember its early days. *The New York Times,* in its obituary on *Look,* showed a reproduction of the cover of its first issue, which displayed the following blurbs and visuals: PAROLE SCANDAL; WHY SO POPULAR?; a picture of the idol of that time, FDR; JOAN CRAWFORD, BEAUTY X-RAY; KEEP INFORMED, 200 PICTURES, 1,001 FACTS; the big photograph was Goering, Germany's fat and jolly-looking air minister. *Look* was originally conceived as a kind of potpourri of information, much as *USA Today* publishes. It was a kind of American Sunday-London paper.

The idea that photo journalism is through is a lot of nonsense. The idea that television and high costs put *Look* out of business is, in my estimate, also a lot of nonsense. *Look* was boring when it took itself very seriously. People don't want fourteen pages on the World Bank. It isn't the province of every magazine to be a responsible journalistic medium. That's fine for the *New Statesman* or *The Guardian.* But if you're going after mass circulation, you must have mass appeal. At the end, *Look* lacked mass appeal and went out of business because of unplanned obsolescence.

The resurrected *Vanity Fair* under Tina Brown's brilliant editorship and, in the mass market, Time Inc.'s *People* prove general-interest publications can flourish in today's world if imagination and talent are applied.

Movies have always been male; so has the business, until recently. The idea that the male "buddy" picture is something invented by Paul Newman and Robert Redford is not true. Tracy and Gable and Bogart once ruled the screen, as did the Marx Brothers, Laurel and Hardy, and Victor McLaglen with other male stars. True, Madonna, Cher, Midler, Streep, Close, and Griffith are changing things, but no more than Crawford, Harlow, Garbo, Shearer, and Monroe did in their time. The big action is still with the men. Eddie Murphy, Ford, Stallone, Hanks, Cruise gross more than all the women stars combined. There are still not enough scripts written for, or by, women, movies' prime customers. Women's stories still tend to wind up in television miniseries. Why aren't these popular women's stories finding their way to the big screen? There are too many male chief executives who decide what pictures should be made. Those women executives with the big titles still have only the power to recommend. The switch that turns on the green light approving a picture for production is firmly held by a man.

In Hollywood, ego is billing. Billing in Hollywood has to do with the positioning of the names of stars, writer, director, and producer in advertising. Years ago at Twentieth Century Fox, the commissary began to name sandwiches after stars, as did some New York and Hollywood restaurants. There was a Don Ameche sandwich, an Alice Faye sandwich, and an Orson Welles (by contract, his had to be a steak sandwich). The front office soon put a stop to this, reasoning that if stars start to select the food which bears their name, some will demand a caviar sandwich, others will ask for a sturgeon sandwich, and humble ham, chicken, and bacon-and-tomato sandwiches will go nameless.

Melvyn Bragg's superb and richly annotated biography of Richard Burton makes much of Burton's drinking. Drinking has never been as frowned upon in the London theater or British cinema as in America. British studios served whiskey while American studio commissaries remained dry until growing deficits forced them to offer beer and wine. The British did not recognize alcoholism as a disease so much as a form of gluttony and bloody bad manners to get drunk, you know! A chap was supposed to be able to hold his liquor.

My favorite story of drinking while onstage concerns a well-known actor who is weaving and slurring in the first act of a Shakespearean play. A dowager in the first row exclaims to her companion, "Why, I believe the man is drunk." "Yes, madam, you are right," whispers the actor as he leans perilously over the footlights, "but wait till you see the duke of Gloucester."

When Darryl Zanuck left for Paris to take up a new life of wine, women, and song, some of his Hollywood pals felt abandoned. Nunnally Johnson, the witty screenwriter and author who wrote many pictures for Zanuck, was asked by Zanuck's daughter whether he thought her daddy would ever see his old friends again. Nunnally said, "Only when he becomes impotent."

When Stanley Kubrick's film *2001* was previewed in Washington, D.C., in March of 1968, the response was ominously mild. The then chief executive officer of MGM, the company which financed *2001*, was Bob O'Brien. *2001* cost a lot of money, and the word that night was that he was out of a job. At the end of the preview, marked by scattered applause, mostly from MGM executives, word also came that Lyndon Johnson would not run for reelection, whereupon the chief publicity officer of MGM gathered some of his group around him and said solemnly, "Gentlemen, tonight we have lost two presidents."

Robert Wagner, former mayor of the City of New York and a distinguished lawyer, is a raconteur of note, particularly of Irish stories. His wife, Phyllis, is equally witty. Together, they are a delight. If the conversation during a weekend at their Mount Kisco estate were recorded and put to paper, it would make a five-foot shelf of marvelous anecdotes.

Frank Sinatra is especially fond of them, as he was of Phyllis's late former husband, publisher Bennett Cerf, himself an irrepressible storyteller. Sinatra is known for his innovative gifts but this one struck me as outstanding.

The Wagners like to serve hot dogs and hamburgers for lunch. They are cooked over a barbecue pit. While Francis Albert was spending the weekend, he became increasingly agitated as lunchtime approached. He was about to indulge in one of his dangerous outbursts when quite suddenly he relaxed and smiled. In the distance, up a winding path, came his house gift pushed by three perspiring men. It was a shiny, new hot-dog stand of the kind seen only on Manhattan streets, where sidewalk vendors use them to feed passing pedestrians. There it was, complete with stove, hot dogs, hamburgers, buns, sauerkraut, and mustard, all ready to eat. It has served the Wagners ever since.

One of my favorite Bob Wagner stories has to do with the funeral of an especially hated man in an Irish village. Nobody could be found to deliver a eulogy. Even the local priest refused to dispatch the man with the church's blessing. In despair, the funeral director addressed the few who attended the services, more to make certain he had died than to mourn him, pleading, "Is there nobody here to say a good word for the deceased?" "Yes," came a voice from the back, "his brother was worse."

You may never have heard of Elmer G. Letterman, but in the 1940s, Elmer Letterman was the world's most famous insurance man. He insured Jimmy Durante's nose, Marlene Dietrich's legs, and Mae West's boobs. One of his books was titled *The Sale Begins When the Customer Says No.* It seemed to me he was the perfect subject for a magazine article. I never sold the article but Mr. Letterman sold me insurance, which I still have.

Nobody is rich enough not to be put down by someone richer. The subtler the putdown the more absurdly painful. It happened while my wife and I, among others, were being shown the extraordinary Charlottesville, Virginia, estate of media mogul John Kluge. Cardinals of the press, media, and industry were gawking at the perfection and grandeur of Albemarle Farms and its newly built Georgian mansion, which hundreds of years hence may well be perplexing to archaeologists because of its state of preservation. They may not know it was built over two hundred years after the Georgian period.

We drove around more than ten thousand acres of rolling hills which the Kluges had acquired and landscaped. The only comparable property nearby was Thomas Jefferson's Monticello. As we entered the stables, where Holsteins and Arabian steeds stood contentedly in sumptuous stalls, my walking companion, himself almost as grand a tycoon as John Kluge, was telling me about the rare antique chandelier he had acquired for his apartment in New York's Pierre. "There are only three of them in the world," he boasted, and then, glancing at the ceiling, exclaimed, "Shit! There are the other two. In John's stable!"

I saw Salvador Dali at lunch almost daily at Laurent, an excellent New York restaurant off Park Avenue. His entrance was signaled by the sight of his flowing black cape and silver-topped stick. Madame Dali arrived first and then Dali, often with two or three beautiful women. Madame Dali was addicted to increasing Monsieur Dali's net worth. I appealed to her base instinct by persuading Dali to create an advertising poster for a Twentieth Century Fox film titled *Fantastic Voyage.* The idea appealed to Dali and the price to Madame Dali. Dali proceeded to paint the poster. A Fox executive named Harry Sokolov interrupted the work to give Dali a telephone message. Irritated by this intrusion, Dali proceeded to paint Sokolov's suit. Sokolov, equally irritated, turned in a ninety-dollar cleaning bill to Fox. "Idiot." Richard Zanuck chastised Harry. "You could have sold your suit for a hundred thousand dollars instead of collecting a ninety-dollar bill on your expense account. Don't you realize it was a Dali original?"

Jacqueline Susann, author of *Valley of the Dolls,* invented the author tour. A former actress, she performed brilliantly on talk shows. Her ad-libs were merciless, although she staggered a bit when Truman Capote described her as a "truckdriver in drag." Actually, she was beautiful—dark-haired, lithe, and sensual. In a discussion of authors on one talk show, she was asked what she thought of Philip Roth, who had just published *Portnoy's Complaint,* his ode to masturbation. "I like him," Jackie responded, in what has become a classic put-down, "but I wouldn't want to shake hands with him."

Helen and I became close friends of Jackie and her husband, Irving Mansfield. Irving was the mastermind of Jackie's tours. He was obsessed with her success and, in the course of accompanying her on book tours, learned as much about the book business as most publishers. No bookstore or thousand-watt radio station was ignored in their pursuit of bestsellerdom. He demanded and got star treatment on the road for his wife . . . suites, champagne, limousines. It paid off. Jackie herself knew every important bookseller and never left town without dispensing gifts to them. The marriage was a curious but good one. Jackie, although a swinger in her time, was quite possessive. Once, she wandered into Irving's office when he was producing *Talent Scouts* for CBS and noticed a letter on his secretary's desk. His secretary was out to lunch. "Dear Mr. Mansfield," the letter read, "I am Sally May and I would do anything to be on your show, and when I say anything, I mean *any*thing." Jackie sat down at the typewriter and replied as follows: "Dear Sally May, I have read your letter to Mr. Mansfield. I am Mrs. Mansfield and I do everything for Mr. Mansfield and when I say everything, I mean everything."

As close as we were to the Mansfields, we had no idea Jackie was dying of cancer or that they had a retarded child in an institution.

Behind the glitz, theirs was a sad life. Jackie was enormously generous to her friends. She pledged her own considerable earnings to force a publisher to pay Helen overdue royalties. We last saw the Mansfields walking hand in hand down Park Avenue after a screening we attended together. After her death, Irving had the good fortune to find a woman who would love and care for him during his last years, which were all too few.

A film intended for Christmas release was in production. The cast included a herd of reindeer. The two weeks that the reindeer were available to the production company turned out to be the two weeks in the year when they were growing new antlers. Ordinarily docile, sweet, and easy to direct, reindeer apparently go berserk during antler-growing season. This unfortunate production company was getting nothing on film except some very angry, thrashing around, horny (sorry) reindeer. The script had to be rewritten to cover this new interpretation of Santa's helpers, and the turbulence he experienced from Dasher, Dancer, Prancer, Vixen, Comet, Cupid, Donner, and Blitzen. It's only one example of the imponderables of making a motion picture and not in the least an extreme one. Who would have even asked if there was a season when reindeer were not jolly and sweet?

Most actors are professional and not at all difficult if the script and director are good. One actress, who would sue if I named her, was so difficult that three different endings were devised in the event of her likely removal from the film. The revised script provided for her to be (1) murdered, (2) abducted and held for ransom for the duration of the story, and (3) run over. When the revised script with alternate endings fell into her hands (by design), she gave no further trouble.

In 1970, John Huston made a movie titled *The Kremlin Letter.* At the sneak preview, members of the audience asked, "What is the Kremlin letter?" There was no letter in the movie. "Damned if I know," Huston replied. "I've never understood that part of it." Neither Richard Zanuck nor I could explain the title. We turned to Noel Behn, the author of the novel on which the film was based. "Yeah, that confused me too," said the man who had thought up the title and written the book.

Mel Brooks is a certified funny man of movies. His film *The Producers* is a classic, as is *High Anxiety.* He is perhaps best known for *Blazing Saddles,* a hit of such proportions as almost to propel him onto *Forbes* magazine's list of the four hundred richest Americans. How and why Mel Brooks came to produce, direct, and write a great deal of *Blazing Saddles* is a Hollywood story of more modest proportions. Early in 1971, a synopsis reached my desk at Warner Brothers in New York with the unpromising title of *Black Bart.* It was the story of a Texas governor who lost a bet that he could make a black man sheriff of a redneck Texas town. The reader's comment on the synopsis was brief. "If you don't buy this, I will," it read. I glanced at the reader's name. She was the daughter of one of the principal owners of Warner Communications. I suffered "high anxiety" that she could and would buy *Black Bart* and bought it instead. Judy Feiffer, my savvy story executive, came up with the idea of enlisting Mel Brooks to direct it, and Dick Zanuck and I persuaded Warner Brothers to go forward with the film.

I have been taunted and criticized about my overtipping. I do overtip, outrageously. Perhaps the most amusing comments about this trait are those of my friend Gene Shalit, on the occasion of my being honored by New York's venerable Dutch Treat Club. Said Gene:

> What does David know from Dutch treats? It's very peculiar that he should be honored by the Dutch Treat Club. He has grabbed more checks than Willie Sutton and made more friends doing it. David's idea of a Dutch treat is to go to Holland and treat everyone in the country to dinner and then tip the royal family on the way out. David is well known as one of America's most prolific and giving tippers. Skycaps at airports have been injured crashing into each other in their frenzy to grab his bags when they spot him coming. When he appears in an elegant restaurant, maître d's have strained themselves snapping their fingers over their heads. He has left ten dollars in an empty coat checkroom in the heat of summer so the girl will find it when she returns in October. He figures it isn't her fault he didn't wear a coat. One of David's best friends is the bon vivant Steve Birnbaum, America's most famous and ubiquitous travel expert. Steve has a splendid house in upstate New York and recalls inviting David and Helen Gurley Brown up for the weekend. Now, David is a city boy, the consummate urbane urbanite, who lives in a quadriplex with a back door where groceries miraculously appear. So now David comes to the country and Steve says, "I'm going to the super-

market. Would you like to come along?" So David, for the first time in his adult life, is in a supermarket. Steve is dumbfounded, when he gets to the check-out counter, to discover David is trying to tip the bagger. Here's the kid trying to put herring into the bag, while David is trying to shove five dollars into the confused kid's hand. Steve told me that he had planned to take David for a walk in the woods, but was afraid David would try to tip the trees.

Well, I suppose some of that's true.

Sam Cohn, an extraordinarily interesting show business agent, represents such formidable talents as Meryl Streep, Woody Allen, and Mike Nichols. He is the only agent who has been profiled in *The New Yorker.* Little wonder. In addition to his undoubted gifts as an artists' representative, he is a genuine eccentric. In thirty years of lunches with Sam, we did scarcely any business. Moreover, lunch was hardly an expense because Sam ate paper. I mean paper matchcovers and paper napkins. He devoured them. His paper-eating compulsion almost did him in at Los Angeles International Airport, where he consumed his parking ticket after leaving the area. Several days later, he was destined to search the vast expanse of LAX's parking areas for his rental car and then somehow prove his right to reclaim it.

The story I've told about my friend Sam Cohn may suggest that he is a man given to anxiety, manifesting itself in the nervous ingestion of paper products. Such is far from the case. He is actually calm and imperturbable, as this next story demonstrates.

Sam was a half-hour late for an appointment with Bill Bernstein, executive vice-president of Orion Pictures, and found Mr. Bernstein occupied on the telephone when he arrived. Never mind. Sam made himself comfortable on a couch and fell asleep. When Mr. Bernstein emerged to greet him, he observed how peacefully Sam slumbered. He decided not to awaken him but instead pinned a note to Sam's lapel stating he would see him after lunch. Sam was gone when he returned. The reason for the appointment has never been disclosed and no mention has ever been made of the incident until now.

When Catherine Marshall wrote a best-selling book titled *A Man Called Peter,* I sought the film rights. It was a wonderfully moving story of a sensual woman who felt God was getting in the way of her marriage to a minister. It was produced by Samuel G. Engel, directed by Henry Koster, and starred Jean Peters. What is not generally known is that God had a hand in granting Fox the film rights. A condition of the agreement with the author was that the option for the film rights not be exercised unless God approved. This was to be made known to us by prayer in Sam Engel's office. There we were, on our knees, Sam Engel, Catherine Marshall, and I, after several scotches, seeking a sign from above. It came as a series of earth tremors, measuring about 4 on the Richter scale. Catherine accepted this as a divine manifestation, and we gave loud thanks after several more scotches. Our prayers were answered at the box office.

Of all the celebrities I've met, the one I would have liked to know better is Frank Sinatra. His torch songs were my lullabies. He is one of the few stars whose energy flashes like lightning through every room he enters, and turns every head in a Hollywood commissary, where stars are commonplace. Part of his appeal is the sense he projects of being dangerous (which he is). He wanted to star in *The Verdict.* The lead role, played by Paul Newman, called for an actor to portray a womanizer who drank too much. "I'd have no trouble with that," was the message Frank sent. We were uncomfortable turning him down, wondering what retribution lay in store. Such is the menace of Sinatra.

Yul Brynner starred in *The King and I* almost to the day of his death from lung cancer. He owned the role since his debut opposite Gertrude Lawrence and his Academy Award performance in the movie. My wife and I saw him often during his last days, when he was in intolerable pain during each performance. His audiences never saw him falter. When we dined with him at the Russian Tea Room, he told us that he continued to rehearse his role daily despite the pain and the fact that he had played it for over twenty years. He could have played it in his sleep, but he discovered new meaning in the role each time he performed it. When he realized he would die from lung cancer, he filmed an antismoking message to be shown after his death. The King was dead—needlessly so, he reminded his viewers.

There is an unshakable belief in Hollywood that a script that is quickly written can't be good. Back in the fifties, Irving Lazar suggested that Romain Gary, author of *The Roots of Heaven,* adapt his own novel for the John Huston production of the film. Darryl Zanuck quickly agreed. Three days later, Lazar, who was Gary's agent, called me to say, "Listen, I've got a problem. Gary has finished his script. It's great. If I give it to you now, they'll think it's no good. Should I wait three months to turn it in?" I advised him against waiting, declaring that we were above such prejudices against quick delivery. I was wrong.

I met Clare Boothe Luce long after her days as editor, playwright, and ambassador. She was living in a villa on the grounds of the Arizona Biltmore. We were discussing a television series idea when, to make a point about her financial independence, she pointed to a large painting of the newly constructed Time-Life Building in New York, saying, "Harry [her husband, *Time* founder Henry Luce] gave me this. The building, not the painting."

The Sound of Music, which was to save Twentieth Century Fox, was turned down as too risky when a deal for the film rights was first presented to Fox's board of directors. Only after Fox's president, Spyros Skouras, received a call from Irving Lazar, representing Jack Warner and offering Fox a $250,000 profit to turn the property over to Warner Brothers, did the board relent and approve the deal. The film did not go forward until years later, after Skouras had been deposed and Darryl Zanuck became president. Richard Zanuck put the film into production with Julie Andrews as its star and Robert Wise directing. Although it became the most successful film of its day, the premiere in New York was a wake. Judith Crist assassinated the film in her *New York Herald Tribune* review. *The New York Times* did not endorse it. Director Robert Wise was so disconsolate that he walked through Central Park hoping to be mugged. The film opened to undistinguished business, but it built and stayed forever at a profitable but not outstanding level. After a year, it still attracted as many moviegoers as it did during its opening weeks. A woman in Scotland wrote to say she had seen *The Sound of Music* ninety-seven times and hoped to qualify for the *Guinness Book of World Records.* Pauline Kael, later the ball-breaking critic of *The New Yorker,* was fired from her job on *McCall's* because of complaints from readers who were outraged by her criticism of *The Sound of Music.* Eventually, it was canonized as a classic and the bad reviews were forgotten.

Why do we enjoy disaster, particularly when it befalls the rich and powerful? I think we like to see power destroyed, subjugated, humiliated. We humans are primitives still. Or are we terminally jealous of those who have achieved more, and yearn for their demise?

This is about our afternoon in 1966 with the then richest man in the world, reclusive Jean Paul Getty, at his home, Sutton Place, in England. It is probably more accurately described as a manor house, just this side of being a castle. The house was originally a gift of Henry VIII to (as my wife put it in her *Cosmo* column) a favorite whose head he didn't cut off. Mr. Getty had called my wife at Claridge's and asked whether she would come by for dinner. When he discovered America's then sex symbol was married, dinner was downgraded to tea. We couldn't have dined with him anyway, as we were going to the theater. Helen later recalled, "Mr. Getty's butler and dog (dog? a buffalo with long, shaggy fur) met us at the door. Shawn (that was his name) snarled, growled and woofed. I went in to meet Shawn's master. Mr. Getty is tall, friendly and . . . yes . . . a charmer. We talked about movies, magazines, men, women, love, oil, and committees (he's only against the last item). After high tea, which I poured, after managing to figure out which forks went with which tea cakes without a Rosetta stone or an Emily Post, the seven of us—Mr. Getty, David, Shawn, three Norwich terriers named Winnie, April, and Mickey, and I—went for a walk in the gardens. The moon was up when we left."

My version goes like this: Mr. Getty asked Helen to serve tea, which she did with grace and elan. Then we got down to conversation. I was full of questions about oil stocks, the relative value of gold, silver, and uranium, hoping perhaps for some tip from the Almighty as to how to make a killing on Wall Street or in real estate. It was soon evident that Mr. Getty preferred to talk about sex. Why else did he invite Helen Gurley Brown? He asked her, "Why is it that I can't have a successful relationship with a woman? I've had so much success in business, and I've merged corporations, but I don't seem to be able to merge myself successfully." I think he had had four wives by then and was now alone. Helen's advice to the world's richest man: "Why don't you find someone closer to your own age?" Getty, a very correct and rather stately man, said, "Mrs. Brown, I've thought about that. You know, if I brought a woman of perhaps forty who'd be suitable for me to this house and I received an urgent telephone call from Saudi Arabia or Los Angeles and I had to be on the telephone for an hour or two, she would be annoyed. She wouldn't roam around and take care of herself. I'll give you a better example. Suppose we were driving in my car. I think that if that kind of woman were to be jolted by a hole in the road and bumped her head, I would hear from her solicitor. The youngster would think nothing of a little bump on her head."

Mr. Getty took us around his home. We noticed the enormous tapestries, some of them dating back to the fourteenth and thirteenth centuries. The house was awesome in its beauty and grandeur. Mr. Getty spoke of Los Angeles where his principal residence, now the Getty Museum, was and said that he didn't go there anymore because of his emphysema. He couldn't take the smog even out at Malibu. He carefully described all of the features of his house on a two-hour tour and I was at a loss to express my gratitude to this man who didn't know us but had invited us into his home. I said, "You know, Mr. Getty, I don't know if this will ever be possible for you, but we'd love to have you come for dinner to our house in New York when you travel there. Of course, it's only an apartment." Whereupon Mr. Getty said, "Mr. Brown, before I lived in this Sutton Place, I lived in your Sutton Place. I would be delighted to dine with you in your apartment." He was referring, of course, to Sutton Place in Manhattan. As for his difficulties with women, Mr. Getty finally acknowledged that he might be a rather difficult man and conceded it was possible that women might be attracted to him for reasons other than love. Or if for love, love of money.

Howard Hughes was never outclassed as an eccentric. This brilliant, reclusive billionaire cared little for what the world thought, caught up, as he was, in his own dementia. Consider how he dealt with an attempt in the early 1950s by a group of bankers to buy up his empire. The catalyst was Darryl Zanuck, one of Mr. Hughes's few intimate friends. Mr. Hughes was accustomed to coming to the Twentieth Century Fox studio at three or four in the morning, a time when Zanuck was winding up viewing the previous day's output of production companies and rough cuts of the movies Fox was churning out. Knowing Zanuck's close relationship with Hughes, the bankers, headed by the Lehman Brothers group (Fox's bankers), approached Darryl to see if Hughes would be interested in selling his entire empire, which then consisted of TWA as well as the Hughes Tool Company and other important businesses.

Hughes indicated that he was interested, but he was as eccentric in dress as he was in manner. Darryl implored, "For Christ's sake, Howard, get yourself a decent suit. You look like a bum." Howard promised to buy a Sunday suit. Dates were set for the bankers to come to California and they came from everywhere—Boston, Wall Street, Cleveland, Atlanta. Mr. Hughes put them up in the most luxurious bungalows the Beverly Hills Hotel could provide.

Gradually, the meetings took place. Hughes's accountants were brought in. Lawyers were assembled. Additional accountants were flown in from the East. Every division and subdivision of the vast financial empire was minutely examined as experts pored over books, assets, plants, inventories, liabilities, loans, tax rulings. After weeks and then months of elaborate scrutiny during which nights were indistinguishable from days, the bankers established a price they were willing to offer.

When the offer was relayed to Hughes, he announced perfunctorily that he was not interested in selling. Zanuck was stunned, and so were the bankers, some of whom were nearly as rich as Hughes. After everyone had departed in considerable agitation and frustration, Zanuck asked Hughes, "How could you do that? How could you allow all those people to work for months and then say you're not interested? I don't understand why you'd put yourself and everyone else through such an ordeal." Mr. Hughes said, "I just wanted to find out how much I was worth."

Hughes was generous to his friends and lent money readily. One of his friends, the Hollywood director Preston Sturges, received fifty thousand dollars. Years passed and Mr. Sturges noticed that long after he sent Mr. Hughes a check for fifty thousand dollars as repayment, the check had never cleared his account. It drove him and his accountant crazy. Where was the check? Had Hughes received it? Was it lost in the mail? Should he stop payment? He didn't know. After four and a half years of carrying this check as uncleared, Sturges saw Hughes walking alone down Fifth Avenue. He caught up to him, tugged at his arm and said, "Howard. Did you ever receive my check for fifty thousand dollars? I paid you back, you know. Do you remember whether you got it?" Howard replied, "I really don't know, Preston. I never open my mail."

My wife, who was a secretary at the Foote, Cone and Belding advertising agency in Los Angeles in 1943, is the authority for this Hughes story. The agency then serviced the RKO Pictures account. Hughes owned RKO, and Jane Russell was both his star in the RKO film *The Outlaw* and under personal contract to him (until beyond his death, as it turned out).

He would come frequently to the Foote, Cone and Belding offices to look over the advertising which, as anyone old enough will remember, was quite flamboyant even for those times. Miss Russell was displayed provocatively in a haystack.

One executive worked tirelessly for seven or eight months on the RKO account and received accolades from Hughes for his efforts. Speculation, somewhat grounded in fact, swept through the office that this executive would be in for a very substantial gift if he was patient. Patient he was.

Two years passed and word—unofficial, you understand—was leaked from Hughes's headquarters that indeed he was in for a handsome bonus.

Finally, on Christmas Eve, the call came. He hurriedly left his fireside, his Christmas tree, and his family to go down to the Hughes mansion on Rossmore Street. Howard Hughes was there and wanted to talk about the advertising. Hours passed. It was nearly dawn of Christmas day and the exhausted account executive, now quite depressed by the absence of any largesse, was dismissed.

As he was shown to the door, Hughes shuffled up and said, "Oh, by the way, there's something I have meant to give you for quite a while." He then produced an envelope. The executive thanked him and attempted to restrain himself from opening the envelope until he reached the street.

There, in the early light, he found a check all right, a check for $954,000 made out to the order of the Mellon National Bank of Pittsburgh. Obviously the wrong check. It took eight and a half months for him to persuade the Hughes Tool office to accept the stray check and obtain permission from Hughes to forward it to its rightful payee. Nobody at Hughes knew anything about a check for him, and evidently no one dared to take up the matter with Mr. Hughes. Certainly not the executive, who never believed in Santa Claus again.

Hughes was aware of the value of money, even small sums. Once, while he was having a business conference in the wee hours of the night—as usual in a battered twenty-year-old Chevrolet on the corner of some God-forsaken acreage on the outskirts of Los Angeles—he asked his associate to stay over another day. The man said, "Howard, I'd be happy to do it, but I'm flying back to New York tomorrow." Hughes asked, "What flight?" "TWA—Flight Ninety," the man replied. Howard said, "Just a minute." The sole owner of TWA left his car and went to a phone booth. Anxious, the man asked, "Why did you have to make a telephone call at this hour?" Howard replied, "I wanted to cancel your reservation. That's cash business for my company, you know."

In addition to John Kluge, there are only two other men I've known who enjoyed their wealth and felt no guilt in displaying it. They are the late William Randolph Hearst and the ever-present Malcolm Forbes. Neither was crass nor vulgar nor mindlessly competitive, although few could compete with the splendor of their possessions. Donald Trump comes close, occupying one of the finest private homes in America, Mar-A-Lago in Palm Beach.

Other superrich are more modest in the way they live, although investment banker Henry Kravis, conglomerator Ron Perlman, Hartz Industries chief Leonard Stern, financier Saul Steinberg, publisher/realtor Mort Zuckerman, retailer Milton Petrie, and real-estate magnate Harry Helmsley are not slumming. Only chain-store owner Sam Walton, sometimes dubbed the richest man in America, lives in a manner more suited to one of his employees, but that is his particular brand of reverse snobbism.

Malcolm, John, and in his time Mr. Hearst, however, exhibited such joy in their toys that one can scarcely summon up one scintilla of jealousy. Malcolm Forbes has a townhouse in Manhattan, an estate in New Jersey, a château in Normandy, a palace in Tangiers, a Christopher Wren house in London, a ranch with thousands of acres in Colorado, and an island in Fiji. I have been to several of them and never felt intimidated. The same is true of visiting Pat and John Kluge. When I first talked to John or, years ago, to William Randolph Hearst, I found they were soft gentlemen in their demeanor, disliking pretense and pomposity and avoiding self-promotion. I have no problem with the rich, only with those who have a problem being rich.

In 1959, Nikita Khrushchev came to lunch at the Fox studios. At that lunch, there were more stars than there were in heaven (to borrow an old MGM motto). The Soviet chief wanted to see as much as he could of the United States and why not a movie studio? And so, with the help of the State Department and the Motion Picture Association, Twentieth Century Fox was designated to play host to Mr. and Mrs. Khrushchev and a Soviet delegation of novelists, poets, and members of the KGB.

We gathered in the historic commissary, whose walls contained murals of old Fox stars and a youthful Darryl F. Zanuck presiding over his flock—all very art deco. We were told to be there early, about 11:30 in the morning, to await the arrival of the Soviet delegation.

Television monitors had been set up so that we could see them on closed circuit as they approached the studio, turning off Pico Boulevard onto the lot and driving to the very steps of the commissary. Soviet secret police inspected the flowers at each table with metal detectors; others were in the kitchen tasting food; still others were looking over the lavatories, the shrubbery around the commissary, and everything along the route that Khrushchev would be taking.

I sat at a table across from Marilyn Monroe, Josh Logan, and George Cukor. Henry Fonda, earphones plugged into a portable radio, listened to a baseball game during the proceedings. Frank Sinatra was at a table seated next to Mrs. Khrushchev and Mikhail Sholokhov, author of *And Quiet Flows the Don.*

Sinatra was drinking in those days, and he went up to the head table to sample the Russian vodka, available only to Khrushchev, Fox President Spyros Skouras, and a few other dignitaries. The rest of us had to make do with American vodka.

When Skouras arose to speak, he told Nikita Khrushchev that he had come to America as a poor boy from Greece, worked as a busboy in St. Louis, and with the help of his brothers had become one of the greatest entertainment moguls in the world, president of Twentieth Century Fox Film Corporation, proving the opportunities that existed in the United States, a free country.

General Secretary Khrushchev came to the podium and said, "You have progressed to be the head of a corporation, Mr. Skouras, but I, in a communist country, have become head of one of the world's greatest powers. You began working when you were thirteen, I began working when I was six. I rose in a socialist state to this position of power."

As I watched Khrushchev, I thought what an able capitalist, corporation head, or entrepreneur he could have been if he had emigrated to the United States. He seemed a likable man, a passionate man, but as it turned out a man bound for oblivion by the very nature of his unique charismatic personality. He was not enough a bureaucrat and too much a Western-type leader to satisfy his masters in the Politburo. Nikita Khrushchev and Spyros Skouras had much in common: They were passionate about life and their jobs.

Khrushchev's only recollections of movie stars were Deanna Durbin and Gary Cooper, who was there and whom he did recognize, quipping, "Yup." He didn't know who Marilyn Monroe was but knew about her husband, playwright Arthur Miller. Although his words were translated almost instantaneously by an interpreter, one had the feeling that he understood a great deal more English than we were led to believe.

After lunch, we milled over to a soundstage where *Can Can* was shooting. It was a mob scene. The secret police lost Khrushchev in the crowd. Once found, the Russian leader was unimpressed by the dancing. Russian dancing is four-star. It was as though we had taken a four-star chef to McDonald's.

Skouras, little known today, was more colorful than most Hollywood moguls who are remembered. He ruled Twentieth Century Fox from 1942 to 1962. Spyros and I were associated for many of those twenty years of epic turmoil. Fox itself was the greatest show on earth. Its boardroom drama and political and sexual intrigue were more spellbinding than most of its pictures.

Spyros Skouras was noted, and truly so, for his daring and his courage as well as for his compassion. While Darryl Zanuck ran production in California, Spyros, in his gothic, cathedral-like office in New York, backed Darryl's showy creative ventures and made similarly flamboyant deals on his own. The decision to change all Fox films to wide-screen CinemaScope was an example of one that paid off. There seemed to be no risk these two were not prepared to take.

Finally, as it must to all risk-takers, defeat came to Spyros, who was forced out, ironically, by Darryl, when Darryl took over the company from him in its financial crisis. Darryl's demise came a little more than seven years later when he was ousted by those money men whose names will never be recorded in the history of motion pictures.

While the show went on, Spyros's eccentricities were the subject of almost endless storytelling. Once, on a visit to the studio following an economy wave, he had a dreadful toothache and was in no mood for staff shortages. When he discovered that the studio dentist was among the missing, he summoned the studio manager and demanded to know why. "But, Mr. Skouras," said the manager, "you told me to fire everyone and so I fired the dentist, too." "You did right," Spyros responded, "but you used bad judgment."

During another economy wave Spyros, who used cables and telegrams the way ordinary people used Kleenex, advised his worldwide organization—fifteen thousand employees—to discontinue the practice of signing office communications with the words "Kindest regards" since every word cost money. His edict was sent, naturally, by domestic telegram and international cable to all concerned. "In future," it read, "omit kindest regards from all communications. Kindest regards, Spyros."

Spyros's Greek accent was often impenetrable. When his male secretary, a former journalist named Ulrich Bell, had difficulty in making sense of what he was told, Spyros attributed it to the fact that Bell was hard of hearing and ordered him to wear an earpiece. Bell dutifully complied and reported that he could now hear Skouras, but still could not understand him.

Spyros, stung by this rebuke to his clarity of speech, decided to address a Greek organization in his native language. He was dismayed to be told that his audience could not understand him because of his heavy accent . . . in Greek.

Spyros called me to report that his barber had told him about a young singer named Elvis Presley. "Never heard of him," I said, and, in 1955, none of our "wise men" at the Twentieth Century Fox Studio had, either. Spyros insisted that he was hot, hot, hot, and so we were ordered to find a story for him. On the shelf—a euphemism for the place where dead scripts are stored—there was one called *The Reno Brothers.* A young producer named Robert Jacks had developed it. I can't remember what it was about, except that it was a Western. And somehow, another young producer named David Weisbart had a notion that it could fit the talents of Elvis Presley (Weisbart had heard of him). The film was titled *Love Me Tender* and the record and title song of Elvis's first movie went on to make music history and Elvis Presley a star to this day, long years after his death. The film recouped its entire production cost within a single week of its release in 1956.

Presley's rotund manager was a Southerner named Colonel Tom Parker. Colonel Parker didn't bother reading scripts that were submitted to Elvis. "Just send me a million dollars, never mind the script," he'd say, "and Elvis will do the picture." And indeed we did, and indeed Elvis did, many millions of dollars ago.

An example of Skouras's comically shrewd story instinct was his comment about Stephen Vincent Benét's epic poem *John Brown's Body,* which the studio acquired but never made into a film. "Dave," he lectured me, "no film about the Civil War can possibly succeed unless the South wins." Think of it. In *Gone With the Wind,* the spirit of the Confederacy remains triumphant among the ruins.

Truman Capote's major work in the sixties was *In Cold Blood.* Capote was writing a screenplay at Twentieth Century Fox when I was there and for some reason did not offer us the screen rights to *In Cold Blood.* When Darryl Zanuck heard of this, he was incensed, considering it gross disloyalty for Truman not to have given the studio that was paying him to write a movie an opportunity to bid for his new book. I had no explanation, but I suggested that we immediately make an offer for the book to follow. Zanuck, still angered, said, "By all means. I was riding with the son of a bitch on an airplane to Paris and he never mentioned *In Cold Blood.*"

I called Irving "Swifty" Lazar, Truman's agent, and said we wanted to buy the rights to his next book. Truman had only the vaguest idea of what he would write next, but he had a very specific idea, through Swifty's eyes, of what he would need in the way of money. It was arranged that I visit Capote in Lazar's apartment at the Ritz Tower in New York. I was to listen to Capote but not take notes. Capote would tell me the story of his next book, very briefly, and I would take my recollection of what he said at that meeting back to my apartment, rap out a synopsis, and get back to Swifty with our offer.

There he was, Truman Capote, diminutive, sitting on a beige chair, his feet scarcely reaching the floor even though the chairs in Irving Lazar's apartment were low, for he is as small as Truman was. Truman told me, in his treble voice, the story of a very rich man on a flight to Paris, seated with his elegant society wife, determined to tell her during this flight of his love affair with someone she knew, when unaccountably she confesses her own infidelity. That was the beginning of it. It was supposed to be patterned after Jock Whitney, the New York society figure and owner of the *New York Herald Tribune.* There were few other details of what this book, which was to be called *Answered Prayers,* would be about. Hardly enough to fill a page, but I filled a page on my Remington typewriter when I returned to my apartment and immediately telexed this wisp of an idea to Darryl Zanuck, who authorized me to acquire the film rights at once. Lazar was startled by this, unaccustomed as he then was to selling unwritten books. He sold Fox the film rights for $275,000, shaking his head with incredulity at it all.

Years passed, with no delivery of the work by Truman Capote. Not only did years pass, but managements of the studio passed, including my own. No longer employed by Fox, I left behind the contract with Truman Capote for a book which had never been delivered. Capote had been paid in full, by the way. Another administration exhumed the contract and demanded the money back from Capote. Providentially, I had negotiated a condition in the contract that in the event of nondelivery, Capote would return what had been paid him with 6 percent interest added.

Capote paid back all the money plus interest, at Lazar's recommendation, because Swifty, by that time, felt he had sold the property for far too little, not realizing that Capote would not live to see the work finished. *Answered Prayers* went unanswered, but for a time fully paid for.

Funny Business

I have always found show business's ethnic jokes irresistible and inoffensive, as they are usually told by a member of the ethnic group. I often wonder who thinks them up. Here are a couple I have heard over the years, often more than once (as perhaps you have).

The first is about three men waiting at St. Peter's Gate for entrance to heaven. One is a Catholic. He advances to St. Peter, who asks, "How have you suffered, my son?" The Catholic answers, "I have been tortured, endured all kinds of religious persecution, suffered in the name of Christ for thousands of years." St. Peter nods and says, "I know, my son. Now tell me, how do you spell God?" The Catholic spells "G-o-d" and St. Peter points to the gate and says, "That way. Welcome to Paradise." The next man, a Jew, approaches and is asked the same question and replies, "You know how our people have suffered. For over five thousand years, we have been victims of incredible torture and persecution . . . the Spanish Inquisition, Hitler, and even discrimination in America." St. Peter interrupts him, asking, "How do you spell God?" and the Jew spells "G-o-d." St. Peter says, "Fine. That is wonderful. Right through that door. Your ordeals are over." A black man advances and is asked the same question. "Have we suffered?" he replies. "You must be joking. You know how the black man has suffered. We have been persecuted, discriminated against, been made slaves, whipped, been taken away from our homes in Africa and put on slave boats. Nobody has suffered more than we." St. Peter says slowly, "Yes, I understand. Now I must ask you, how do you spell Albuquerque?"

The next is about a rabbi who implores his rich and fashionable congregation to realize they are as nothing before God, that they are as dust. To make his point, he invites members of his congregation to get up and tell how unimportant they are in the eyes of God. A banker in the rear of the congregation wails, "I am absolutely nothing in the face of God. I am but a grain of sand, if that. I am nobody." A woman in a sable coat gets in the mood and screams, "Oh Lord, I am nobody. God knows I am nothing. I amount to nothing. I am nothing at all." And so it goes as one member after another of the congregation rises to profess humility and insist that he is nothing at all. Nobody. Heads of multimillion-dollar businesses grovel before the rabbi, saying how little they are really worth and how they too are nobodies. Suddenly the temple janitor bursts through a side door and, in the spirit of the occasion, advances toward the pulpit and exclaims, "I too am nobody. I am nothing at all. I am nobody." Angry at the intrusion, the rabbi shouts, "Who told *you* you are nobody? *Look* who's a nobody!"

This story has been told in other versions. Like all good jokes, it comes down through the years in many garbs. In my version, a highly gifted but commercially unsuccessful director has died at an early age and gone to heaven. St. Peter is extremely compassionate. "Poor lad," he says, "You never had a hit but you always received great notices. Here in heaven you need not concern yourself with grosses. Every film is a hit up here." Overjoyed, the director asks whether he can organize a production of *Hamlet.* "Of course," says St. Peter. "You can even have Shakespeare for rewrites. As for Hamlet, we have Barrymore, Booth, Maurice Evans—almost all the great ones are available here." "Then I have total cast approval?" exclaimed the director, overjoyed. "Yes," says St. Peter. "I'd like Maude Adams for Ophelia," says the director, by now ecstatic. "Oh, about Ophelia," St. Peter responds carefully, "I need a favor. You see, God has this girl . . ."

Have you had difficulty getting a reservation in a really good restaurant, one of those snooty haute places that make your teeth rattle when you come in the door? This will please you. Years ago a man reliably reputed to be a mob leader and mad-dog killer engaged a public relations firm to polish up his image. He and his girlfriend, a flashy blonde of the Las Vegas variety with her skirt up to her navel, wanted to go to La Grenouille, one of New York's most exclusive restaurants. The public relations man was instructed to get him in and at the right table. He made the reservation for noon, thinking that the early hour would help his client's chances of being properly seated. When the maître d' observed this bizarre trio, he quickly escorted them to the table nearest the kitchen. There was no other table occupied in the entire restaurant. Mr. Mob turned to the maître d', picked him up with one arm, with the other arm placed the maître d's pudgy hand on the cold steel barrel of his gun in its shoulder holster, and hissed, "I want that table," pointing to the most desirable table, just to the right of the entrance. The maître d' whimpered, "Of course, monsieur." He was let down and ushered Mr. Mob, Miss Mob, and their trembling public relations man to table number one. That is one way to get a good table.

Some restaurants just *look* sophisticated. At the fashionable (and otherwise excellent) Fairmont Hotel in Dallas, before a preview of *Jaws,* Dick Zanuck and I suggested to the haughty maître d' that we split a salad between us. He promptly brought us a salad and two forks. The staff of the even haughtier La Tour d'Argent in Paris ought to have known better, but its maître d' was carrying on as though my wife and I were country bumpkins. My wife deflated him by crooking her finger and directing his attention to her salad where a fat worm was wriggling out from under a leaf of lettuce. The hasty removal of the offending salad silenced him for the rest of our dinner.

California: The 1930s

Period note: In 1933, when I attended Stanford, tuition was $115 a quarter (there were three quarters in an academic year). I traveled there from New York by ship. Passage (taking nearly three weeks by way of the Panama Canal) was eighty dollars, including meals and other expenses except for tips and drinks. Martinis were twenty-five cents. At Stanford, meals and lodging at a dormitory cost nine dollars a week. Sex at a San Jose bordello was two dollars. You could sign a non-interest-bearing note for the tuition, but not for the sex. AIDS was nonexistent but condoms were de rigueur. The greatest sexual fears were unwanted pregnancy (abortion was illegal and dangerous) and venereal disease (incurable then).

There were two courses which counted toward a Stanford degree in those years that are not in the curriculum today. One was called *Business of the Theater* and was taught by a young instructor named George Wilson. It was a rule at Stanford that when fewer than three students were enrolled in a course, the course was discontinued. There were but three students in *Business of the Theater.* When one of us became aware of this rule, George Wilson became our hostage. Whenever he talked of giving a difficult or arduous assignment, one of us, by prearrangement, would threaten to resign from the course, which would, of course, have put Mr. Wilson out of work. It turned out to be a very easy course.

Even pleasanter was the course in *Psychic Phenomena.* Mrs. Leland Stanford had been a spiritualist and her will stipulated that such a course be given. The idea was to do research in all phases of psychic phenomena and write a paper stating our findings. The subject was also taught at Columbia until a famous medium, Eusapia Palladino, was caught under a table helping it levitate. Our course was unaffected by this and we continued holding seances in dark rooms, making contact with heavenly bodies of co-eds through hand-holding, which caused a certain amount of man-made levitation under the table.

The motto of Stanford University was, "The winds of freedom blow." It was inscribed in German on the university shield, curious in view of the fact that the winds of freedom were dying down in Germany at that very time. They did not blow for eminent economist Thorstein Veblen, author of the classic *The Theory of the Leisure Class.* He was a professor of economics at Stanford who was excommunicated not for his radical economic views, but because he was living with a woman on campus, a woman who was not his wife—shacked up, as they used to say. So Veblen left because the "winds of freedom" did not blow over his illicit love affair, although they countenanced his most unorthodox views, political and economic.

Another acerbic and uncompromising professor was Marjorie Bailey, professor of English at Stanford University in the thirties, a legend in her own time. Marge Bailey taught Elizabethan English and was a formidable figure, with long gray hair and a rather voluptuous body, of an indeterminate age (we thought she might have been thirty-eight or thirty-nine; that was indeterminate in those days). Marge Bailey was noted for such comments as one she made about a professor for whom her contempt was freely expressed. She said, "I never believed in the Immaculate Conception until I saw Professor Schwartz's child."

It's hard to realize now that Southern California, so economically vibrant in the era of the Pacific rim, was a grim and forlorn place throughout the thirties, the Depression years. The All-Year Club of Southern California sought tourists by taking out beguiling advertisements showing the beauty of the southern part of the state. Each advertisement carried the warning, "Come to California for pleasure but do not come seeking employment. Employment opportunities are severely limited." Before World War II, the aerospace industry, and Silicon Valley, California was an economic desert except for the movie industry.

In America, it seems an upper-class British accent can get a girl anywhere. It suggests beauty, elegance, and haute pleasures. Not so in the thirties. Nobody knew about British accents except in dopey movies. In those faraway times, a southern accent made a girl instantly wanted for dates and jobs. Those southern, dulcet tones caressed the ear and traveled south. A southern female voice on a switchboard could talk a landlord out of two months' rent in that Depression era.

The King of Columnists

Walter Winchell was the best of the three-dot columnists in the thirties, forties, and early fifties. They were called three-dot columnists because their items were separated by three dots. Winchell wrote for the *New York Daily Mirror,* which syndicated him to hundreds of other newspapers. On Sunday nights at nine, America tuned in to his fifteen-minute radio program, the *Jergens Journal,* named for its sponsor, Jergens Lotion. Power-crazed, manic, maniacal, kinetic, he was a newsboy with a staccato voice. He pounded a telegraph key to underscore the urgency of his spiel. Beginning his career as a child actor in 1910 in Gus Edwards's *Kid Cabaret,* he toured America for two years with Eddie Cantor and Georgie Jessel and worked in other acts until 1920. Winchell came from the Lower East Side of New York as did many show business immortals, including Irving Berlin and George Burns. His career as a columnist began on the *Vaudeville News* in the early twenties, and took off on June 10, 1929, when his column appeared on page one of William Randolph Hearst's new tabloid, New York's *Daily Mirror.*

In his glory days, Walter Winchell liked to think he could make or break anyone, and too frequently succeeded. He had his enemies and his heroes. One of his heroes was J. Edgar Hoover, director of the FBI, with whom Winchell sat almost every night Hoover was in New York at a corner table in the Stork Club, while others came by to pay tribute. It was Winchell who popularized the expression "G-man" for Hoover's FBI agents ("Machine Gun" Kelly originated it), Winchell who glorified John Dillinger by making front page news out of his movie theater capture by the G-men, and Winchell who traveled with a police radio at night to the scenes of crimes and persuaded the notorious Lepke to surrender to him. He wore a snap-brim, gray fedora, was married to a former showgirl named June, lived in a carefully guarded country estate in Bedford, New York, but mostly occupied an apartment at the St. Moritz Hotel in Manhattan. Winchell had more scoops than any gossip columnist before or since. I learned about my impending divorce from my first wife in his column before I heard it from her. "The David Browns are in Splitsville," he reported, the night before I received her lawyer's letter.

Walter Winchell's ego was as big as his mouth. Before World War II, he wrote in his column that the real villains of the Third Reich were not the German people but Hitler and his henchmen. When British Prime Minister Neville Chamberlain made his declaration of war in September of 1939, he said that Britain was declaring war on the rulers of the Third Reich and not on the people of Germany. Winchell promptly crowed, "Following this column's advice, Neville Chamberlain is not declaring war on the German people."

I was with Winchell the night Fritz Kuhn, notorious Nazi head of the German-American Bund, entered the Stork Club. Winchell, who carried a gun, handed it to a companion, fearing he might use it on Kuhn.

Ernie Lehman wrote what has become a classic, a novella titled *The Sweet Smell of Success.* It was about a gossip columnist and a fawning press agent who would do anything to get a client into his column. I purchased the story for *Cosmopolitan,* but had to retitle it "Tell Me About It Tomorrow," because my editor, Herbert R. Mayes, could not abide the word "smell." The original title became part of the language as well as the title of an outstanding movie based on the novella, starring Burt Lancaster and Tony Curtis. Lehman had once worked for Irving Hoffman, a press agent who was one of Winchell's chief sources of column items. Winchell assumed Lehman's story was about *him* and Hoffman, and Lehman was given the enemy treatment. He was so intimidated by Winchell's taunts that he went to Tahiti to escape such venomously false column items as "The Ernest Lehmans are writing their own unhappy ending."

Winchell also gave the enemy treatment to Barry Gray, the veteran New York radio interviewer, who permitted columnist Ed Sullivan to attack Winchell on his radio show, calling Winchell "a small-time Hitler." Barry was thereafter referred to in Winchell's column as Borey Pink, Borey Gray, and Borey Lavender. He was beaten up twice by unknown assailants. According to Bob Thomas's excellent book *Winchell,* Winchell reported, "The list of Barry Gray's assailants has been narrowed down to a thousand suspects." Barry survived the attacks and Winchell, and is still a major broadcaster.

In 1940, I was writing a column for *Pic* magazine which I titled "Gabble." It was much like *The New Yorker* end-of-column items calling attention to errors and inadvertent humor in various news stories. Winchell used to tear out my column and send it to me with suggested items. He wrote in longhand. He asked me to write an article about him, which I did. He wanted it to be known that he was more than a gossip maven, that he was a serious political writer and humanitarian. He did found the Damon Runyon–Walter Winchell Cancer Fund. Damon Runyon, one of Broadway's most gifted writers, died of cancer. Ironically, reports Richard Blackburn in an essay on *The Sweet Smell of Success,* Winchell never went for a cancer test himself and cancer was what killed him.

Until the SEC intervened, Walter Winchell was so powerful he could move a stock up or down five or ten points by reporting a corporate rumor. Winchell did not profit from these items, but those close to him could and did. The films in which he appeared, mainly musicals for Twentieth Century Fox, were mere divertissements, but as his fame and power grew, Fox provided an office for him in its star dressing room building, where he hung out while he was in town. He was the victim of hopeless little flings with girls half his age.

A poet named Phillip Stack, who signed his work Don Wahn, was a frequent contributor to his column. He wrote wonderful torchy Broadway ballads for the column, mainly sad, lonely laments about lost love. Bob Thomas, in his book, says Stack was a clerk at the Brooklyn Edison Company when he started writing. Winchell never paid him.

I remember the day Winchell discovered a cure for impotence: He told the group in the Twentieth Century Fox executive dining room that very young women cured impotence in older men. As though he had discovered a cure for cancer, he shouted, "All you need to do is find a very young girl, and you won't be impotent anymore." He assumed everyone else was impotent. "You know," he ranted, "impotence is all in the mind. The way to cure it is to find someone thirty years younger than you are."

He also discovered tranquilizers and carried on about their magic properties in a strident, untranquilized voice.

Only Darryl Zanuck was unafraid of Winchell. He could scream as loud as Winchell, "For Christ's sake, Walter, you don't know what you're talking about," when Walter would go on with his latest theory about the German general staff which he had heard on a news broadcast just before he came to lunch. But he *was* a phenomenon, and I miss his column. It was never boring. Many of his Winchellisms survive, among them "blessed events" (newborns) and "don't invite 'ems" (people you don't invite to the same party) and "debutramp."

Winchell was known for his cruelty to those who misled him. His idea of a retraction was to print the correct item and add, "The source just killed himself."

He once printed an item suggesting that Bette Davis had a dread disease. When her press agent called his secretary, Rose Bigman, to report that Miss Davis did not have that disease, Rose is reported to have told the press agent, "Want some advice? Tell Miss Davis that if she doesn't have it, to *get* it."

Asked by Jerry Wald, then an obscure columnist and later a major Hollywood producer, how to become well known, Winchell advised, "Pick the most famous person you can find and attack him."

Still, Winchell's plugs could be as powerful as his pans. Sherman Billingsley's Stork Club became an immediate success because Winchell's column tagged it "the New Yorkiest place in town." Olsen and Johnson, two zany but unfashionable comics, owed the record-breaking run of their show *Hellzapoppin,* to Winchell's repeated raves, shouting down the derisive comments of Manhattan's snooty drama critics.

Once a month, during the war years, Winchell, in the uniform of a commander in the United States Naval Reserve, traveled to Washington to whisper the nation's juiciest gossip (too hot to print) in the ear of his commander-in-chief, President Franklin D. Roosevelt. FDR loved it. On the hit parade was a song titled "I Want to Be in Winchell's Column (Gee, If He'd Give Me a Line)".

* * *

I last saw Winchell, more than eighteen years ago, in Danny's Hideaway Restaurant in New York City. He was sitting alone in a booth, going over clippings and old photographs. He waved Helen and me over. He didn't have a *Daily Mirror* column anymore, or a radio show. Even his column in weekly *Variety* had been canceled. His power was broken when his publishers and broadcasters tired of his paranoia. Worse, his public was getting bored. Soon, the once-feared Winchell was being openly attacked. Columnist Ed Sullivan, already better known than Winchell because of his television show, again denounced him, this time as a "charlatan" and "cheap terrorizer." The man who once wrote "Be nice to the people you meet on the way up—they're the same ones you see on the way down," had not taken his own advice. He was through. All he had were his bank books, which he carried with him. Like the old vaudevillians—he had been one of them—he had money in banks all over the country (only recently the name Robert [Bob] Hope turned up in an unclaimed bank account list). After having to pore through memorabilia of his power days, we finally left him on Forty-fifth Street, near the building which had once housed the *Daily Mirror.* Winchell looked around, put his coat collar up against the night chill, and walked away, a solitary figure with no place to go. Soon after, the king of columnists was dead.

Somebody will make a movie about this complicated and amazing man who lit up the sky for a few years, like a blazing comet, and vanished.

Winchell's chief source of gossip, Broadway press agent Irving Hoffman, never fawned on him, unlike the press agent character in *Sweet Smell of Success.* Hoffman was recklessly independent of opinion with his clients, idiosyncratic, and eccentric. Celebrities doted on him. His office was in a scruffy off-Broadway building above what used to be Billy La Hiff's Tavern, a hangout for the show business crowd of the forties, and across from the original Pearl's, a Chinese restaurant that was also a hangout. Hoffman hated letters. His defense was to reply with an elaborate form consisting of dozens of categories which could be checked in answer to a letter. Some of the categories were: "Mr. Hoffman has been confined to an institution. Your letter will be forwarded to his psychiatrist." Or "Mr. Hoffman has been declared sterile by a committee of doctors." Or "Mr. Hoffman's wife has forbidden him to marry again." Or "Mr. Hoffman is bankrupt and can no longer give money to anyone." Whatever the request, Hoffman had a box for it.

He also sent copies of highly personal letters he thought would interest his small, trustworthy list of friends. A widely circulated letter might be from a girl complaining about the sexual performance of a Hollywood braggart. Irving knew the girls who consorted with the famous and the girls told Irving everything.

Hoffman was himself afflicted with satyriasis, male nymphomania, and had hordes of young women attending to his considerable needs the world over. He was not a procurer. Call him a consumer. Hell, he was more than a consumer; he was a market. His satyriasis may have been hereditary because his father was equally horny and demanded part of the action. This life-style was not without its hazards. He became the victim of the monomania of a woman who left humiliating messages with his friends. Examples: "Mr. Hoffman never wants to speak to you again." "Mr. Hoffman thinks you're a shit." "Mr. Hoffman's prostitute is available to you, courtesy of Mr. Hoffman. When can I come up?" Or whatever it was that would embarrass him. Hoffman settled this through the good offices of J. Edgar Hoover, director of the FBI, who determined that the offender was a Catholic, had an agent get in touch with her priest, and set her on the right path. She turned out to be one of the operators at Hoffman's own telephone answering service.

Outtakes

I think we have within us a psychic clock. Once, as I left for California, I felt tensions building to a dangerous level of anxiety. What was my antenna picking up? Was it a combination of things? My son was in a hospital for a knee operation with the prospect of piling up medical costs. My wife, Helen, jealous perhaps or perhaps correctly, had said, "Why do you subsidize this boy of twenty-eight? What Indian sign has he got on you?" It all came to me. Helen was the one who had an Indian sign on me. She could make me feel like a wrongdoer. I was anxious and that ain't good. Besides, things weren't going well in my career. I felt a great wave of apprehension.

Then, within four or five days, I had a meeting which convinced me that things were actually going better in my career. My son, I learned, would be in the hospital for only a few days. My wife's fear of overextending herself by producing a British edition of *Cosmopolitan* turned out to be exaggerated. "All your fears are foolish fancies maybe." I remembered the lyric of "Melancholy Baby."

I have since learned to let troubled waters roll over me—short of drowning. To put it another clichéd way, I have learned to roll with the punches. Most fears are unrealized. There are times when you feel terribly exposed, terribly anxious. At those times, it's best to remember the Eastern proverb "This too shall pass."

This is how fear fuels my marriage. On vacation in the south of France, I had the responsibility of checking to see whether all our bags were stowed in the automobile that was to take us from Les Beaux in Provence to the Hotel du Cap d'Antibes on the Riviera. When we arrived at du Cap, having driven more than four hours, an important piece of baggage was missing. It contained my wife's entire wardrobe, which included everything she would be wearing at a gala that evening. I remonstrated with the porters, insisting that the bag must be downstairs. "Non, monsieur," was their response. My wife's response was that it *better* be there when she woke up from her nap or the gift shop, noted for its exorbitant prices, would have a new customer that afternoon. I continued to insist the bag would be found but a light bulb went on in my head and I could see the bag in a room I neglected to check back at Les Beaux. I said nothing of this to my wife, of course. Panicked, I telephoned Les Beaux and, in my awkward French, established that "le bagage rouge" was there, and arranged for a taxi to bring it from Provence to Antibes, another four-hour drive. Forget the cost. The cost in anxiety and recrimination was higher. While my wife slept, I paced the pebbled driveway of the Hotel du Cap until—voilà—a small taxi appeared as the sun was setting. After doling out thousand-franc notes to the overjoyed driver, I took the bag to our room. As Helen opened her eyes to behold it, she had no idea that a new wardrobe from the gift shop would have cost less.

It always astonishes me how many people fail to respond to mail and telephone calls. Everything has speeded up in the world except getting telephone calls returned. Responding promptly is the mark of a gracious and elegant person. One of my great friends was the late Peter Gimbel, sportsman, filmmaker, and adventurer. He expressed delight and astonishment that when I said I would call him on Wednesday, I called him on Wednesday. Lew R. Wasserman, chief executive officer of the entertainment colossus MCA/Universal, always returns telephone calls on the same day or arranges for someone else to do so. You may only get thirty seconds of Mr.

Wasserman's time but he is listening. If he feels you are wasting his time, he will let you know. What is happening to people who are afraid to take telephone calls or reply to letters? Can it be they are simply inept or uncouth? Or afraid?

The late Robert Goldstein, onetime head of Twentieth Century Fox, falls in the latter category. Notorious for not replying to telephone calls, he accidentally picked up the telephone at his home in Palm Springs and, hearing my voice, said, "Just a moment" and never returned.

I've experienced this form of rudeness many times in my life. It's also a form of fear, evidence of inability to make decisions. A friend telephoned a literary agent but was unable to reach him, although she had important information for him. She was story editor of a motion picture company. She continued to call, reprimanded the secretary, sent notes, left plaintive messages—all to no avail. She even sent him a quarter to telephone. At last, she reached him and they made a luncheon engagement which he broke at the last possible minute. Then followed other broken engagements. When he telephoned a third time and said he would have to cancel still another luncheon engagement because he was utterly fatigued, having just flown in from California on a "red-eye" flight, she would have none of it. "No you don't," she shouted, "you will not cancel again. I will not have it. You will come. I don't care." Somehow she bulldozed him into keeping the engagement. She talked loudly to him about the business matter she needed to discuss but he heard not a word of it. Halfway through the first course, he fell asleep. Those who do not wish to keep engagements or respond to telephone calls do not, of course, wish to hear, and their defenses are unassailable.

I abhor the lack of manners that too often characterizes show business power. It's boring. I recently bought the film rights to a novel about a writer who threatened to kill a movie executive who did not return his telephone calls. As for answering their mail, forget most movie executives. One explanation may be that they cannot read. That doesn't excuse stars, who are the worst offenders. We are still waiting to hear from Jack Nicholson to whom Richard Zanuck and I submitted a script more than eleven years ago.

Social engagements with many of those in show business are subject to change without notice. A producer with whom I had a luncheon date at the Russian Tea Room was late. I took pains to get the right banquette because he wanted to talk. I reached him on the telephone from the restaurant. Obviously still asleep, he said, "Can we cancel for today? I'm so tired." I would have dragged myself out of bed to have kept any date out of respect for the other person, much less respect for a friend. His behavior was typical of the spoiled children who constitute a significant portion of the show business world, a world in which children often dominate adults.

Helen Brown's own diatribe about her unfavorite people is worth noting.

> There are some unfortunate people—maybe 72 percent of all people—who simply don't receive messages from other people. I don't mean spoken messages. I'm referring to another kind of language which indicates in a not-so-subtle way that you don't have much time. I get these messages frequently, from people more important and driven than I am, and I know when to cut my conversation short. A man in my company who approves budgets is always beleaguered by those who need two thousand dollars here or six thousand dollars there. You so rarely have a crack at him, so once you get him on the phone you're tempted never to shut up. You want to keep on with things you've been saving up for him all year. Well, I can immediately sense when he's had about all he can take of me. I put the rest in a memo or await my next chance on the telephone. Let's just say one of my small talents is to be able to receive messages from people as to how far I can go, both in person and on the telephone. But I constantly talk with people who don't seem to get any messages at all from me. There's a woman I know in public relations who occasionally books me on television shows. Well, this one tells you what she's worked out for you, and you say OK, Jane, that's terrific, I'll talk to you soon. I think that's enough to let anybody know that you want to get off the phone. But no. This poor lady starts all over again to tell me what she just told me. I know she's probably nervous and anxious and eager to please and wants to make sure I understand. I want to tell her to get hold of herself and listen to what others are *not* saying. There are people I don't call back from one week to the next, because I haven't time for conversation that cannot be ended except by dropping the phone.

Sooner or later, many superachievers wind up dispirited and defeated. Not many survive success. Either they get too old and have to be forced out of their positions of power or must peacefully relinquish them to make way for successors. The head of one large corporation said at a dinner party that he thought power was something to be given up—not only for one's own good but also for the good of an institution or company or government. My wife disagreed, saying, "That may be good for the institution or company

Richard Burton, Richard Zanuck, and I in France on the location of Staircase *in the late 1960s. Burton's headdress was part of his costume and not the result of a hard night.*

With Irving Lazar on the Île Saint-Honorat in the south of France

On the set of The Sting *with Robert Redford and Richard Zanuck.*
I appear to be having an out-of-body experience.

On the Orca, *our picture boat for* Jaws, *at Martha's Vineyard in 1973. The young man between Richard Zanuck and me is Steven Spielberg, and Robert Shaw is behind us.*

Helen and I on the set of Jaws 2

Richard Zanuck, Elizabeth Taylor, and I receiving an award, apparently oblivious to the lawsuits we had been firing at one other a few years earlier during the making of Cleopatra

Gregory Peck as General Douglas MacArthur beams down at us on the USS Missouri, *which was taken out of mothballs to enable us to film the Japanese surrender ceremony where it actually occurred.*

Gene Hackman and I negotiating for a tie on the Hamburg docks during the production of Arthur Penn's Target

Members of the cast of Cocoon *at a preview party hosted by producers Richard and Lili Zanuck*

Barbara Walters interviews Helen and me for ABC's 20/20.

Photograph by Ann Limongello

A 1985 book party for author Liz Carpenter given by columnist Liz Smith. Diane Sawyer, Helen, and I are flanked by these worthy ladies. Liz Carpenter had written about her close association with President Lyndon Johnson and Lady Bird.

The dynamic duo, Zanuck and Brown, at the Cannes Film Festival sometime in the mid-1970s

Photograph by Jonathan Becker

Vanity Fair caught this glimpse of me on my terrace, the only place I'm permitted to smoke a cigar.

or government but it's very bad for the individual." We thought of the many people we knew who had to be dragged from their posts. For example, de Gaulle hung on to his power, but was that good for France? Even after death, his power was long felt through successors who were disciples of his political philosophy. I think the reason to give up power is to prepare for death or a second life. If one learns to live without it, then he has succeeded in life because anyone can live with power. It takes a great man to live without it—having had it.

The Triumph (and Tragedy) of George Stevens

George Stevens started directing comedies early in his career. They became classics. He enlisted in the army during World War II and photographed the invasion of Europe. Later, he arrived at Dachau as the Allied troops liberated the survivors of the concentration camps. What he saw moved him so profoundly that he would never make a comedy again. He took photographs at Dachau, which were discovered in a garage years later by his son, George Stevens, Jr., who used them in his award-winning homage to his father, *A Filmmaker's Journey.* What came through in that film was Stevens's intense feeling about human suffering. George Stevens was not a Jew. When some of the Holocaust survivors touched him, he involuntarily recoiled. Shocked by his reaction, he said, "I realized at that moment that in every one of us there is a potential Nazi." When he returned home, he produced and directed *The Diary of Anne Frank,* the poignant story of a Jewish girl in hiding from the gestapo. He spent a long time on it. Although not directly threatened by the Nazis, he could never forget what they did.

George Stevens, Jr.'s, *A Filmmaker's Journey* belongs in every film student's cassette collection. I knew George Stevens, and that film is not only an homage but is also an incredibly powerful and truthful re-creation of the man.

George Stevens, Jr., says that the 1965 failure of *The Greatest Story Ever Told* made his father unbankable to major studios for the first time since he directed Katharine Hepburn in *Alice Adams* in 1935. *The Greatest Story Ever Told* was a five-year job for George. He wanted desperately to do it and worked on it with more than his usual attention to detail. Researchers were dispatched to find out, so far as could be determined, what was happening in every civilization during the time of Christ. In Abyssinia. In China. In the Indo-Scythian Empire. Wherever. Charts surrounded his office walls indicating what was taking place before and after Christ's crucifixion. He wanted to know the context of the greatest story ever told, the story of Jesus Christ.

I worked on that film with George. I was then, in 1962, executive story editor of Twentieth Century Fox and the studio was going through an uneasy period while its production head, Buddy Adler, was dying of cancer. Spyros Skouras attempted to rule the studio from New York, but was wary of Adler's power until Buddy's last breath and would make no decisions.

Stevens was asking for budget approvals and needed a multitude of other decisions. I telephoned Buddy at the UCLA Medical Center to try to get him to focus on these problems. His wife, Anita Louise, answered the telephone and said, "Take it up with New York." Spyros Skouras said, "Take it up with Buddy." The problems were later solved when the production was sold to United Artists Corporation; it was a godsend for Twentieth Century Fox, which could ill afford the millions the picture would lose. Before that occurred, I was involved with the preparation of the production and development of the script.

George had decided he was going to make that story into a film almost immediately after reading the book by Fulton Oursler. The book was a re-creation of the New Testament written in a contemporary style that made the book a huge best-seller, although not so huge a best-seller as the Bible itself.

Stevens decided he wanted to shoot the picture in the American West. We talked about it as we were flying over the Rockies. "This is where I want to make the movie," he said, pointing down. "Jordan and Israel do not look at all what they looked like in biblical times." Of course, there were no mountains in Israel the size of the Rockies either, but somehow George was always ready to overlook detail in favor of some grand design. Our flight from Los Angeles to Chicago resulted from a meeting George Stevens, Jr., his father, and I had to discuss who would write the screenplay. Ivan Moffet, who had worked with Stevens on *Giant,* had done some excellent work, but Stevens felt we needed someone who could write believable dialogue for the character of Jesus. "Whose dialogue," Stevens asked, "could be as majestic as that contained in the King James version of the New Testament?"

I could have bit my tongue afterward but I suggested Carl Sandburg, the famous American poet who lived in Chicago. Stevens thought that was a swell idea. How could we get him? I called Lucy Kroll, Sandburg's agent, and she said she thought that Sandburg might be interested. It was necessary, however, to set up screenings of all George Stevens's pictures. We had to rent a Chicago theater to show Sandburg the films.

Finally, the word came down that yes, Carl Sandburg would be interested in discussing this with Stevens and me. George and I flew to Chicago, went to Sandburg's spartan hotel apartment on the Near North Side, and talked to him about the assignment. Sandburg said he would be delighted to take on the job. It was up to me to make a satisfactory financial arrangement with Lucy Kroll, but we knew we had Sandburg. This impassive man, George Stevens, began to weep. A few tears came down his cheeks as we walked the wintry streets of Chicago, stopped at a bar in the Drake Hotel and had enough drinks to encourage us to walk the frozen beaches of Lake Michigan that night, drunk and happy.

I had known George Stevens for several years before *The Greatest Story Ever Told.* We met when he was trying to interest a studio in making *Giant,* an appropriately titled, outsized novel by Edna Ferber. I had tried to persuade Darryl Zanuck to acquire the film rights. It had wonderful characters and a great canvas. *Giant* was the precursor of all the massive TV maxisoaps—*Dallas, Dynasty,* and the like—but exquisitely crafted with credible, larger-than-life characters. One look at the movie and you can readily see how many television clones owe their lives to *Giant.*

I had heard about *Giant* from Henry Ginsberg, a former head of Paramount Studios who was then out of a job. He controlled the Edna Ferber property, wanted to produce it, and had attracted George Stevens to direct it. I went back to Zanuck, presenting *Giant* with George Stevens as director, but got nowhere because word was circulating that a movie called *Shane* had been directed by Stevens and was considered unreleasable. So afraid of *Shane*'s box-office reception was its distributor, Paramount, that it offered to sell the movie to Howard Hughes, who almost bought it. Unable to dispose of it or bury it, Paramount grudgingly agreed to release it. It became a box-office triumph and is now considered a movie classic.

Before *Shane* was released, George Stevens, Henry Ginsberg, and Edna Ferber had to offer to work for nothing and throw in the book rights for nothing in order to persuade Jack Warner, ruler of Warner Brothers, to make *Giant.* He did agree to give Stevens, Ferber, and Ginsberg one third of any profits from the film. They made more money from their share of this immensely successful film than any of them had previously made on any other enterprise in their lives.

George Stevens lived in a remote house in the Hollywood Hills. I spoke to him about the problems of getting *Giant* made. Stevens said, "If you examine the books of the motion picture companies, you will discover that no big company has ever made a profit in production according *to their bookkeeping.*" He emphasized the last three words—this was before present-day "creative accounting." It was during the golden period of big studios. Stevens also said, "No successful movie has ever been made—except over the dead bodies of studio executives." How true, then and now.

The last film George Stevens directed was not included in George Stevens, Jr.'s, *A Filmmaker's Journey.* That was *The Only Game in Town,* starring Warren Beatty and Elizabeth Taylor. George wanted to make this film but it came at the lowest point of his career, after the failure of *The Greatest Story Ever Told.* Richard Zanuck, then president of Fox, was intensely loyal to established talent, whether in or out of favor in the marketplace. Stevens convinced Dick that he was still able to operate economically; after all, he had started in the business making inexpensive two-reel comedies. Since those days, however, Stevens had acquired a reputation for prodigal consumption of exposed film to a degree that was unreal. Sadly, he was unable to prove his point about being able to operate on a limited budget on *The Only Game in Town,* although the extravagances of that production had less to do with Stevens than with the demands of his stars.

Richard Burton and Elizabeth Taylor were superstars. Dick Zanuck and I had acquired film rights to two plays, one titled *Staircase,* about two homosexual barbers in London, and the other *The Only Game in Town,* a love story set in Las Vegas. Burton was cast in *Staircase,* to be directed by Stanley Donen, and Taylor in *The Only Game in Town.* Neither could work in England or the United States because of tax considerations. Their contracts and desires required that they never be separated. Therefore, *The Only Game in Town,* a story that took place entirely in Las Vegas, and *Staircase,* whose locale was London, were both shot in Paris, in neighboring studios.

Staircase, a rather affecting play, also starred Rex Harrison, who didn't mind in the least working in Paris. *The Only Game in Town* was a good picture—Stevens could do no less—but it didn't work with the audiences. Beatty was a touch too young for the glamorous Elizabeth; originally her role was to be played by Mia Farrow, but

Stevens thought he could recapture the magic of *A Place in the Sun* with Elizabeth Taylor. Beatty and Taylor would have done anything for George and they did, by agreeing to work on the film almost on command. When the picture failed at the box office, George was once again deeply distressed, as were we all. It was his bid to get back to work in a modest, credible way, and perhaps he suspended some of his usual severe judgments about the kind of material he needed. It was, as he said to Richard Zanuck, "an effort to prove that I am capable of doing what I did in the old days."

After George Stevens directed and produced *The Greatest Story Ever Told,* Darryl Zanuck also became fascinated by the Bible, this time the Old Testament, in a film produced by Dino De Laurentiis and directed by John Huston, who also played Moses. The film, not at all surprisingly, was titled *The Bible.* Darryl backed it with the enthusiasm of a man who had just discovered the greatest story ever told. It occurred to us later that he probably had never read the Bible and came upon this unforgettable work for the first time. Audiences had not forgotten it. They knew the story only too well.

The Way It Was, as It Now Seems

Diary entry, May 16, 1973:

I was tired last night and went to bed at 9:35 P.M., Pacific Daylight Saving Time. I woke up at 2:05 A.M. This was the precise moment my father died in a hospital three thousand miles away—5:05 A.M., Eastern Daylight Saving Time. I have moved one rung up on the ladder to eternity. This man, who had begged me not to keep him alive if he was comatose, was being kept alive artificially. Just before I had left for Los Angeles, I had had my talk with the medical director of the hospital. The life-prolonging machines fell silent and so did my father. When one is dying, it seems as though one will live forever. The expression "lingering death" is all too true. It's as though Death will never call. To have seen this man breathing in desperate gasps, his eyes and mouth open month after month while snow falls outside his window, and when trees are greening, and still later when summer is upon us, is to have withstood an endless vigil. And then one morning, a little after five in New York, he breathes his last breath of eighty-seven years, and perhaps sighs. He dies alone as most of us do, without the comfort of a hand or a kiss. Who knows the thoughts he had, what sudden consciousness surfaced at that final moment?

* * *

One day a few years ago, I traveled to the small estate I owned in Southampton, Long Island. It had once belonged to my father, purchased by him with the winnings of an Irish Sweepstakes ticket. One of our houses was being rebuilt after a fire. Next door was the studio where my father and stepmother spent many summers surrounded by the flowering trees, grape arbors, formal gardens, and spacious lawns of the property they called *Stepping Stones.* Now in the bare studio was the debris of my father's eighty-seven years of life. Lying on a tattered couch were his two U.S. Army officer hats, resplendent with braid when they first came from Brooks Brothers, but now sadly faded. He had been a colonel in the General Staff Corps of the United States Army, chief liaison officer with the Soviet Army, a good job for a Wall Streeter. Scattered on the floor were copies of *Yank,* the army weekly, of various dates in 1943. There was also a copy of *Collier's* containing an article on the Persian Gulf command, the headquarters of which were in Teheran, where he was long posted. Fragments of a lifetime: old checks, blank checks headed for the junk pile; no place to put everything, complete sets of *Scribner's* and the *Century* magazine (now *there* was a magazine) from the 1850s onward. Maybe we'll find a place for those in the town library or with some rare-book dealer, I thought. There was also an autographed copy of a book by my father's friend Montague Glass, who created those memorable characters the "cloak and suiters," Potash and Perlmutter, big-selling books of the twenties. Montague lived in the south of France in a beautiful villa far from the madding crowd and the pushcarts of Seventh Avenue.

After poking around in the ruins of this studio in Southampton and seeing all the books my father loved, I turned away, realizing that most of them would have to be thrown out or given away. I drove westward toward Manhattan, not on the Long Island Expressway but along Route 27, following the South Shore of Long Island through Hampton Bays, Quogue, Westhampton Beach, Center Moriches, and finally to Nassau County where I decided to have another look at the old house I lived in at number 132 Pine Street, Woodmere. I'd been there once before since I drove by with Ernest Lehman. That was one winter day when I parked my car and gazed at the trees I climbed and the rooms in which I grew up. I had never asked whether I could enter the house. This time, as I drove up and parked, a young couple came out of 132 Pine Street and asked if I was looking for someone. I said, "No, but I lived in that house more than sixty years ago." The young lady responded, "You must be David Brown. Would you come in?" Oh would I and did I! The young lady's mother had written me years ago about an interview that appeared in *Newsday,* the Long Island newspaper. In that interview, I had reminisced about the house. The present owners had written me a note saying, "Why don't you come out and see your old house; we've found some of your toy soldiers and a secret hiding place." I wrote a polite note but other matters seemed more pressing. And now, on August 17, 1985, sixty-three years after I first entered that house as a child of six, I entered it again. The year 1922 was only four years after the end of what was then known as the Great War. The enormous oak tree in front of the house was the first thing I had noticed as a child.

As I walked into the house on that August day in 1985, there was no longer a smell of tar, and the porch was now enclosed. The living room, dining room, and foyer were all one space instead of being partitioned by doors. I lingered in the kitchen where our cook had let me scrape the pot whenever she made chocolate frosting. I can taste it even now. The outdoor stairway to the cellar was closed off because there was no need for a coal bin in 1985, but in 1928 it was near that very coal bin that I heard Governor Alfred E. Smith's voice from a radio upstairs broadcast one of his first campaign speeches. "Let's look at the record," he rasped when he was running unsuccessfully for the presidency. That cellar is also where I hid when I told my parents I was running away, hid and cruelly listened to their worried conversations when they couldn't find me. I finally took pity and reappeared.

Outside was the place where I had buried my dog Trixie, replaced a few years later with a St. Bernard who proved to be too big. He would jump joyously on me when I came home from school and knock me down. He ate five pounds of beef a day. He was from the Bide-a-Wee Home, a place for pets which still exists in Manhattan. I also remembered a pet bird I buried on the edge of the Woodmere Country Club. I revisited each of the rooms I once lived in. Down the hall was my mother and stepfather's bedroom. There were still the old sconces, candle-lit in my time but now electrified.

I told the young couple, barely in their forties, what life was like in the twenties. Then, driving away from my childhood house on Pine Street, I passed houses on nearby Central Avenue. I remembered each of the girls who lived in those houses. I saw one of them only a few years ago, who still possesses the great legs and saucy, inviting look that excited me then. Odd how those memories cling. Walking through that house, going to the attic where I cut my thigh trying to climb out a window, the scar still with me, I recalled vividly the details of my life of sixty years before: my love affairs;

my introduction in high school to the exciting worlds of physics, chemistry, and biology; my beautiful Latin teacher, Miss Patterson, who even now occasionally drifts through my dreams; and my homosexual physics teacher, "Pops" Corell, who does not.

Slow Fades

It has been determined by the current rulers of the motion picture industry that the business is safer in the hands of marketeers than producers. They may be right, but it makes it infinitely more difficult to get a film made and decidedly less pleasant than it used to be. It took Richard Attenborough twenty years to get Academy Award-winning *Gandhi* made and he had to sell rights to Pakistan and India and everywhere else to raise the money. *The Verdict* took us two and a half years to get on, and there are films we haven't yet made but have profoundly believed in for ten years or more. Academy Award-winning *One Flew Over the Cuckoo's Nest* was rejected by studios for more than eight years until Kirk Douglas, by then too old for the leading role, had to turn over the rights to his son, Michael, to see it made. It's not pleasant dealing with research-minded, demographic-crazed marketing "experts," the same "experts" who decreed that *E.T.* was utterly unpromising and would appeal only to small children. It took *two* research companies to make that error. Fortunately for posterity, another studio took it on and saw it become the highest-grossing movie in film history.

Another deterrent to rational filmmaking is the short shelf life of production executives. Production executives usually rank lower than marketing and distribution heads who, while disdaining to read scripts, actually decide which of them will be produced—without reading them, you understand. They are influenced most by the choice of a director or star rather than the subject matter, although directors and stars often have abysmal records in choosing their own material. Executives take few risks, rarely discover new talent, and compound their errors by going to the same small group of actors and filmmakers, bidding up the cost of making pictures. The game is getting perilously expensive and nobody knows what may happen when the industry runs out of sequels.

On the good side, there's a more eclectic quality to movies coming out of the United States, mainly from the smaller production companies. In olden days, you could tell an MGM, RKO, or Columbia movie by the way it looked. The same was true of a Paramount or Twentieth Century Fox picture. Each studio had a supervising art director whose stamp was on his company's product. The subject matter was also a clue to a film's origin. Warner Brothers specialized in gangster movies, Bette Davis, and patriotic war films. MGM was famous for lush musicals and down-home Andy Hardy films. RKO was great for comedy, Cary Grant, Rosalind Russell, Irene Dunne, and Fred Astaire and Ginger Rogers. And Zanuck's Twentieth Century Fox was the social conscience of the industry with *The Snake Pit, Gentleman's Agreement, Viva Zapata,* and *Pinky.* Columbia made one great picture a year with Frank Capra or George Stevens and a slew of "cheapies." Paramount had Bing Crosby, Ray Milland, Alan Ladd, Martin and Lewis, and a varied story mix. David O. Selznick was the rajah of high-taste classic movies based on great novels and starring Ingrid Bergman, Joan Fontaine, and Laurence Olivier. Sam Goldwyn had Eddie Cantor, Danny Kaye, the Goldwyn Girls, and an occasional masterwork such as *The Best Years of Our Lives.*

Producers ran the studios. When I first went to Twentieth Century Fox late in 1951, those of us in the front office made the movies. The producers were surrogates of Darryl F. Zanuck, who reigned supreme as head of production. He bought the stories, cast the scripts, selected the directors, producers, and screenwriters through a well-organized, highly efficient staff of specialists of whom I was one. No sales, advertising, or financial executive was allowed to attend dailies or see an uncompleted film on pain of being fired. Movies then were show business. Today they're simply business. That's the difference.

Thomas Berger's dark novel *Neighbors* was adapted for film and was the last film in which John Belushi starred. Richard Zanuck and I produced it. Dan Aykroyd, drop-dead beauty Cathy Moriarty, and some gifted comedic actors appeared in this movie, which was shot in New York City. *Neighbors* was not only dark in content but also dark as a production experience, in fact a nightmare. Although the film was successful, it was a struggle from the first hour of filming, and even before that. *Neighbors* was the story of a family held hostage by an outsider, played by Dan Aykroyd. It was an extraordinary tale of what can happen to an ordinary family when a stranger appears and makes them all crazy. Belushi and Aykroyd decided not to play the roles one would think were right for them. Belushi played a bland, passive minor executive, who came home every night with an attaché case and was married to a pleasant, conventional woman, played by Kathryn Walker. Aykroyd played the crazed outsider with panache and skill. John Belushi was in the twilight of his life—drugged, troubled, brilliant, suffering from self-imposed pressures of celebrity and sudden affluence. Married to a saintly girl named Judy, he lived on Morton Street in New York's West Village. John was making more money than he had ever made in his life and reveling in his celebrity, which began with his first appearance on *Saturday Night Live.*

At the beginning of production, the word was good on John. During almost all of the production cycle of *Neighbors,* he not only was there and worked hard, but he also kept other members of the company off drugs. We stationed a perimeter guard, since we were shooting at night on Staten Island, to keep pushers and junkies away from the set. John's work was outstanding, but he was at war with John Avildsen, the director. Avildsen is maddeningly calm, and his apparent lack of emotional response to Belushi's taunts only pushed Belushi closer to the edge. He threatened to punch out Avildsen almost on a daily basis. As if that were not enough, Gerald Hirschfeld, the cameraman, was also at war with Avildsen because he felt Avildsen supervised too much of the photography, leaving Hirschfeld to do nothing but operate the camera. Hirschfeld came over to tell me he was quitting, while I was being interviewed on the set by the *Los Angeles Times.* I managed to keep him aboard by having Gerry explain to Avildsen why he was unhappy. John hadn't a clue. As for Belushi, Aykroyd was the peacemaker. He kept Belushi from attacking Avildsen physically. He worked with Belushi to keep him up. Cathy Moriarty developed severe skin eruptions and gum trouble two days before she was scheduled to commence shooting, which made it impossible to film her on schedule. There were other parts we could not photograph. Miss Moriarty would not show her ample breasts, as the script required her to do. We offered to use someone else's body for the nude shot, photographing her below the neck. Ah, the Screen Actors Guild no longer permits doubling in nude scenes without permission from the actresses. So, Cathy Moriarty was covered up in what was supposed to be a sexy scene. It turned out to be even sexier, a reminder that often in erotic scenes, less is more.

John Belushi worked on the movie tirelessly, always trying to improve a scene. He and Aykroyd continued to disagree with Avildsen's direction, although they followed it. They had wanted to replace him before the picture began, although they acknowledged he was a good director. He had, after all, won an Academy Award for *Rocky.* They felt he was wrong for this picture, that his comedy sense was different from theirs. Avildsen compromised by allowing the actors to have their own take of each scene after he had completed his. Except for one or two nights when John was out of it, photography continued without incident. When Belushi reached the danger zone in anger, he would leave the set and visit his mother for an hour or two. He was a wonderful actor, a compassionate individual, and I loved him. It was difficult to love him at times. When the film completed shooting, he became obsessed with the idea of using a really horrible, metallic, heavy-metal kind of punk band for background music. He broke into music-scoring sessions with his demands and once walked into the office of the head of the music department at Columbia Pictures and, with one karate chop, cut the amazed, elderly music department head's desk in two. John was now on a swift downgrade. He was at his best in New York and his very best on Martha's Vineyard, but Hollywood unraveled him. His only peace came with death.

Joseph H. Moskowitz, the Fox executive who sent me to Hollywood, was not educated but inexplicably was placed in charge of Fox literary operations in New York. He developed a crude but effective method of evaluating material, relying on his New York story head, Bertram Bloch, and Bloch's subordinates, Henry Klinger and Duncan Boss. When Bloch gave both men a raise and they became assertive, Joe, never at a loss for a graceful phrase, said, "See what happens, Bert, when you take the wrinkles out of their bellies?" He described Klinger as "only a clog in the machine." Duncan Boss, unknown to Joe, was an elder in his New Jersey church and never told his neighbors he worked for a movie company, lest he be excommunicated. It was not a happy ship. Bloch was so upset by Joe's niggling that his wife, Edythe, regularly set an extra place at her dinner table—"For Moskowitz," she said, because all Bert would talk about when he came home was the latest Moskowitz horror. "He might as well be here," she complained, filling the absent guest's soup bowl.

Joe married his faithful secretary, Kay Sullivan, who was helpful at smoothing out his faulty grammar and sometimes crude mannerisms. He was, however, capable of an occasional gem of expression, so fitting that it could not be bettered by Oscar Wilde. Example: When an executive named Peter Levathes was first dispatched to the Fox studio by Spyros Skouras while the man he succeeded, Robert Goldstein, was still in office, Moskowitz explained his position thusly: "He's going out there to share the no authority with Goldstein."

Sam Goldwyn was celebrated, of course, for his malapropisms ("We've got Indians fresh from the reservoir," "This picture will go right up the toilet," "I've been laid up with intentional flu"). Some of the best and funniest "Goldwynisms" were the creation of press agents, although I doubt not that Sam did well on his own. I never heard him misspeak except for an occasional flaw in pronunciation. For example, he called me his fav*orite* (pronounced *favor-right*) editor. After all, as editor of *Liberty* magazine, hadn't I written an editorial praising *The Best Years of Our Lives*? Our rave review would have sufficed. But then Sam was merciless about publicity. Lynn Farnol, his Eastern publicity chief, told me that Sam once arrived in New York to find his desk piled high with press clippings praising his latest movie. Sweeping them to the floor unread, he turned to Lynn and exclaimed, "What are we going to do about getting some publicity?"

Pioneers don't do well, as a rule. David Sarnoff, founder of RCA, never made the money his corporate predators did. Neither did Adolph Zukor, who organized Paramount Pictures. He lost most of his fortune by investing in his own company's stock. Too bad he couldn't hang on until Gulf + Western bought it, but he waited as long as he could. He died at 106. William Fox went broke dreaming of the wide-screen movies and television that would make his successors rich. His buying spree which almost won him control of MGM *and* Fox broke him, an early example of takeover excess and its dangers. In his case, one hundred million dollars in bank loans came due at once. Jesse Lasky also saw his dreams fade. One of the founders, with Cecil B. De Mille, of the motion picture industry, Jesse also wound up broke. I last saw him in the early fifties when he was trying (vainly) to interest studios in a film about a small-town band. *Music Man* proved him right. D. W. Griffith died poor in a furnished room in Hollywood. Both John Ford and Orson Welles could not get a picture going in their last years. Neither, for that matter, could David O. Selznick, producer of *Gone With the Wind.*

Hollywood is replete with stories of writers' credits. Among the more bizarre is this one. The credits originally proposed for *A*

Midsummer Night's Dream read: by William Shakespeare with additional dialogue by Sam Taylor.

What Does a Producer Do?

A producer is, in many respects, a double agent. He needs the support of his cast and crew. He must also have the backing of their natural enemy, the studio. He is the one who must interpret the organized chaos of a motion picture production to those who put up the money. "What are all those people hanging around for?" someone from the studio asks. "Nobody is doing anything." Right. They may be rigging a shot for six hours and some people may be lying around sleeping. But like musicians in a symphony orchestra, they each have a part to play and it may be a while before their instruments are heard. The people supposed to be doing the work are at it.

The producer's first job is to find the property that is to be produced and persuade some innocent lamb to put money in it. He or she then goes through the horrible process of trying to get an acceptable screenplay. Never in the nearly forty years I have been in the motion picture business have there been more than seven or eight men or women who could be relied upon to write a screenplay without the intervention of other writers. More than once have screenplay writers met for the first time when they received an Academy Award, because they weren't working on the picture at the same time. After the script is written, and sometimes before, the search for a director begins. When, or usually before, you have your script, director, cast, and budget, you have to get a movie company to put up the cost of production. Finally, if you're fortunate, someone in charge at the movie company says, "Make the movie." He also says it must cost this much and no more. OK, you've got that. He or his minions say we want changes in the script. You try to please them. They refuse to pay what some of your actors and key technicians cost. You agree to replacements, even though you have promised jobs to people for a year but have never been able to assure them that they will get those jobs because the picture could be called off at any moment, and often is. Sadly, they understand the nature of the business. Finally you have your cast and crew, and are off to your location. You assemble them and start working as a family.

The period of photography is anxiety-ridden. Someone may die or become ill and halt production, necessitating cast changes and long delays. The wrong decision about a stunt can cause death or injury, and it has. There is potential for disaster in every shooting day. Everybody cheers the dailies, but will they cut together and make sense? Midpoint in a long shooting schedule on location there is usually a "down" period. Cast and crew are bored, homesick, out of sorts. Parties must be scheduled to perk up morale. It's a dangerous time. Finally, it all comes to an end and at the wrap party everyone swears to be friends forever. You never are friends forever. But during that intense period of production, you forget everything but your small world, because all you think about is filming. You get up before sunrise. After seeing the dailies at the end of shooting, you eat and pile into bed, usually beat.

As the production crew says good-bye, dozens of new people come aboard whose work starts when the picture ends. They are the post-production crew. You're home again or wherever editing, rerecording, dubbing, and scoring are to take place. The hours are long, but more relaxed. The film is in the can. You may have forty or fifty technicians working in the dark with those images that were created and trying to make sense out of what you have been doing through those months of shooting. New anxiety builds. Will the film, as put together, be successful? No longer is there the camaraderie of the shooting company. The director is still on the show, but his brow is furrowed. So is the editor's. After weeks or months, they show you a rough assemblage of the movie without music or sound effects. Almost invariably, you are appalled. Is that all there is? When Richard Zanuck and I showed *Jaws* without sound or music to the executives at Universal, there was silence when the lights went up. Finally, we asked, "What do you think?" The reply from the studio chief was a decidedly unenthusiastic, "Pretty good."

If you had the right script, you could get Robert Redford or Paul Newman, as we did with *The Sting,* without ever inviting them to dinner. What's more, they didn't want to be invited and probably wouldn't have come. Brando was the first of the truly antisocial stars, but John Garfield and Bogart did not court executive favor either. Brando, however, hated the star image and the royal treatment. He preferred to invite a secretary on the Fox lot to dinner, and not necessarily the most attractive one. If she appealed to him as someone he might have a conversation with, he'd ask her, and there was no feeling of, God, what am I doing with her, or Who is she?

How much creative control does a producer have today? As little as possible if he's got the right director. Witty superagent Sue Mengers suggested that Sidney Lumet direct *The Verdict.* Being Lumet's producer during the shooting schedule was like a month in the country for Richard Zanuck and me. Once we had Lumet, he selected, among the many scripts we had developed, the one we first thought least of, David Mamet's. He explained why he thought it was the best, and provided an ending which Mamet had declined to supply when we requested it. Our role at this point was to hear whom Lumet wanted to cast in the film and offer suggestions or arguments with which he occasionally agreed. Dick and I had always operated by consensus, rather than edict. The only argument we won with Sidney was about music. Johnny Mandel did a fine score for *The Verdict,* but we thought there was too much of it.

For example, when Paul Newman sat down on a hospital bed to photograph a victim of malpractice, there was music as his Polaroid film developed. We suggested it might be more powerful for the audience to hear the hospital breathing machine, without music. Sidney also chose to use music during the scene in which Newman turns down the money offered him by the bishop. Finally, he wanted music beginning with Newman's summation to the jury and through the filing in of the jurors. We convinced him that the footsteps of the jurors were all that was needed. He agreed, but not until we showed the movie to an audience, with and without the music cues. No quarrel with that.

Like most good directors, Lumet dislikes sentimentality. We prevailed on him to allow Jack Warden's hand to linger on Paul Newman's arm after Newman returned from making his masterful summation. Sidney said audiences might applaud. We urged him to let them applaud.

Nevertheless, when you have George Roy Hill or Sidney Lumet or a director of comparable sensitivity, you don't usually fool around trying to exercise control. The only time you do it is when your director becomes obsessed with length or doesn't respond to what the audiences are telling him at a public preview. Attention must be paid, for example, to unintended laughter at a line or scene, or impatient shuffling of feet during an overlong speech.

Mostly, if you have the right director, your creative instincts won't be as good as his, and you respect that.

Producers find stories almost anywhere. I found one at a New Year's brunch. A man named Phil D'Antoni told me about a script that had been turned down everywhere. The subject interested me and I asked him to send it on to me. It was *The French Connection,* which became a major hit and won an Academy Award.

Producers rarely find good scripts unless they have developed credible relationships with the people who write them. I like to think I've been hospitable to talent because I revere and protect it. When you've been in the business a long time, people come to you with their projects. And if you keep your telephone open, and "waste" hours hearing about projects, you're bound to find one. It takes a long time. The mortality rate is horrendous. You have to read a lot of stuff. It's like mining for gold in a used-up old stream.

Richard Zanuck and I are among the few producers who promoted our films throughout the world. I preferred the Southern Hemisphere: Latin America, Australia, South Africa. I also favored the Far East, including Hong Kong and Japan. Richard Zanuck traveled to those sybaritic cities of Europe: Paris, Rome, London. The areas of the world I chose were more interesting to me. Besides, I liked the long transpacific flights that afforded me thinking time in which to sort out my life.

I developed a network of journalistic friends south of the equator. When I arrived in Australia, South Africa, or Latin America, I was interviewed by men and women who had interviewed me many times before. In countries such as Argentina and Brazil, it was not often that anybody important from the American film industry visited them and they consequently gave major press attention. I made many lasting friends there.

With the intense interest in films in those parts of the world, there was an opportunity to talk about movies in general instead of merely flogging the film about to be released. Still, the distributors who put up the money for those hotel suites and dinners and sent us around the world first class obviously felt it was worthwhile. It most certainly was when you had a good picture, if only as ego salve.

When asked what else producers do, I usually reply that they are in charge of box lunches. Sometimes upgrading the food on location is the best way to improve the performances of actors and enhance production efficiency. Next to story and cast, selection of a caterer for the set may be one of a producer's important decisions. Some European crews want to be served individually and demand tablecloths and wine. U.S. crews line up for chow buffet-style. Shooting in the tropics is toughest on caterers. I solved it once by getting food from the huge kitchens of an airline—before it was frozen—and flying it in. In Antigua, on *The Island,* we had a mixed crew—French, American, Australian, British, and Spanish. They ate under trees on a beach. The French and Spanish had their wine, the Australians and Americans their beer. When the rains came, as they did suddenly, they had to get out of the shelter of the trees because poisonous sap would drip from the drenched trees onto their plates.

The producer looks beyond the shooting day. I was in Paris in 1985 where Arthur Penn was directing *Target.* I tried talking to him about Texas, where we would be shooting in four weeks' time. He did not want to hear about Texas until he finished in Paris. That would be too late, I told him. He agreed, but it was still my problem. A producer is a wailing wall, a buffer, a conduit to the studio. He has the studio's confidence, and the artists' confidence, although neither has confidence in the other. Producers such as Richard Zanuck and I deal with the concept of the movie: We have the dream, the vision, and sometimes the nightmare. We are the first ones on the show and the last ones to go.

The producer must be all over the lot. When Zanuck and I were partners, one of us was usually on the location of every film we produced. If things were going well, we paid two or three visits to the set in order to find out about the box lunches and whether the director had problems. We were the buffers with the distributor, the studio, and the press. That's the reason I spent six months in Germany and France on *Target* and my partner spent equal time with his wife, coproducer Lili Fini Zanuck, on *Cocoon* in St. Petersburg, Florida. We were always there and always available when the money people wanted to know what was happening on the picture.

No producer who isn't there can give an authoritative answer. The producer is not all-powerful, nor is the director or the writer. The producer is powerless without a script, a director, or money. Obviously, the director needs a script and money. So do the actors. We are all interdependent, but the producer gets the picture made. A good producer can see that it all happens. While a producer is a double agent because he has the trust of the studio, basically his fidelity is to the film. The ultimate power—to pull the plug or keep shooting—is with the man at the studio who can say yes or no.

Bright young men and women by the thousands want to be in the movie business. Why, I wonder, do they seek work in this scruffy business, where only a few survive, mostly by wit rather than by brains and taste? I can only recall how different it was when I entered the business. In the forties and fifties one went to Hollywood only to make money and get the hell out to write an honest book or play. Movie work was déclassé. The operative phrase was "selling out to Hollywood." I think the industry is still unkind and unreceptive to young talent although hardy ones like Spielberg and Lucas triumphantly slip through. Note, though, that when they do, they quickly grasp and never relinquish artistic control, so that know-nothing executives cannot brutalize their work.

One of the best parts of being a producer is being able to program your own life. It's a long time between pictures and there are periods when the writers are off preparing screenplays and I am able to do other things. My wife and I have lectured on the *QE2* while sailing down the East Coast of Africa. We have traveled in Egypt, Israel, Turkey, China, Botswana, South Africa, Morocco, and Australia, in addition to the Soviet Union and all of Western Europe. I am an amateur radio operator (call letters W2IOY) and keep in touch with the world through my own broadcasting setup in New York. I like the excitement of urban living. Although I spent my early years in Woodmere on Long Island, I am now fearful of nocturnal country sounds. I prefer the screeches of traffic and wail of sirens to the terrifying sound of a twig snapping in the woods.

A newer generation of studio chieftains—primarily lawyers, talent agents, businessmen, and other noncreative types—has come in, and old-timers scoff, asking, what do they know about making films? Some of these new bosses don't see dailies (the day's work on film) and couldn't evaluate them if they did. They surely can't or won't read scripts. These new men and a few women mostly place bets on directors and stars in making their creative decisions. They do watch budgets. They are sophisticated observers of the marketplace. They judge projects not by reading scripts but through "coverage" (story summaries) and market tests to determine if the subject matter and probable cast of a film have sufficient box-office appeal to return a profit. The jury is out on this practice of corporate distancing from the creative process. The most "hands-on" studio in Hollywood is Disney, where executives still read. It is assuredly one of the most successful. A project submitted to Disney on Friday can be decided on by Monday, or even Friday if there is an urgent need for a decision.

The movie business is alive and well in Los Angeles, where the production power structure is centered. Television and the VCR were believed to be the enemy of movies, but turned out to be their savior. Without income from cassettes, television, cable licensing, and production for television, no studio would be economically viable. Moreover, they ultimately increased rather than, as feared, diminished the appetite to see movies in their natural habitat, the theater. Still, there isn't the enthusiasm, fun, glamour, and verve of Hollywood's earlier years, although it's easier now to climb over the studio walls if you have talent, perhaps only because not every studio is behind walls. Some production companies are more likely to be lodged in high-rise office buildings in Century City on Santa Monica Boulevard.

The new honchos of Hollywood are young—thirties or late twenties—their dress neither preppy nor Italian but quietly smart; they are well spoken and healthy. I see few paunches among them. Iced tea has replaced scotch. Drugs are out; use of them, like booze, marks one as part of an older de-generation. Boring salad and mineral water are de rigueur for lunch. Cigarettes are mostly gone and cigar-smoking producers are extinct except for me. Harvard, Yale, Princeton, Stanford, and Oxford are their universities. Partying is passé; children are obsessively "in" and, God help us, executives schedule playtime with their kiddies in place of a power breakfast at the Bel Air or Polo Lounge.

What has changed Hollywood most, in my opinion, is the Creative Artists Agency and the rulers of Disney. The men and women of CAA, as it is known, are the Koreans of the industry. They're in early, work fiercely, and collectively know more about the business than most of the clients and studios they serve, and the pace of other agencies has quickened as a competitive response. While somewhat in the style of the old MCA agency, the first to require its agents to wear dark, conservative suits and affect a dour business-oriented style, the CAA talent agents are silkier, more innovative, and stealthier than their predecessors. Their ayatollah is Michael Ovitz, who purports to disdain publicity, which serves only to whet the appetite of ordinarily inaccessible publications like *The*

New York Times and *Forbes* for stories about him, possibly the design of his public relations man, Howard Rubenstein. Ovitz collects fine art, and looks more like a nonindicted investment banker than the representative of most of Hollywood's star power.

However, star power and agency power are sometime things. CAA, sullied in 1989 by a contretemps with a defecting writer-client, must fight more fiercely, and yet more delicately, to prevent incursions by ICM, run by the crisp, still-preppy Jeffrey Berg, and his star counterpart in New York, the sweatered, tieless Sam Cohn. Now privately owned, ICM is on combat alert. Triad, Bauer Benedek, and the William Morris Agency are also bestirring themselves.

Disney's Michael Eisner and Jeffrey Katzenberg are no-nonsense empire builders who do not indulge in the pranks and high jinks that Jack Warner, Darryl Zanuck, and their fellow power players enjoyed. You will see no girls on their arms, other than their wives, and smell no booze on their breath, even after working hours. They are more likely to see their movies in theaters on Saturday night while munching popcorn with the regular customers than in posh projection rooms—sometimes even standing in line. These are family men and women, more in touch with St. Louis than St.-Tropez.

Katzenberg is said to arrive at work at five in the morning. When one of his executives petitioned to stay home on Saturday to attend his son's birthday party, Katzenberg is alleged to have said, "In that case, don't bother to come in on Sunday." At least two other studio heads are now showing up at five in the morning, hoping, no doubt, to catch the Disney worm.

When I visited Hollywood in the forties, Mark Hellinger, not atypical of the producers of his time, was pleased to display in his office a book-lined wall which swung out to reveal on its reverse side a fully stocked bar. Studio talent schools were filled with girlfriends of executives, and prison pictures were routinely approved for production to enable executives to keep campaign promises of getting an occasional girl into the movies. Prison pictures could handle the overflow by allowing girls to be cast as wives of inmates on visiting day—giving one day's work to any girls who were promised a small part.

There were also real-life prison officials in Old Hollywood. When I became a story executive at Twentieth Century Fox in 1952, two former guards were on the producer roster. They had been especially kind to a studio executive who was serving a prison sentence in the federal penitentiary at Danbury, Connecticut, and were rewarded with producer contracts on his release. Oddly enough, they were successful in their new occupations, as were another executive's former ski instructor and French teacher. So much for qualifications to become a producer.

New Hollywood's producers are more likely to be former agents, lawyers, television programming executives, and failed production executives. The life span of a new Hollywood executive is often no more than that of a fruit fly, while old Hollywood executives had to be routed from their jobs with flamethrowers after decades of entrenched power. New Hollywood, albeit well schooled, is a bureaucracy, while old Hollywood was a dictatorship, production decisions being made by a single man, the films the reflection solely of his taste.

Small digression about the new Hollywood. Now in the 1990s, there is hardly a wife-stealer or drunk or con man, although I can think of one throwback producer who has been accused of spending quality time with hookers in his office, the hookers booked by his eager-to-please assistant. Mostly, however, they're upright citizens who have attended Harvard or Middlebury or Oxford. Disney President Frank Wells is a Rhodes scholar. Other moguls are Harvard or Stanford Business School graduates, a far cry from the industry's barely literate, immigrant forebears. Perhaps we could use some of the ingrates and fakers who made early Hollywood colorful and creative.

The beginning and end of a film are especially important, the end more than the beginning. There are many great beginnings of movies. Perhaps the most memorable was Darryl F. Zanuck's *The Desert Fox,* where action before the main titles was used for the first time. While a great opening sequence can hook an audience, it can also be a trap. If there is nothing following it, audiences soon catch on that they've seen the best part of the film and the picture never recovers. A great deal of money used to be spent in devising opening titles which too often proved to be the best part of the movie. The ending is what audiences take home with them. If they like it, they think with pleasure of everything that led up to it. That is why it's important for a film to end in a dramatically satisfying way, if possible in a way that makes people feel better. It is pleasurable when a character they liked has escaped from some harrowing experience or situation or otherwise redeemed himself. Endings need not be conventionally "happy"; they can be dramatically satisfying when they are bittersweet or even sad, as in *Camille* or *Love*

Story. What audiences don't like are downbeat, hopeless endings. An unsatisfying ending can be terminal to the fate of a picture at the box office.

The real life of a movie starts after all the scripts are written and rewritten, casting and budgeting are completed, and the company assembles for the first day's shooting. Then come the dailies, the film representing the day's work, which the principal actors (some are not invited; others occasionally do not find it constructive to see too much of their work) and key crew members see the next night and every workday evening throughout the shooting schedule. After the director has his rough assemblage of the film (weeks and sometimes months after the end of shooting), he may bring in a few friends and colleagues to see the work in progress and make suggestions—carefully selecting those people who are knowledgeable, and will not be thrown by a first cut without music, optical effects, and titles, often with unbalanced color and missing inserts. The director goes on from there, refining the cut, rerecording dialogue, adding sound effects, working with his post-production crew, his editors, and sound technicians. He can lean on them as they are usually supportive. The composer comes along and sees the first cut and his opinion is important. He is seeing the film for the first time, having had scant previous connection with it (perhaps having read the script and met with the director once or twice); if he likes what he sees, that keeps the director going for a while. Finally, a release print is being projected and if the guys in the lab don't say something, the director and producer start worrying, even though nobody sought their opinions. If you're the producer, you start asking the various projectionists what they think. Some of them lie, some are noncommittal, but most say they like it (which may also be a lie). The first critics come to screen it, and the publicists try to "read" their reactions, usually to no avail. You find out soon enough. The first previews are an ordeal at best because you have no idea how the picture has turned out until you see it through the eyes of a paying audience. Then you may discover some dumb misjudgments. Soon enough come the opening day's grosses, the reviews, and the first weekend's figures. Too soon perhaps. Immediately comes the period of mourning, of desolation, or, miraculously, of disbelief and euphoria that accompany a box-office triumph.

The pressures on a filmmaker are enormous. Getting a movie made at all is a feat of endurance. Convincing anyone to put up money for so foolish and risky a venture requires the talents of a world-class confidence man. Equally daunting is trying to get a good script, an accomplished director, and a talented cast in the first place. The period of photography is filled with dangers to the production, the actors, and the crew. For all this trouble and expense you don't have a clue as to what you have accomplished until it is too late to change anything.

For success in show business there is only trial and error. You learn as you go. If you lived to be a thousand, you would be learning more and more about how to avoid failure. How to achieve success is more mysterious. Still, there are some givens. It bodes well for your film if the subject matter is exciting visually, subliminally, emotionally. Forget intellectually. No committee, research institute, or computer can foretell the success (or failure) of a film, play, or book. For movies, you need to ask yourself whether the material lends itself to storytelling by the camera. Will people understand it? Will anyone give a damn?

The difference between a good and a bad script is often the lack of a fresh idea or a durable old idea served up in an innovative, elegant style. Predictability puts audiences to sleep. Drama is surprise, and if you are ahead of the projectionist, why hang around? A sympathetic lead character is also essential. A sympathetic character in jeopardy is even better, especially one who is overcoming impossible odds. That's box office insurance. *Rambo* and *Rocky* are classic examples. As noted but worth repeating, without a good beginning, you may lose your audience in the first ten minutes, but when the *ending* is disappointing, your audience will surely tell their friends not to come.

If you have a film that truly engages the emotions, you can get away with murder at the ending, and have all sorts of unbelievable things happen, because the audience wants to go along with you. But it must be satisfying.

Before you have a workable shooting script for a movie, you discuss with the writer the material on which the script is to be based. Once you're in accord on the direction of the script, based more on the writer's ideas if you have a good writer, the writer goes to work. Weeks or months later he presents a first draft, although there can be discussions as he goes along. You may ask him to prepare an outline of his story or script before he begins writing the screenplay. If it's based on a complex or long novel, I prefer a dramatic treatment of perhaps seventy or eighty pages, outlining the master scenes and indicating what's been left out. At this point it is desirable to involve a director because, not infrequently, if the director is not involved at the inception of a project he wants to start all over, frequently with a different writer. That's part of the whole business. Many drafts are written and rewritten before producers and directors are satisfied; at this point, you submit the script to the studio or your financial backers. They may offer suggestions for further changes. Finally, the money men want to know whom you can get to star and how much the picture will cost to make. The answers to these questions pretty much determine whether the movie will be made. In addition to a detailed budget, a production breakdown of each scene and a shooting schedule are prepared. Key crew are hired. Locations are surveyed. You make whatever further adjustments in the script and budget are necessary. If you have important actors or actresses, other script changes may be required of the writer to satisfy them, or even to attract them. Finally you have a shooting script, and sometimes even with a shooting script, you have a writer in residence on location to make whatever changes are necessary on the set. On both *Jaws* and *Jaws 2,* a writer was in residence to make changes for the actors and accommodate the locations and the temperamental shark. It is a great communal effort when actors themselves get into the act in rehearsal to hone the script so it "plays" perfectly. Improvisation can result in important and beneficial script changes.

One of the many problems of the scriptwriting process is that while you can tell a writer what troubles you, or what doesn't work for you, you can't always tell him how to fix it. He may adopt some of your ideas. If he is a good writer, he will respect your opinions because writing is a solitary craft and at this point you are his only audience. If you or the director or an actor say you don't understand something, he will know something is wrong, and not with you. One of my colleagues was the distinguished Henry King, who directed 105 films in fifty-five years. He was honored with a special retrospective at the Museum of Modern Art in New York. The first film shown in that retrospective was *I'd Climb the Highest Mountain,* written by Lamar Trotti. It was a successful, inspirational film about a country minister. Henry told me that Lamar Trotti had been a very religious man and wrote his script while under contract to Twentieth Century Fox. When he submitted the first draft to the studio, Darryl Zanuck read it and asked why the hell anybody would want to be a minister. He said the script didn't answer that question. Lamar was shocked by his reaction and told Henry that Darryl hated the script and couldn't understand why anyone would want to become a minister. The project is a lost cause, he complained. Henry said, "Wait a minute, now, Lamar. I haven't read your script but is it possible that he is telling you something about the script? *Does* your script tell why a man would want to become a minister?" Lamar said, "No no no, but that wouldn't help. Darryl just hates the idea." That Sunday, King attended church and the sermon was titled "Why I Became a Minister." King whipped out a pad, and started to take notes. On Monday he brought them in and said to Lamar, "Put this in your script if you haven't got it." Lamar read it, rewrote the script to include King's notes, and resubmitted it to Zanuck. Zanuck exclaimed, "Well, this is what I was trying to tell you. Now it's *great*!"

That's the best example I can give of how a producer or director can help a writer by being "dumb" and demanding, by suggesting transpositions, new endings, or a few lines of dialogue that clarify, enrich, or that work better. A producer has got to be the writer's first audience.

If there is one thing that makes a producer crazy it is a wife or girlfriend who wants a part in his movie. It's all right as a courtship come-on but after marriage, no. She pesters him night and day to get a part. A producer friend once entreated a studio head to allow him to cast his wife in a minor role in his own film on pain of divorce if he didn't. Unfortunately, she would have had to replace the studio head's actress wife who had already been promised the role by the director. The studio head refused the request by saying *his* wife would divorce *him* if she didn't keep the role. My friend's marriage ended. The studio head's didn't.

Women who court producers often do so because they want to get into pictures at any cost. Once, while traveling with Darryl Zanuck to Los Angeles, his love of the moment, Genevieve Gilles, sidled into the seat next to me and begged me to try to get her into a film. "Darryl doesn't know that's what I want," she said, "he'd kill me if he did." That evening I dined with Darryl and his girlfriend and agent Charles Feldman and his beauteous companion. "The wonderful thing about Clotilde," boasted Feldman, "is that she has absolutely no interest in acting." Zanuck chimed, "Genevieve actually *hates* the idea of being in pictures. Of that I am certain." To which Feldman responded, "Aren't we lucky?" I sat there silently, remembering my conversation with Genevieve on the airplane. She did ultimately have her way with sad results, while Clotilde stayed out of harm's way.

Nunnally Johnson was wise. We had a memorial service for him at the Academy of Motion Picture Arts and Sciences on December 9, 1986. One of those present quoted from a book written by Tom Stempel called *Screenwriter: The Life and Times of Nunnally Johnson,* in which Stempel said: "Nunnally Johnson writes screenplays actors can act. This is not so simple as it seems. Many writers, particularly those who work primarily in prose rather than in some dramatic form, have great difficulty writing lines that can not only be spoken, but acted. Johnson's lines move the story forward, but they also provide the actors with some emotion or attitude to put across while saying their lines."

Nunnally himself had some advice for writers. One of us read an excerpt from a letter written by him to the composer Robert Emmett Dolan in November 1971:

> Dear Bobby, I hope you haven't too heavy a hang-up on the pure mechanics of writing. I understand your concern with sentences and paragraphs, I suppose all writers have that concern, but there is a way to cope with it. There ought to be no question in your mind about your ability to write—I mean to convey thoughts in a graceful and intelligent form—for your letters are ample proof of that. No one who writes the letters you write needs to doubt his gift of communication. Myself, I rewrite and rewrite and rewrite. And so, I'm sure, do you. So why don't you forget the esthetics of sentences and paragraph structures in your first draft, giving all your concern to the narration, and do all your rephrasing and your restructuring in a second draft? After all, the grace of writing should come second. The first concern is the story telling.
>
> The odd thing about this suggestion, which I know is good, is that I never follow it myself. Like you, I become concerned with the shape of the sentences and the structure of the paragraph. So instead of finishing a day's stint and then examining it, I do the rewriting then and there, slowing everything down and holding up the progress of the work. Pure stupidity. Nearly all writers that I know anything about do it the way I have suggested. It's obviously the most sensible way of handling it, and I swear to you that in my next incarnation that's the way I'm going to do it from the very beginning.

Do studio heads read? You may judge for yourself by this story. Joseph Janni, whose films include *Darling* (1965) and *Sunday*

Bloody Sunday (1971), arranged a meeting with the head of Twentieth Century Fox studios some years ago. I have mercifully omitted his name. Janni told the studio head that he had a novel by Frederic Raphael which he would like him to consider. The studio head, hearing what the novel was about, expressed enthusiasm. He said, "Of course I want to make that movie. I want to buy the rights to the book immediately and engage Mr. Raphael to write the screenplay." Janni said, "You own the rights to the book and Mr. Raphael has already written the screenplay for you. The purpose of this meeting is to get you to read it!"

The Production Code is a set of rules by which the motion picture industry once governed its morals. Scripts and films were routinely submitted to a Rating Administration which culled out obscenity, lascivious conduct, and any suggestion that a man and woman might occupy the same bed. Things have changed. There is still a Production Code but God knows what it rules out, judging from what it allows.

In more innocent times, however, even the glimpse of a woman's inner thigh was decreed to be sinful and the admonition of the Production Code would occasionally fly in the face of history. I received, for example, a warning that the illicit relationship between Cleopatra and Mark Antony, as well as Caesar, could not be tolerated in the movie *Cleopatra.* Not mentioned was the off-screen illicit relationship between Cleopatra and Mark Antony (Elizabeth Taylor and Richard Burton).

Once a director is shooting, he can usually focus only on that day's work, all of which has been carefully planned with the actors, sets, and props on hand. The scenes to be shot are all he can absorb. He is an athlete in motion, a pilot in flight. You don't talk to him while cameras are about to roll except in emergencies. You have to grab him after the day's work to discuss changes in the schedule.

In the case of Arthur Penn's *Target,* the story began in Dallas, in the autumn of 1985, but our plan was to shoot the film almost entirely in Europe. The script called for a Texas lake. We found one near Paris, France. We shot interiors of a Dallas home on a set in a studio in Paris. When we returned to Dallas, after shooting in Europe, there were only four days in which to shoot what were supposed to be autumn exteriors. It was still autumn but there were eight inches of snow on the ground. This wouldn't work at all. We had a whole picture shot based on autumnal foliage. There we were with our big company in Dallas, Texas, looking for any place in Texas that didn't have snow. This was the winter that snow seemed to cover the entire Northern Hemisphere, even the south of France. We finally found a snow-free location in Corpus Christi, on the Gulf of Mexico. On a Saturday night, we flew to Corpus Christi, and on Sunday scouted all new locations. On that same Sunday our equipment trucks rolled south to Corpus Christi, and we started shooting on schedule on Monday, matching all our locations to what we had previously found months earlier in Dallas. Had we waited for the snow to melt in Dallas, one of our stars might have had to be paid an extra hundred thousand dollars a week because his contract would have expired after the four days originally scheduled in Texas, and he would have been on contractual "overages." Until you get a movie in the can, you are always in potential jeopardy. There can be illness, fire, death, or almost anything to destroy the progress of the movie. Director Arthur Penn had only the weekend after a long flight from Europe to become involved in the new logistics. On Monday he was shooting and could not be disturbed.

Shop Talk

When Academy Award-winning director William Wyler wanted to retake a scene, actors would ask what was to be done differently. The director would reply, "Just do it better."

Everybody in a movie is part of a family that can never be invaded by outsiders, including real family members. Some call it summer camp. For others it is like marine boot camp. Making a movie is also like a war, an intense, emotional experience for cast and crew. Each day you press on. There is no standing still and going back is expensive and dangerous to the common effort.

Script supervisors are among the most important and least publicized members of a motion picture crew. They are the memory of the movie. It is their responsibility to know every camera or cast movement on the set, every shot and item of clothing, the way someone is standing, makeup, hair, exit and entrance directions, and every prop that is filmed. They log every incident in the course of shooting; who walked off and when, the exact time of the first and last shot, the timing of every scene and the number of scenes filmed to the fraction of a script page. The director cannot be expected to recall every detail of the preceding scene of the movie, which may have been filmed weeks before, but script supervisors can and do, saving the producer, director, and cameramen embarrassment, shooting time, and considerable sums of money.

Scoring movies is an arcane art and a great deal of serious thought goes into it. Most producers and directors are musically illiterate and selecting a composer is done on the basis of what the composer has previously scored. "Get me John Williams or someone like him!" says the producer with a fat budget. Not so with *The Sting.* Director George Roy Hill was fortunate enough to have a teenage son who knew the music of Scott Joplin. That's how Joplin's music, adapted by Marvin Hamlisch, became the memorable score of *The Sting.* Never mind that Joplin's music was composed in the teens and *The Sting* took place in the thirties. It fit perfectly. George is an accomplished pianist and played the Joplin music as Richard Zanuck and I viewed a rough cut of the movie. "You can't afford me," said George when we suggested that he score the film. That's how we got Hamlisch who today is far pricier than George would have been.

I believe in every relationship one tests the other. In movies, the director tests the producer. Each has territorial rights. Early in the shooting schedule of *Target,* Arthur Penn, the director, engaged a still photographer. This decision is the producer's to make. I rescinded his action and engaged the photographer of my choice. There was a moment's anger. I had been tested. A director's testing period occurs on the first day of shooting when the actors and crew determine, however unconsciously, if they can be governed by him. When a director shows strength, everybody settles down, but if the director doesn't, there is trouble. You earn respect by showing strength, in life as in the movies.

At the rushes (another term for the dailies), you first get the awful feeling that the picture isn't going to work. It happened on *The Girl from Petrovka,* a love story set in preglasnost Moscow. The film began to sweat failure. It is something that permeates the set. It started when we were thrown out of Yugoslavia—where we were supposed to shoot—and had to complete the picture in Hollywood. The actors, Goldie Hawn and Hal Holbrook, were marvelous, but performances suffered by not being on location. Shooting on location is different from shooting in a Hollywood studio. Actors do not usually remain in character when they go home each night if the story they are filming takes place elsewhere. Woody Allen goes home each night but his films take place in New York. The love story that attracted Goldie Hawn and Hal Holbrook and our talented director, Robert Ellis Miller, came to life on the page (of the script) but not on the screen, possibly because we were shooting in the San Fernando Valley and not in Eastern Europe. Or perhaps, as Ernest Hemingway might (and did) say, isn't it pretty to think so?

It's weird how often hairdressers are mentioned in Academy Award acceptance speeches, while the most important people are ignored. Neither Julia nor Michael Phillips nor Tony Bill, producers of *The Sting,* nor George Roy Hill, who directed it, mentioned Richard Zanuck's and my contribution to the film in their acceptance speeches. All we did was acquire the screenplay, engage George Roy Hill to direct, serve as executive producers, and get the picture made. As executive producers, we were not asked to receive the Oscar. That is sometimes the only difference between executive producers and producers. The title "executive producer" is also often given to the "line producer" who is directly involved with the day-to-day production operations or, just as often, to a star's personal manager or agent who has no responsibility for the film and is never present on the set or location. And that is why there is such a fight to be designated as producer. We lost that fight.

Glossary. A few terms used in Hollywood:

To solve an adaptation problem, you "break the back" of the story. The poor little story is lying there, its writing writhing.

"I want a story with a beginning, a middle, and an end." Don't give me *Waiting for Godot.*

"No third act." A transplant from the theater. The story doesn't pay off.

"No rooting interest." Character is unsympathetic.

"What we have is an approach." It doesn't work.

"A germ of an idea." Something so fragmentary that it cannot be discerned through a microscope.

"Notes." An executive's script comments which have been cribbed from a reader's report.

"Pitch." A verbal presentation of a story not likely to be remembered by the buyer or the teller (or the audience, if the picture is made).

"D-Girl." Female development executive.

"Development executive." Someone with the power to reject, reshape, and otherwise harm a story she or he does not have the power to buy.

"Story analyst." A reader who prepares a synopsis or "coverage," as it is known, on a story submission. The ultimate power in Hollywood. The opinion of a forty-dollar-per-synopsis story analyst in the San Fernando Valley can result in a million-dollar purchase or a costly rejection by a studio boss who has neither the time nor the ability to read anything but box-office grosses.

"President of the film division." Usually can make only development decisions. Must seek approval from his boss, the chairman, before a picture is green-lighted.

"Pass." You've flunked. A rejection. The opposite of what it means in school.

"We need to punch up the script." Another writer is waiting in the wings.

"The rewrites work." Another writer has already been engaged.

Richard Zanuck and I lunched often with Alfred Hitchcock, M.S. (Master of Suspense), in his opulent bungalow on the Universal lot during the eight years we were at that studio. On one such occasion, Hitchcock recounted his theories of suspense while munching his customary rare minute steak and sipping a glass of world-class claret. "I never make a whodunit," said Hitchcock. "I always let the audience in on the killer, usually in the first act. Whodunits are intellectual and cold. For emotional involvement, one must know who 'done it' early on. The audience is most attentive when it is given information that the characters in the film do not have. That lets the audience in on the crime."

This had been Hitchcock's secret, plus the fact that he precut his films. That is, he shot with the cuts already planned. When he turned his film over to an editor, every cut had been precisely designated.

Hitchcock illustrated his theory of suspense. "Suppose," he said, "those of us sitting around this luncheon table (there were four that day) were characters in a film and were unaware that there was a bomb under the table. For effective suspense, the *audience* would have to know there was a bomb, but *we* would not know. The audience would have information we didn't have. We might be having the most boring conversation—about baseball, for example—but if the audience knew there was a bomb under our table and if perchance one of us kicked it in such a manner as to suggest it might go off, the audience would be on the edge of their seats." The unforgivable sin of suspense, according to Hitchcock, would be to permit the bomb to go off while we were all around the table. "For maximum suspense, it's necessary," he said, "for one of us to be brushing up against it, or somehow feeling it, or perhaps seeing and grasping it at the last possible moment and flinging it out the window. The audience would be cheated if we were all blown to hell."

Hitchcock didn't believe in photographing talk. By illustration, he mentioned someone who was involved in larcenous and low activities. Hitch said, "You know, I was acquainted with this man years ago. He was at a dinner party. I happened into the dining room before the guests were assembled and saw him, a guest, changing the place cards around. I knew then he was far from trustworthy. A very, very sticky fellow. Changing the place cards so that he would be more advantageously placed. All that one had to do is photograph that interesting bit of business for the setting up of a low character. No dialogue was necessary."

Hitchcock said that he had never looked through a camera in his life. He believed that the work should be in the screenplay. One of the film students to whom he once lectured asked whether he ever improvised on a set while he was shooting a film. Hitchcock snapped, "Never." Once a film was being photographed, he never improvised. He followed the shooting script exactly. He did his improvising on paper while the screenplay was being written.

He compared a film director to the conductor of a symphony orchestra, saying it would be as unseemly for a director of a film to improvise on the set as it would be for a conductor of a symphony to depart from the orchestration and order a musician to play different notes. "If music can be recorded on paper, so can a film. After all, music is aural and yet it is preserved on pieces of paper with key signatures, bars, clefs, and the rest of it. A film is but a script translated to the photographic medium of film."

Hitch was mystified by the most commonplace bodily functions. The Master of Suspense, who had directed hundreds of beautiful women, had never heard of a menstrual period. When Eva Marie

Saint in *North by Northwest* informed him that she was indisposed because of her period, he had to be told what that was. It was probably the only flow of blood with which he was entirely unfamiliar.

It's tough to find a star who will accept your script. Stars have their own sensitivities. Producers propose and studios dispose. If you can't get the first star, you try for a second or third choice. The latter choices often turn out better. Zanuck and I worked on *Patton* on and off for twenty years. It was started and dropped a dozen times. A book by Ladislas Farago titled *Ordeal and Triumph: The Story of General George Patton* made us start up all over again in 1965. After working on half a dozen scripts, we attracted William Wyler as director. Champagne flowed because Willie was the best. Then, as on *The Sound of Music,* he dropped out after he couldn't get Burt Lancaster or John Wayne or any of the stars he wanted to play Patton. When Darryl Zanuck said, "What about George C. Scott?" it was far from a first choice. Scott had been brilliant in *The Hustler* and a few other pictures, but he was no star. Still, he resembled Patton and it seemed like a good idea. We were years into the project and hundreds of thousands of dollars had been spent on scripts, when Scott said he'd only commit if we got a satisfactory script. We were ready to cancel the project again when his agent, Jane Deacy, said, "In that load of scripts you sent Scott, he sort of liked a first draft by a man named Coppola."

"Will he commit to that?" I quickly asked.

She replied, "I'll ask him." Within the day, she telephoned to say, "Yes, if you go to script number one, he'll commit."

The script by Francis Ford Coppola won Francis his first Academy Award, along with his cowriter, Edmund North, who made revisions which Coppola was unable to make because he was already directing a movie.

Like shaving off layers of paint to reveal a long-hidden mural, we spent months restoring everything from the original Coppola version that other writers had obscured in the six years since he had worked on the project. They had even rewritten the speech before the flag at the opening of the film, a speech written not by Coppola, but by General George Patton himself, in which he exhorted his troops to make grease balls of "those Krauts." Scott never wanted to film that opening because he thought if we started that high, we'd never get back to the peaks. Well, we did. We asked him to shoot it at the end of the picture and never told him we'd use it at the beginning.

Paul Newman does not like violence. In fact, he abhors it. When we were preparing *The Eiger Sanction* in 1975, he expressed interest in being in it and we worked with him for months on revisions in the screenplay. All to no avail. Mr. Newman realized he would have to kill some people . . . in the movie, that is. He decided he would have to withdraw from *The Eiger Sanction* because of his commitment to nonviolence. Understood and respected. But where did we go for another actor?

Clint Eastwood, where else? Yet Clint, too, abhors violence. He is a peaceable man by nature, with a decidedly intellectual streak in his film philosophy. There is a morality footnote in all his films. You may have to dig, but it's there. He'll tell you where. Eastwood doesn't make his day by mindlessness. That may surprise some, but not those who have the pleasure of knowing him and working with him.

Put me in someone's office whose hand signs my check or who is convincingly authoritative and I am instantly deferential. Have you had an experience you wished you could replay, with different dialogue? I had one with George C. Scott, the actor. When Dick Zanuck and I planned to make our film about General MacArthur, George C. Scott was considered for the title role, which was ultimately and magnificently played by Gregory Peck. A meeting was scheduled with Scott in New York at which were present Sidney Sheinberg, president of MCA/Universal, Zanuck, and I.

As soon as we sat down, Scott looked at Zanuck and me and asked Sheinberg, "What are *they* doing here?"

"What are you talking about, George?" said Sheinberg.

"I had the most unpleasant experience of my life with those men," responded Scott, "on two films, *Patton* and *Rage*." (*Rage* was a film Scott made for Warner Brothers; he directed it and starred in it.)

As Scott continued his tirade, he became increasingly abusive. Zanuck finally broke in, "George, I think you had a very successful experience with *Patton.* As for *Rage,* that was your movie. You also directed it. You refused to edit it. You wouldn't even attend the screening of the rough cut. We were left to edit it."

Later, I thought, why didn't we also say that we gave him the role of *Patton* over the opposition of the entire Fox board of directors, the role for which he won (although refused) the Academy Award, and say further that the scene in front of the American flag, which he staunchly resisted, turned out to be the most memorable scene in the movie? As for *Rage,* why didn't we remind him that we begged him not to make the film? We've thought of other versions of our office encounter in which we humiliate Scott. Dick's version is that he lands on top of Scott, which actually happened sometime later at the Bel Air Hotel in Los Angeles, when Scott angrily rebuffed a peace offering from Dick and began a scuffle in the bar.

Stars know exactly what they can do and can't do as actors, however far they reach for something different from what the public expects of them. As a rule, they are shrewd and perceptive about scripts. It is no longer how large the part is, but the balance between their roles and the others and, more than ever, their ability to get into the head of the character they are being asked to play. Goldie Hawn is an exceptional actress, as she demonstrated in *The Sugarland Express,* a Zanuck/Brown production and the first theatrical feature directed by Steven Spielberg. Goldie should have won an Oscar for her performance, and Spielberg for directing her.

Musings

Life hands out blows, and those at the top have further to drop, as Stephen Sondheim reminds us in his lyric from *Follies:* ". . . the greater the height, the greater the drop." I came upon Muhammad Ali at a party celebrating the Festival of American Film in Charlottesville, Virginia. Ali was seated with one of the sponsors of the event, Mrs. John Kluge. As others left the table to dance, Ali and I were left alone. He was quiet, obviously not in the best of health, but not disoriented. I said, "You look fine, champ." He fixed his eyes on me and said, "Oh, I'm just an old, washed-up bum." I protested, "You're still young, and there are other careers. You know better than anyone that careers in the ring are short. Everyone who has followed you will also have to decide what to do with the rest of his life." I continued, "Look at me. I'm seventy-two. I've started a new company. I'm starting over." He became slightly animated and said, "What you're telling me is the best thing I've heard in a long time. It makes me feel better." And I said, "Well, you should. You were the greatest." He looked at me quizzically and said, "Tell me something. You still look at women?" "You're damn right I do," I replied, gazing at one in particular on the dance floor. He smiled and asked, "How is it when you do it? Is it good?" I answered, "Yes. It's less but it's still great." He said, "Now I *really* feel good."

Mike Nichols was celebrating the triumph of his film *Who's Afraid of Virginia Woolf?* Ernest Lehman, who wrote the screenplay and produced the film, was reading one rhapsodic review after another to Nichols, when Mike looked up at him pensively and asked, "But Ernie, we still have to die, don't we?"

Those who lie have, for a time, an advantage. We tend to believe what we hear and especially what we read, unless the source is clearly discredited. Unfortunately, liars can go undiscredited for a long time. Adolf Hitler boasted of the efficacy of "the big lie"—the bigger the fabrication, the more likely it is to be believed. Rumors are its finest form. Gossip is a lesser one. The liar believes he is truthful when he lies. Some lies are benign—the so-called white lies of politesse. "I've had a wonderful time," one says when one hasn't. Why hurt the hostess? "I'm so sorry," is often said when one isn't. Anything to get out of there. The lie is usually a form of one-upmanship. It is the next step up—or down, as I see it—from bragging. I don't like liars or braggarts, although on occasion I am guilty of being either or both. I regret any traces that may have found their way into this book. They are inadvertent and my hope is that they are also invisible.

Recently I've had a minor skin ailment and I am driven wild by itching. In scratching, I've experienced the nearest sensation to sexual satisfaction short of the act. The feeling of being violently scratched provides great, inexpensive, and safe pleasure. It was Plato, I believe, who said happiness is the absence of pain. I think true happiness is the removal of itch through scratching.

There is no assured happiness. One man I know has over sixteen million dollars, is at his professional peak, but has no one to check in with when he comes home. Another is married to one of the most glamorous women in the world, but suffers excruciating back pains and is constantly in traction. There's a catch to everything. Once you grasp that truth you needn't worry too much about being a malcontent. One is not supposed to be happy. One's life is like a building that requires maintenance, an airplane whose engines are periodically in need of repair, whose aging skin must occasionally be repainted or peeled off and replaced, and whose interior is never quite finished.

Fear of Flying

Super-agent Irving Lazar is one of those flyers who wants to go to sleep and wake up at his destination without experiencing the fright of flight. Once, years ago, Lazar was seated next to Darryl Zanuck on a sleeper flight from Paris to New York. Irving knew that Zanuck had a powerful, possibly illegal, suppository which rendered him unconscious from takeoff to landing. Lazar, who was not shy about asking for things, importuned Zanuck to give him one of these suppositories. Fade out. Fade in. When DFZ was disembarking, a stewardess said, "Mr. Zanuck, it's too bad what happened to your friend." The concerned Zanuck learned that in the middle of the night, Lazar was found peacefully sleeping in a snowbank with his glasses broken. The plane had stopped for refueling in Gander, Newfoundland, and somebody had left a passenger door open. Lazar had to go to the toilet and while sleepwalking, climbed out of his berth, mistook the open door for the lavatory, and plunged through it into an Arctic snowbank, where he continued sleeping until he was lifted back on board, somewhat dazed, chilled, but otherwise unhurt.

I do not claim to be a fearless flyer. Nobody was as timid, I think, as I was on airplane flights. My very first flight was over Lake George in the year 1918, when I was but two years old. I loathed flying. As I got older, I found myself listening for every particular sign of imminent disaster. I would cancel flights because of a bad dream or some vague premonition. I felt I would surely wind up on a mountaintop with the tail of the airplane sticking up, marking the place of my demise along with hundreds of other passengers. For many years, I imagined what it would be like to be in the cabin of an airliner quickly descending to the ocean or to some canyon remote from all life and to be the last resting place of all of us. Then, as life became more complicated and troubles grew, particularly in early years, I found a certain peace aboard an airplane. No one could get to me and I was helpless, totally under the control of the pilot and his crew and the plane itself, its logistics and its aerodynamics. Alcohol was a great savior in the early days. I drank in the cocktail lounge at the airport and in the airplane. My anxiety soon was numbed by martinis, Cuba libres, and scotches.

Soon, but not too soon, after years of safe flying, I began to give up the drinking and the Valium and the prayer on takeoff (a silent prayer, although you could read my lips). Now I rarely think about these things on takeoff and on landing. Just as well.

Among noted nonflyers to this day is Stanley Kubrick, the film director, who lives in London, not far from Heathrow International Airport. Stanley Kubrick will not go aloft in an airplane, although he is said to be a licensed pilot. Perhaps that is the reason. He stays in his compound in England and makes the films there. He brings the locale to his earthbound studio. He even brought the Vietnam War there for *Full Metal Jacket.*

My friend Gene Shalit, so far as I know, has never been in an airplane and does not expect to be. I have never asked him why. He simply will not fly and does not wish to be interrogated about it. He is the only film critic I know who has never been to Hollywood. Too far to go by train and forget flying there. Hollywood stars fly to Gene for his memorable interviews, and you can see Gene in Hollywood only on KNBC, Los Angeles. The closest Gene has come to any kind of flight other than one of fancy was when he was in love with an airline flight attendant. He would have flown with her, I think, but then the romance crashed.

Ray Bradbury neither flies nor drives. The distinguished science-fiction author rides a bicycle in Los Angeles. At least, he has until recently. During my years in Los Angeles, Ray did not drive a car and could not be persuaded to fly. Neither could Irving Wallace, until some years ago. He traveled to Europe by train and by ship, while his wife, Sylvia, flew. Irving now flies.

Aaron Spelling, the television producer, will still not fly. He will engage a private railway car to transport his wife and family from Southern California to New York and there board the *QE2* on his infrequent visits to Europe.

Add Isaac Asimov to the list of those who do not fly. Isaac, like Ray Bradbury, has a mind that encompasses the heavens, an imagination that goes beyond the farthest star. Although Isaac does not fly, his imagination soars beyond the reach of any aircraft or satellite.

And finally, and perhaps the most bizarre nonflyer, is Sam Shepard, the actor who portrayed Chuck Yeager, the indomitable test pilot whose exploits in the air are legendary. Sam would not fly in the film *The Right Stuff.* His flying was accomplished by a double, while he portrayed Chuck Yeager on the ground. On one occasion I offered Sam Shepard a role in a film that was to be made in Australia, and was told by his agent that the travel time, during which he would be on salary, might be several weeks. He would travel to the location by ship.

These are a few of the stories of those nonflyers in the world of supersonic and soon-to-be-hypersonic flight. Bless them. There is a certain courage in not following those of us who choose to be shot across the world in metal capsules at greater than the speed of bullets.

What do celebrities do when they're trapped with a talkative seatmate on an airplane? Frank Sinatra used to purchase the seat next to him and the two behind. That was before he bought his own airplane. It's an extravagant way to avoid talkative companions, but the pain of listening to a garrulous civilian can be severe. It is not only a problem for celebrities. You're on a flight. You want to rest or read or be alone with your thoughts. Here comes a tool manufacturer from Indianapolis who wants to talk for five and one half hours. Goldie Hawn told me of being on an airplane with someone who talked all the way across the continent. She's a polite girl, a sweet woman, and wouldn't rudely turn someone off. My wife is also sweet and considerate, but more protective. I asked Helen what she would have done in Goldie's situation. She said, "The best way is to feign sleep. That deprives you of reading, of course. Another way is to say, 'Look here, I have a speech to memorize. Would you be terribly insulted if I didn't talk?' The foxiest way, if you're Goldie Hawn, is to say, 'You know, I have this terrible problem. Everybody mistakes me for Goldie Hawn and I'm actually Kate Lipschitz from Leonia, New Jersey.' " Of course, Kate Lipschitz, being as beautiful as Goldie Hawn, would still get considerable attention. I once sat next to a celebrity and said nothing for five hours. I simply gazed at her legs. She was Marlene Dietrich. Although it was more than twenty years ago, I can still remember the seat—1B—and, of course, the legs. Oh, the legs.

The Verdict: A Very Special Movie

Producers have died and worms have eaten them before they were able to induce Robert Redford to read one of their scripts. The elusive, reclusive Redford is known to cross to the other side of the street if he sees a producer approaching with a script. I had no such difficulty, thanks to my friend Jay Presson Allen, the intensely gifted playwright, novelist, and screenwriter who wrote one of the many drafts of *The Verdict.* The story was about a lawyer down on his luck and fighting for his one client in what seemed to be a hopeless medical malpractice case.

Jay was engaged to write a new draft of *The Verdict* after David Mamet first wrote a screenplay, brilliant except for the omission of a verdict. Jay undertook the job after warning Dick Zanuck and me that we had a perfectly good script from Mamet (we did, as it turned out), and that Mamet surely could be persuaded by a director to include a verdict (he was).

We nevertheless persuaded Jay to write a script faithful to the book by Barry Reed on which the movie was supposed to be based. Mamet's version had departed from the novel. "Tell me exactly what you want," Jay insisted. "I don't like to give surprises or get them." What Jay did was get five hundred thousand dollars for writing a screenplay in three weeks, containing to the millimeter everything we had requested and never eventually used.

Dissolve first, however, to an afternoon in Roxbury, Connecticut. Robert Redford was at the front door of Lewis and Jay Allen's country home, wanting to know if their house was for rent. Who would not show Robert Redford their home, for rent or not? While roaming through the rooms, Redford noticed the script of *The Verdict* on Jay's desk. Could he possibly read it? Could the pope bless you?

"Bob, this is something you should direct," Jay said, aware that secret discussions were underway with Dustin Hoffman to star. Within three days, Redford telephoned me to offer to commit to the role *without* director approval by him, an unheard-of accommodation for a star of his stature. His offer was designed to get Hoffman out of the way since Hoffman had insisted upon approval. Neither actor got the part and, as Jay predicted, the script that was used was Mamet's *with* a verdict and with Paul Newman in the starring role, which she had also predicted would occur after a few waltzes with the golden Redford.

The Verdict turned out to be more about the redemption of a man than the indictment of a system. We know there are corrupt judges. We also know (as David Mamet wrote in the film script) that the rich are powerful, the poor are powerless, and that we have begun to doubt our institutions. Still, even Milo O'Shea, portraying a corrupt judge, turns out to be a reasonable fellow when the jury confronts him with the verdict. If anything, the film is an endorsement of the American judicial system. It shows that the same judicial system that brought down a president, through the House Judiciary Committee, can protect the poor and powerless. Not often, but occasionally.

Nearly everyone connected with *The Verdict* was off his usual track. Zanuck and Brown were involved in subject matter unlike anything else they had previously produced. It promised to be a grown-up thinking person's movie, with all the commercial hazards and esthetic rewards that lie within those boundaries. Paul Newman was attracted to a role antithetical to his superstar image. He was playing a broken-down man, defeated by life, fighting the church, a powerful law firm, and the medical establishment. He was an alcoholic. A womanizer. Someone who had really had it. A man who shuffles at an early age, and who wheezes. Everything Paul Newman does not do in real life, he does in *The Verdict,* including chain-smoking cigarettes. He wanted that role because it extended the boundaries of his acting. He's a most serious actor.

As Hitchcock did, Sidney Lumet camera cuts. Unlike most directors not schooled in live television as he was, he shoots only the cuts he uses. There's very little editorial discretion. When he shot Newman making his summation to the jury in *The Verdict,* he deliberately did not move his camera in on him until the last possible moment. He wanted to show *him,* his helplessness, his plight, against the overpowering, massive background of the courtroom. A little man facing overwhelming odds.

One of the most favorable reviews of *The Verdict* we received was from the influential Catholic newspaper *The Tablet.* It held that the fact that it was a Catholic hospital in the film was of no relevance; that it dealt with redemption was of relevance, a Christian theme of which they approved. There was no suggestion in the film that the Church was actually aware that a hospital record had been altered. When the bishop asked his assistant how the trial was going and was told of Mason's triumphs, he abruptly said, "I know that. But did you believe him?" And the camera held on the bishop.

In *The Verdict,* an establishment law firm uses "dirty tricks" to cow its adversaries. There were no protests from lawyers saying that they had been maligned by the film. In fact, at a conservative club to which I belong, a member of a prestigious Wall Street law firm confided, "Don't let anyone tell you we don't employ 'dirty tricks.' Everything in your movie, including the use of a Mata Hari, has been done by the best of firms." In my own experience with corporations employing law firms, I have seen the worst. When Richard Zanuck and I were thrown out of Twentieth Century Fox years ago, we had reason to believe—and some evidence—that the great Wall Street law firm representing Fox arranged to tap our phones, put us under surveillance, and do everything to discredit us. I know this because while we were still executives at Fox, we used the same law firm to employ the very same tactics against someone who was mounting a proxy fight to remove the management, which included us. Years later, when I returned to Fox as a producer, I temporarily occupied the office of the chairman of the company, and couldn't resist peeking at a mass of documents the chairman had neglected to hide. The documents concerned a friend of mine who had accumulated a sizable amount of stock. The chairman and other managers, who had virtually no stock, were trying to get something on my friend. At company expense, meaning the expense of the stockholders (which included my friend), they had assembled what amounted to an FBI report. Every infraction and traffic ticket, details of matrimonial disputes, student misdemeanors, voting records, and friends were revealed here. All done not by the law firm but by an investigative service the law firm had caused to be hired, carefully concealing its own connection to this assignment.

In *The Verdict,* a magical actress named Charlotte Rampling pervades the film with her erotic coolness (yes, eroticism can be cool) with only a few pages of script. It was always Lumet's vision that the role of Laura would be so mysterious that you really would never be sure of her history. We've had people ask whether she was related to the James Mason character. In South Africa, I was asked which scenes between Newman and Rampling had to be cut to satisfy the censor. The interviewer was astonished to learn there were none. They were never seen in bed, although she says she will stay the night with him when she is concerned about his lack of sleep. He replies, "You're going to stay with me?" Cut. That's all there is. The only other scene is the one in which they enter Newman's apartment and he prepares a drink for her and they embrace.

She looks over his shoulder and sees his wife's photograph. He sort of smiles and shrugs and goes over and places it face down. She says that's all right, and opens her blouse. Cut. That's all there is. There is nothing more. Nothing else was shot. That's the relationship. There is no love scene between Rampling and Newman except what is suggested. Are they having an affair? Of course. We know that. After she opens her blouse they go to bed together. But we never see it. It never was shot. It was never seen by U.S. audiences or any other audiences. The reason: It's better that way, sexier. Censors would think otherwise.

There were only two actresses who wanted to play the role: Julie Christie and Charlotte Rampling. Julie Christie was doing a film in India and was not available. Charlotte wanted to do it because the role is all reaction.

In *The Verdict,* the purpose of Charlotte Rampling's character was manifold. It established Paul Newman's sense of maleness in his character. David Mamet said that alcoholics are not wild womanizers. Frank Galvin, the Newman character, wasn't that far gone. He saw that lady in the bar and was attracted to her. She reminded him of his male responsibility to perform when she said, "I'm sorry, Frank, I'm not going to invest in failure anymore." In that scene, we realized a complex character in a compressed area of screen time.

The purpose of the ending which Sidney Lumet devised (Rampling's unanswered phone call) was to remind Galvin that for every victory in life there's a price. When he looks up in the courthouse rotunda after his victory and sees she's vanished, he knows the price . . . and later, when she calls and he watches the phone and decides to let it ring. We don't know then whether they will ever see each other again because, so far as he knows, she betrayed him. But does she love him? We know but he doesn't . . . yet. We saw her tears when James Mason said, you've had your marriage. This is what buys your clothes and liquor and the rest of it. You wanted to come back to the real world, and the work you do. Welcome back. We know from her expression that she's hooked on Galvin. He's a man without a woman. His wife divorced him. Who would have him? She would. When he is disconsolate and believes he has lost, she believes in him but doesn't pamper him. She says, Frank, you told me the case isn't over until the jury is in. You want me to treat you like a little boy. Tell you that you've got a fever and you don't have to go to school. Well, I won't, Frank.

We often wondered how we would cast a role that didn't have more than a few pages of script. What the director and the actress recognized was that the important part of the role was in the silences and in the repetition of words. When Galvin says, "Maybe I can do something right," she says simply, "And is that what you're going to do?" He replies, "That's what I'm going to try to do." They've said all they need say to set up their characters.

Rampling's gaunt, gorgeous looks helped. She appeared beautifully used. Those extraordinary cheekbones, those challenging eyes. The look was enough. And the voice.

As for audience complaints about not being able to hear Jack Warden's remarks about Rampling's background in a scene with Paul Newman on the Boston shuttle, Lumet wanted it that way. He wanted the Rampling character to be mysterious. He succeeded.

Did she begin as a spy when she met Galvin in a bar? Even that at first was obscure, but you learn she was when you see James Mason fix her whiskey and hear him say, "This pays for your clothes and the work you do."

Throughout the film, Charlotte Rampling, playing a spy, never turns down a drink. Every time there's one offered, she quickly says yes. And when Newman fixes her a scotch in his apartment, he asks, "Ice?" and she replies, "No ice." The sign of a drinker.

On *Target*

Target was tough to cast. It called for a Middle-America businessman so nondescript that nobody would know—especially his teenage son—that he was once a CIA agent. When Gene Hackman reported for the film in Paris, I took him to dinner at a restaurant off the Champs Elysées. A group of American businessmen had come over on the same plane as Hackman and were occupying a table next to ours. I listened to these guys from Minneapolis and Kansas City talking about the deals that they were going to make in France. They were not in the entertainment business. Gene was sitting with me and a couple of people from the production company. I thought, "Gene could be sitting with those businessmen; he would fit in completely. He doesn't look like an actor. He speaks the way they do." Hackman has said that one of his greatest advantages is his ability to make people identify with him as a character. It looks easy but Gene works hard at it, and he is one of the world's great film actors.

We needed a beautiful European actress to play the part of Hackman's former lover, both of them portraying onetime spies in the Cold War. While in New York, we heard Victoria Fyodorova read for us. She was beautiful . . . nearly six feet tall, marvelously lean, and with a seductive Russian accent. So far as I was concerned, she had the part. Our director, Arthur Penn, and I traveled to Munich, Vienna, and Berlin to interview others for this role, but in my head and I suspect in Penn's, Victoria was the one. Equally beautiful was Gayle Hunnicutt, who played Hackman's abducted (by the KGB) wife in the same movie. We had seen Gayle, too, and become instantly infatuated. Don't believe producers and directors are blasé about great-looking men and women. Why do you think we're in this business?! We were so taken with Gayle Hunnicutt, who had flown to Paris from London to be interviewed, we took her to dinner and, by the time coffee had arrived, never mentioned the film. "Don't you want to talk about the movie?" asked Gayle. Reluctantly, we went to work.

As for Victoria Fyodorova, she is a good actress and has a remarkable personal story which someday may make a movie of its own.

Victoria was the daughter of a Soviet movie star and an American who had been a Navy flyer attached to the American Embassy in Moscow. For her sin, the Soviet movie star was sent to prison. Victoria was brought up by her aunt whom she was led to believe was her mother.

Before she grew up, her mother miraculously was released. Victoria flew across Red Square to embrace her, still thinking she was her aunt. She tearfully smoothed Victoria's hair and said, "Darling, I'm your mother." Wonderful scene.

Later, Victoria Fyodorova also became an actress and was determined to meet her father who was living in Florida with another wife. She bewitched the clerks in the visa section of the Soviet Foreign Ministry and (to everyone's astonishment) received permission to visit her father in the United States. Victoria instantly recognized her father by looking in his eyes, which were her eyes. When this mid-America flying type cast his eyes on his beautiful Russian daughter, they embraced.

In an interview in *People* magazine, Victoria said she wanted to bring home a dog. A Pan Am pilot on the New York–Moscow run read the interview and offered to fly the dog to Russia. Victoria met the pilot in New York, forgot the dog, and fell in love with the pilot. Instantly. Victoria knew only one English word: "Married?" He shook his head. The dog and Victoria never returned to the Soviet Union. She tends to their establishment in Greenwich and their twelve-year-old son. Only when we cast her in *Target* did she return to Europe and fly with us to Paris, her husband in command of the aircraft. As for Gayle Hunnicutt, the stunning Texan who speaks with an upper-class British accent but can revert to Texan at will, she is married to Simon Jenkins, one of Britain's most distinguished journalists.

Selected Short Subjects

Before you can do battle on film, you have to do battle with the Pentagon to get government cooperation to make a movie. The government insists on prior approval of scripts for movies requiring the use of troops, tanks, airplanes, and ships. The rationale is simple. There is no reason the American taxpayer should pay for a film unless it serves the public interest. One aim of World War II films, in addition to making money, was to keep the public in a state of patriotic fervor so it would support the war effort, and to recruit men and women for the armed forces. If you were producing *Winged Victory* or *Thirty Seconds Over Tokyo* or whatever, Congress, the generals' or admirals' boss, leaned on its Military Appropriations Committee to lend you their arms.

It was a congressman, years later, who almost killed the practice. At Twentieth Century Fox, we were making a film titled *Tora! Tora! Tora!* and needed the cooperation of both the Japanese and the American governments to reenact the raid on Pearl Harbor. Our movie raid may have cost more than the Japanese raid. As a result of a broadcast by Mike Wallace on *60 Minutes,* which revealed that Twentieth Century Fox was receiving free use of ships, planes, and sailors in the production of a movie, the congressman was outraged and forced a change in the policy of the Pentagon. Fox and other movie companies were required to pay the reasonable cost of all government personnel and equipment.

More recently, during the production of *MacArthur,* it was necessary to move the battleship *Missouri* (then in "mothballs" at Bremerton Harbor, Washington), to face seaward for the reenactment of the historic Japanese surrender ceremony. It cost fifty-nine thousand dollars to take the plugs out of the big guns and turn the ship around. In addition, Fox had to pay every serviceman who was used in the movie. It was still a bargain, compared to the price of building a battleship set. We also needed landing barges and the use of Camp Pendleton to reenact MacArthur's landing in the Philippines. Permission was granted us to shoot MacArthur's farewell speech to the cadets at West Point (the women cadets were asked to keep out of camera range). Congress, however, refused the use of its chambers for MacArthur's final ("old soldiers never die") speech, and a smaller room had to be used.

If you want cooperation for a movie from any branch of the federal government today, you must submit a script for approval. It doesn't constitute censorship. It is simply a process to determine whether your film—in the government's view—is in the public interest. If it is judged to be, the use of government resources must still be paid for. Many movies that were denied cooperation were still produced, *From Here to Eternity, The Caine Mutiny,* and *An Officer and a Gentleman* among them.

Patton seemed to be an impossible project when Richard Zanuck and I put it into work. Opposition to *Patton* came not only from the Pentagon but from a highly articulate sector of the public during the peak of antiwar sentiment in the sixties. Film-industry sages asked why we were making *Patton.* They thought it was a terrible idea. They warned that young movie audiences had never heard of General George Patton. We found ourselves preparing a story about a general when everybody of military age was trying to keep out of uniform. Amazingly, it turned out that the movie appealed to both antiwar activists *and* right-wing military hawks. One group saw it as persuasive evidence of the idiocy of militarism and the other, veterans of World War II, myself among them, saw it as an appeal for patriotism and a tribute to a wrongly maligned military leader.

Without the Academy Award performance by George C. Scott, I believe the film would have failed. The role fit him perfectly. He even looked like Patton. He studied his manner. He looked at thousands of feet of newsreels showing Patton in action and sent for all sorts of books on him from the New York Public Library, War Department Archives, and everywhere else that might have material on him. George C. Scott was himself fiercely antiwar. Imagine his astonishment when, after the film was released, he was invited to address the cadets at West Point. Military-academy officials confused the man with his role, the greatest compliment an actor can receive. He did not accept the lecture invitation or the Academy Award. As for the Oscar, he had notified the Academy of Motion Picture Arts and Sciences in advance that he would not accept it. "I mean no offense to the Academy," he explained. "I simply do not wish to be involved." He later said that he did not believe in competition among actors for awards. The Academy voted him the award anyway.

I think what is read is more influential than what is seen and heard even though movies and television reach more people. Have you tried to remember what you saw on television last week? Good movies stay with you longer, but they're not life-changers. Important books are. Moreover, even the film and television worlds are dependent on the written word—whether in a script, a book, or even an ad in a newspaper or *TV Guide* to tell the public where an attraction can be seen. Print has credibility to a greater extent, I believe, than audio-visual media. It's also a reflective medium; one can think about what one is reading without the distraction of images flashing by. The most important advantage of print is that it is portable and permanent, even when it comes out of a computer's printer, as it usually does these days—as did the manuscript of this very book. In fact, if you want to influence people who in turn influence others, there is nothing like the printed word, whether in a newspaper, magazine, or book. Good for starting a religion, a revolution, or a war.

Walter Cronkite accepted a dinner invitation to our house with his beloved Betsy. He could easily have postponed the date because it was the evening his first interview with President Ronald Reagan was to be broadcast. It had been taped the day before. There were other dinner guests. Walter asked that they not watch his interview, but he was overruled. While the others watched, Walter and I swapped jokes in a hallway. Before leaving the room, he said wryly, "Listen, watching that interview isn't going to put you in higher standing with me at all." But watch they did, having passed up the live Cronkite for the Cronkite interviewing the president of the United States. Hollywood style would have had him say, "Oh, I can't make your party because I am on the air with the president," or insist we all watch because he wanted to watch. Instead, his concern was that he might be disrupting a dinner party: an example of the courtesy of a truly important person.

Jack Warner, ruler of all he surveyed on the Warner Brothers lot, may have turned off the lights when he left the studio each night but had no difficulty spending money for his personal comfort. In addition to his walled baronial estate in Beverly Hills and a drop-dead waterfront villa on the French Riviera, he maintained a tower apartment in New York's Sherry Netherland so vast that it contained a waterfall.

One evening, after dining at Trader Vic's, he invited Helen and me to come across the street and see it. As we entered the cavernous digs, heard the rushing water (clearly not from a toilet), and gazed in awe at the three-story drawing room with views of glittering Manhattan from all sides, Warner said, "Be it ever so humble, there's no place like home."

Intermission

When to accept an invitation, how to take reasonable precautions against a boring evening, how gracefully, tactfully, to get out of a commitment when it is discovered to be a mistake, are part of the strategy of social survival. I've always been an advocate of entertaining in a restaurant. Home entertainment may well be more flattering to the guest, but it is also more difficult and often destructive to one's home and peace of mind. One can be stuck for hours at a home-based dinner party because guests won't leave. One can announce the departure time in a restaurant by calling for the bill. At home, servants quit, power fails, and cooks are capable of culinary catastrophe. Such risks are rare in good restaurants. Restaurant gatherings can be organized with a minimum of advance notice and with no advance preparation. One of the best dinner parties my wife and I have ever given was pulled together at the White Elephant Club in London when we discovered that we would have to leave London five days earlier than anticipated. We had to telescope all our social engagements into a single evening. That meant friends who never knew each other were thrown together madly in one group. Our guests loved meeting new people. It worked like crazy.

Further on the strategy of social survival. Hostesses know when you're lying. They are like customs inspectors. They can tell instantly whether you do have 105 fever, and if you haven't they lay a guilt trip on you. I tell the semi-truth by making excuses less dramatic. I never resort to deaths in the family and that sort of drastic circumstance. At receptions, my wife or I will appear and explain that the missing one has been felled by the flu. One doesn't have to go into this too much because your host and hostess or one of their other guests have been through the same sort of thing often, and if you're observed dancing the next evening, it was the twenty-four-hour flu.

This is background for the story I am about to tell. A few years ago, Helen and I accepted an invitation to a small dinner party. We had no idea how small. We were the only guests. That is true captivity. There is no escape. The party does not begin until you arrive. The party is over when you leave. In this instance, the risks were greater for the host than for us. He was unaware of Helen's spectacular aversion to the cadaver of any species. Innocently, he brought forth a living lobster for our appraisal to assure us that the lobster that is alive one moment and boiled the next is better for eating purposes. The moment this unfeeling brute displayed the living lobster, Helen screamed. She screamed again when he explained that lobsters cry a little when dropped into the boiling pot. As he carried the lobster into the kitchen while it was still wriggling, claws and all, Helen raced out the door and ran along East Fifty-third Street in Manhattan for three blocks before I could catch up with her to persuade her to return. Back she came. She fled again when she heard the slight hissing sound of the lobster being boiled and this time she was gone for good. Moral: Research the peculiarities of your guests before you invite them. Or your host, before you accept an invitation.

When people are terminally boring, my resource is to tune out. My wife's defense is to bend a spoon around her finger and hand it to me as a warning to get her the hell out of there. She is a frail woman but has the strength of Samson under these circumstances. The spoon is as tangled as a pretzel around her tiny finger. A famous author's husband and a one-time movie mogul, both noted for nonstop discourses, have been mystified by the sight of spoons being bent out of recognition by Helen in world-class restaurants as I hurriedly call for the check. While my wife does not suffer bores gladly, I dissemble and pretend to be interested. I'm for face saving. I don't believe in scenes. I try—unsuccessfully—to hide the bent spoons.

Mean Stories

These are mean stories.

Julius Epstein, the screenwriter who wrote *Casablanca* with Howard Koch and even better but not so memorable films, told this story about George Jean Nathan, a brilliant critic and raconteur. Nathan lived in the old Royalton, which is across West Forty-fourth

Street from the famed Algonquin. He was known as the most miserable low tipper in the hotel. Author and actor Robert Benchley, a member of the Algonquin Round Table set, knew this and also knew all the waiters at the Royalton, because he lived there, too. While going up in the elevator one day, he observed a waiter bringing a cup of tea to Nathan's room. He said, "I see Mr. Nathan is splurging again." The waiter remarked, "For thirty-five years Mr. Nathan has never tipped more than a dime. He is unquestionably the worst, stingiest tipper in the history of this hotel." Benchley asked, "Why can't you tell him?" The waiter said, "We have a better way to get our message across. This cup of tea which Mr. Nathan will soon be drinking was laced with urine by an appreciative kitchen staff." Three hours later, Benchley saw George Jean Nathan at "21" with his great and good friend, the delicately beautiful actress Julie Haydon. Nathan was making quite a commotion about a cup of tea that had been served to him. He denounced the captain and said, "You call this tea? At ninety-five cents a cup? You should taste the tea I get at the Royalton for a quarter. No comparison."

Charles Lederer was one of those iconoclastic writers of old Hollywood who, like Harry Kurnitz and Wilson Mizner, was often wittier privately than on the page. An example of Lederer's unfettered wit is this discourse he had with a British lady in India just after that country had won its independence. Lederer was admiring her collection of Ming vases. Clearly out of the Raj period, our lady sought to engage Lederer in a sensitive discussion. "You should have known India in the old days," she said. "It was so much nicer, because there weren't any Jews here." "No Jews?" Lederer said. "Do you have something against Jews?" She replied, "Nobody I know really likes them, but no, I have nothing against them." Lederer swept her Ming collection off the table. "Well, now you do," he exclaimed, picking his way through the fragments of shattered porcelain to the nearest door.

In those golden olden days of Hollywood, scandal was easily suppressed. The media could be shut out, even when the media was part of the story. Filmland's feared columnist, Louella O. Parsons, wrote for the Hearst newspapers and was married to "Doc" Martin, a congenial physician who attended to the many and bizarre needs of movie moguls, stars, and their playmates. I suppose he could be described as a Doctor Feelgood of his day. His needle banished anxiety and pain. One night he was feeling no pain when he fell down the stairs of an elegant Hollywood whorehouse, a bottle of gin tumbling after him. "Careful, don't step on his hands," one of his companions shouted. "He has to operate tomorrow."

The meanest boss I knew was one of Hollywood's most visible and powerful lawyers. As a song Sinatra sings has it, he was "meaner than a junkyard dog." The lawyer had hired a new secretary who put his unopened mail on his desk because she did not know whether he wanted her to open it. He summoned her into his office and said, "Young lady, how dare you not open my mail? What if there were a plastic bomb in one of those letters?"

Larry Gelbart is as clever and funny as any of the Algonquin Round Table crowd. When asked recently if a deal between a big Hollywood studio and a Japanese conglomerate was about to be completed, he said, "Let me put it this way: it's all done except for the crossing of the t's and the slanting of the i's."

Larry was equally outspoken at the funeral of comic Marty Feldman. Admonished by Marty's widow to say something funny at the services—anything funny, because Marty would have wanted it that way—Larry rushed out of the chapel before the eulogy was over, explaining to the widow, "Sorry I have to mourn and run."

Quick Cuts

The perversity of fashion is ever fascinating. The best tables in fashionable restaurants are often in the least desirable sections—next to the kitchen at "21," for example. Residential districts that are far from the most attractive inexplicably become the most fashionable. For years, posh Beekman Place in Manhattan faced a slaughterhouse (where the United Nations now stands) and odors of freshly killed animals were wafted on the summer breeze. The elegant Hotel du Cap d'Antibes on the French Riviera occupies a site a beach resort developer would scarcely consider desirable today. He'd say, "But, monsieur, this is nothing but a collection of rocks along the sea. One has to dive into the water. There is no beach and practically no sand." Yet for a hundred years, kings, dukes, grand-dukes, and tycoons from all over the world have come here to swim and sun. The only sands are the pitiful patches which are imported to surround the cabanas. The drop to the Mediterranean is sheer and one has to go down rope ladders to the water if one isn't a diver. Such is the perversity of style that the public beaches at Juan-les-Pins, Golfe-Juan, and Nice are far more beautiful, sanded, with a gentle slope to the sea, and far less expensive.

Here is a cure for hiccups. I heard about it one weekend at Richard Zanuck's home in Newport Beach, California, while I was occupying a bunkhouse with two other men (my wife was visiting her mother in Arkansas). If you occupy a bunkhouse with two other men—or women—a case of hiccups can make you seriously unpopular. Fortunately, one of my chums told me how to cure them. Plug your ears with your thumbs. Plug them so you really can't hear and then, with your forefingers, clamp your nostrils so you can't breathe. At that point someone, if a girl she'd better be tall enough, pours some vodka into your mouth and you take three or four gulps. Voilà, no more hiccups, but you are a little drunk (water may be substituted by teetotalers).

What would happen if everyone told the truth? A woman was about to reveal the name of her lover. I begged her not to do so. Why? Because I've always had the feeling that if you couldn't confide in a woman you liked, the relationship contained the seeds of your own destruction. In time she would blab about you. A girl I knew years ago was privy to most of my secrets. She's dead now. But only when I go will our secrets be safe. Until then, you can never be sure I won't blab.

Fragment from a seminar I gave in Capetown, South Africa, 1979:

Student: People like you seem to have a talent. Do you think that's something you are born with, or something you pick up? And if you have talent, is that enough to succeed?

Me: I think you're born with some of it, but you must learn how to scurry and hurry and get things done if you want to succeed. Having been a Depression kid, I was always running scared, and I think that's helpful.

Student: Does the same thing go for people who are writing and directing?

Me: Yes. Perhaps more so. Steven Spielberg is a man of your generation who is enormously energetic and gets into all sorts of things. He makes mistakes, is sometimes over his head and often all over the place in his creativity, but his willingness to take risks is, in my opinion, part of his special talent. My generation was battered by a success ethic that demanded that we almost kill ourselves to succeed. Spielberg did. I don't think you have to do the same thing. Talent is not enough. It must be backed by energy and the ability to get things done, but there are some of you who will have the talent and be able to follow through, and others of you who won't.

Seeing a movie in a theater is a special experience and unlikely to become extinct because the audience is part of the movie. I think if you saw *E.T.* without an audience, as I did, in a tiny projection room, you would have no idea of its appeal. When I saw it in a theater, it was a totally different experience. Richard Zanuck and I viewed *M*A*S*H* in a projection room and were disappointed. It didn't seem funny. Not until we saw the same film in a New York theater before a wildly responsive audience did we appreciate its extraordinarily comic quality. Filmgoing is a communal experience. Even standing in line for tickets is part of it. Audience participation came to the movies when *Jaws* and *The Sting* lifted theater-goers to their feet and made them howl and scream at images on a screen.

I believe critics exaggerate the virtues of some films and the defects of others. They overpraise and overkill. They see things in films that were never intended by their makers. One critic observed that *E.T.* was really a parable about Christ. Director Steven Spielberg's reply was, "Now why would a nice Jewish boy like me be doing that kind of film?"

Critics do hurt. John O'Hara told me that no matter how much praise he received for a novel, he would brood over the one bad review he got in Boise, Idaho, wondering "whether the son of a bitch was right."

My most distressing experience with critics involved one of the meanest of them. While seeing *The Island,* a film that needed all the help it could get, a lady seated next to the critic threw up on him during a horrific scene at the very moment I observed another woman fleeing the theater clutching her hand to *her* mouth. It is one of the few reviews I have not had the courage to read.

Most movie critics are responsible, if not fair. At least they convey the subject matter of movies to people who can then judge for themselves whether they're interested. There are, in the judgment of movie distributors, good-bad reviews and bad-good reviews. A good-bad review may be so venomous that it impels people to find out why the film is so upsetting. A bad-good review may be one that judges a film to be one of life's noblest experiences and, in so doing, bores readers into staying away from the box office. I much prefer a good-bad review that reviles my movie into a hit.

Consequently, reviewers and film journalists can be good for filmmakers even when they hate the picture. Thirty years ago, the newest boy on a newspaper staff was given a pass and told to go out and see a movie and do a couple of paragraphs on it. "If we have space, we'll run it," the editor growled. Today's movie critics, especially on television, make more money than foreign correspondents . . . for themselves as well as for us.

As for legitimate theater, no play on Broadway has much of a chance unless Frank Rich, all-powerful drama critic of *The New York Times,* likes it. A playwright who shall go nameless because I can't remember it (but be assured he exists) determined to write a play that would contain everything Rich had ever liked and nothing he hated, assuring a favorable review. Using a computer, he programmed seven years of Rich's reviews, separating his likes and dislikes until he had a common strand of everything Rich hated or adored. Using this as his database, he wrote a play carefully constructed to highlight Rich's favorite things and avoid what he abhorred. It didn't help. Rich destroyed the play. Oh well. As Broadway Rose once said, "Go figure."

In 1932 I was at Long Beach, California, when a great earthquake struck. In order to calm the panicked guests, the band at the hotel struck up the only song that was on their music stands, "Why Can't This Night Go on Forever?"

I recently spent a weekend in bed. I don't know whether it was exhaustion, depression, or mental fatigue that kept me there. Sometimes pressures build. There are psychic warnings. Each of us has a vulnerable place. My back began to ache this morning. Someone always has the Indian sign on you: a child, a wife, a boss, maybe even a God. Often the only way to cope is to take to your bed for a while. It's hard to accommodate yourself to the emotional demands of life. Consider jealousy. I don't mean romantic jealousy. That's painful, but jealousy of others' achievements can be lethal. You mourn who you might have been and aren't and never will be. It comes down on you all at once. I am ashamed of those feelings. For selfish, affluent souls such as I, there's not only the fear of failing but also the dread of death. Little wonder people go for yoga, gurus, and old-time religion. In the Marx Brothers' movie *A Night at the Opera* the boys tear up one portion of a contract after another because it's unacceptable. Finally, Chico glances at a section and says, "You can't fool me. There ain't no sanity clause." And indeed, in the contracts that are made for our lives, there ain't no sanity clause.

My knowledge of fine art is dismal, if not abysmal. During my years in California, my second wife, Wayne, brought home some paintings. I cared so little for one of them that I nailed it to the wall of a room we rarely used. After Wayne and I were divorced, she appeared on my doorstep in a state of panic and demanded the return of the painting. No problem. I had no use for that atrocity. Carefully removing the nails from its four corners, I turned it over to her. It was so large that it barely fit into her taxi. The painting was by Jackson Pollock and now hangs, without nails, in the San Francisco Museum of Art. Its probable present value: seven or eight million dollars.

Wayne Clark Brown knew Jackson Pollock and the value of his work or she would not have retrieved it. Obviously, it was on loan to her. As I think back on how well she knew Pollock and how little I knew about art, I wonder why she didn't divorce me sooner.

In 1975, Helen lost the manuscript of a book on which she had been working for eight years. We looked everywhere and even went to her office at three in the morning to search each desk drawer. We wondered whether by some hideous misplacement it might have been thrown in a wastebasket. There seemed to be some strange psychopathology at work. We have always been capable of losing important possessions but invariably we found them cleverly hidden not far from where we began to look. We wondered whether the book manuscript might have been dispatched with other manuscripts to one of the editors of *Cosmopolitan;* it was a forlorn hope. The job of reconstructing this work would have been hopelessly arduous, and demoralizing. The manuscript had been last seen in its orange folder on her desk only a week before. Like parents retracing the movements of a lost child, we kept looking and hoping. Months later, after much of what was lost was rewritten, it was suddenly found amid a mound of papers, the original pages, astonishingly, much the same as the rewritten ones.

Rudolph Giuliani ran for mayor of New York on an anticrime ticket. As United States Attorney, he was particularly successful in putting away some of the Mafia's most formidable bosses. When Giuliani appeared as a speaker at New York's Dutch Treat Club following a prominent diva of the Metropolitan Opera company, he remarked that he had grown quite fond of Italian opera, having heard so much of it on the miles of wire taps he listened to in order to gather evidence against the mob.

I am ruthless in my pursuit of desirable screen stories, having learned that failure to buy the right property can cost a company a dividend or an Academy Award. There is no length I or my empathetic wife won't go to gain an edge. When film rights to Alfred Uhry's (to be) Pulitzer Prize-winning play *Driving Miss Daisy* were being contested—I had heard they had virtually been sold—I telephoned Alfred's agent, Flora Roberts, hourly. At a series of breakfasts, I entreated Alfred to favor the Zanuck/Brown Company. One weekend, I panicked when I could not reach Flora, a brilliant agent who knows exactly when to be unavailable, to find out whether my bid was acceptable. Flora returned my call during the only hour I was not at home. My wife destroyed my negotiating position but possibly saved the day by saying to Flora, "I want you to know that if David doesn't get that property, he'll jump out the window." I might have, too.

Fade to Black

In the course of a long life, one learns about the art of making love. Women don't learn enough about it, I'm convinced. Any moderately attractive woman and even some quite unattractive ones can have almost any man they want, if they study the art of pleasing him. Men today are so insecure, possibly because of women's new assertiveness, that they are easy prey for an artfully aggressive woman. And what's wrong with being "captured" by an aggressive woman who is interested and interesting?

Some women, and not a few men, glory in being covert lovers. I know married men and women who have had romantic affairs in secrecy through long periods of years. The difference today, unlike the past, is that more women inaugurate these relationships (perhaps because of the relative scarcity of men).

Paris truly is for lovers. No girls on earth have quite the sexuality, assurance, and haute beauty as do the French. They drip chic. English women, on the other hand, display an openness in their sexuality which is free, friendly, and undemanding, yet dignified. The French woman is more likely to be thinking of the bottom line, whether marriage or a hundred-franc note, while the English girl is more romantic and less grasping. And yet the French woman, for all her purposeful pursuit, is more exciting. One is pleased to pay.

We're at the Sheraton Wentworth Hotel in Sydney, Australia, on a February day awaiting an interview with Susan Malloy of the *Sydney Morning Herald.* It's summer in Sydney. Temperature in the low eighties Fahrenheit. As I look out the window I see women and men wearing very little clothing. Minis, no stockings, for the ladies, and men in shirts but no coats. Summer in Sydney. Snowing in Manhattan. It's not such a small world, is it?

When I moved to Los Angeles in late 1951, I detected very early that my then wife, Wayne, would not like it. I've never found Hollywood to be hospitable to the kind of woman Wayne was. She was a brilliant working lady, a senior editor of *Good Housekeeping* when I met her, Vassar-educated, accustomed to living in Greenwich Village among the likes of Mary McCarthy, James Agee, and Jackson Pollock. Putting her up in the Hollywood Hills in late 1951 was putting her in exile. She didn't have a job; she didn't like the town or the social life. I thought the only way to save my marriage was to find her a job. I wrote my good friend Margaret Ettinger, then one of Hollywood's stellar press agents, "Maggie, I need you to give my wife a job. My marriage is at stake." Maggie responded at once and engaged Wayne. It worked out well for Wayne but not for our marriage. While on the job, she met Robert Healy, the boss of

Interpublic, Inc., then the world's largest advertising agency, and fell in love with him. In writing Margaret Ettinger to save my marriage by giving my wife a job, I ended my marriage by giving my wife her next husband.

Recently a young lady identified herself as my niece, and said she'd like to talk to me about something that was troubling her for years. She came to New York and visited me at my office. I was wary. I did not remember her. A lovely girl. She said, "You know I've always had on my mind the thought that you might be my father." I told her as gently as I could that I was not her father, although I might have liked to have been, under other circumstances. Months passed and I heard from my first wife, from whom I had been divorced twenty-two years. She said, "I just heard that [and she mentioned the young lady's name] has been saying you are her father." I told my ex-wife that this wasn't true. She said, "I've often wondered why my sister asked me to forgive her just before she died." I think I convinced her that I did not have an affair with her sister. I didn't, but I was touched that her daughter had sought me out as a father figure. I would have liked to have had a daughter. I think I would have been a good father to a girl, but an unwilling father-in-law to her husband. I would have found it hard to let her go.

Even so, the daughter I never had surfaces in my dreams. I see her in her graduation dress, white and swirly, smiling, her hair long and blond, well below her shoulders. I see her as a child, rushing to me, crying because she bruised her knee or fell on the sidewalk or perhaps bumped her nose against the glass. She's there, bright and lovely, and we talk of many things. I think of her growing up to be a strong, independent woman, and of her beaux, intelligent and keen, coming to see her. I think of her smile as she walks down the aisle on my arm on her wedding day, and of her tears on the day I die.

It's a blustery, rainy March Sunday in 1975. New York is at the tail end of a bleak winter, the kind that makes one fantasize about fringed palms on sun-baked beaches. Helen and I are hungry and anxious. We've had a bad night, one caught up in petty anxieties. I ask why we aren't happier, pointing out that we've made more money than we dreamed we could and that she's had an astonishing success as a magazine editor. Now that we've got it, why do we feel the need to prove ourselves all over again? And why is Helen, especially Helen, still maniacal about working, and filling every vacant moment with a task? Helen doesn't know. "Didn't you work in order not to have to work someday?" I ask her. "I thought so," she replies. "That's what I thought, too, but it isn't true. We're on the bread line of success. If somebody gets rid of you or me, we are pitiful people." Helen goes to a psychiatrist three times a week to have him tell her, among other things, why she can never find time for anything except work.

It's touching to find one's wife turning her back on her work to be with her husband for a few hours before he leaves for Los Angeles. I'm not likely to forget the sight of Helen popping into our apartment at 605 Park Avenue one night and finding me writing—what else?—the cover blurbs for the April 1973 issue of *Cosmopolitan.* She was in from Caracas, Venezuela, having stayed there for only three hours to address a sales conference before rushing home to spend only a few hours with me.

When I think of the sadness I've known with women, the heartbreaks, agonies, broken marriages, and unrequited love, it's astonishing that I kept looking for someone who loved back. I still remember my despair over losing a bosomy blonde I was mad about in 1935. I never did like bosomy girls again, and I never thought I'd get over the departures of my first wife, Liberty, and my second wife, Wayne, but look who I found.

How much does she love me? I think quite a bit, as this story illustrates. My wife and I were en route to Tokyo on a business trip when she mentioned the name of the man who would meet us and act as our representative in dealings with the proprietors of Japanese *Cosmopolitan.* He spoke the language, lived in Japan, knew the customs, and so forth. As she spoke his name, my mind flashed back to the time another wife spoke the same name while confessing a rhapsodic affair she had had with him during *her* business trip to Japan. The shock propelled me into a trauma from which I did not recover until I met Helen. I held my peace aboard Pan Am's Tokyo-bound 747 and did not mention the connection until we were safely airborne *leaving* Japan. "If I had known what he did to you," Helen said, "I would have tried to have him fired." "For making love to another wife?" I asked incredulously. "Yes," she replied, "nobody can do that to the man I love."

I am about to see my first wife, Liberty, after many years. It is June 1976. A small incident has arisen concerning our son. It is poignant discussing family business with a lady from whom I separated a quarter of a century ago. I remembered her as achingly beautiful, fragile as a lily, with long blond hair and lean, exquisitely shaped legs that never ended. Her breasts were small and perfect and her green eyes could render a man helpless. They did me. Now reality collides with memory. Beauty has fled to inhabit newer, younger bodies for a time. My youth has fled as well. I hope I will never forget the way we were. The death of memory is truly sad. My memory of my first love is still intact; only the pain is forgotten.

There is a time, usually when one is young, when you wish to freeze the moment and not grow older. For me, that time was my senior year at Stanford. My closest friend stayed on to do graduate work. His name was Charles Zucker. We shared living quarters and experienced that closeness which can exist only between the very young. We talked long into each night about life, love, our future, and the future of mankind. When I graduated from Stanford, Charles wrote me a letter I still have. I was then much in love with a beautiful girl from San Francisco. We were, my friend and I, as close as two men can be. The world was golden and beckoned to us. We were young and, I thought, bright. He wrote that he hoped that time of our life would remain as it was forever. It did for him. He died not long afterward. For me, not growing older would have meant not experiencing most of what you've read here, but it would have been a happy time in which to check out, as Charles did.

There was sadness ahead, but joy too. My only son is grown and we are friends, closer than we've been in years. I love him as I did when he was a child. I'm married to an incredibly wise, loving, seductive woman. What luck. Yet in the happiest moments, I often feel a surge of sadness as I reflect on friends and lovers who are gone, and of my long-dead and beloved mother.

I thought of all that recently at the funeral of my friend Thornton Bradshaw, a year younger than I, and looked around wondering who among us would be next. It was Joe Raposo, as close to me as a brother. His sweet, fine music will surely live on.

I think of the transitory nature of life as the seasons rush by. The many times I have looked down on Central Park to see green and then snow and then the sprouting of spring, to be replaced again by summer foliage and later by falling leaves. What to do about the swift passing of time? Flog oneself to greater efforts, I think. Those who work terribly hard do so to give their lives a reason. Perhaps, too, work is the only therapy, blocking out the inevitable sadness of knowing we must soon say good-bye.

My friend, author and raconteur Willard Espy, who writes elegant books about wordcraft, has a theory about memories which I hope does not apply to this book. "Wede" says he has the most vivid recollections—down to who was there, what they wore, how they looked, what they said—of events that never happened. How does he know? It was the wrong time and place and couldn't have occurred. Yet to Wede, the fraudulent memory seems indisputably real.

As I write this on August 12, 1980, my wife Helen and I have had, for the past eighteen years, a friend whose presence has been an unfailing source of delight, fascination, and occasional irritation. Her name is Samantha. She arrived home for the first time in the front seat of Helen's sports car, a tiny kitten wriggling to get loose and make mischief wherever she could. She was an outside cat then, bringing mice, lizards, and snakes for our inspection and causing us to recoil in revulsion. She was soon joined by another Siamese cat named Gregory and together they played in the hills and canyons around our home for a couple of years until we made the big move from California to New York, where my new job was. I remember the day. We were to travel east by train, having packed our furniture into a huge moving van which would follow us. As we were about to leave 515 Radcliffe Avenue, Pacific Palisades, California, we couldn't find Samantha. We called, hissed, whistled, cajoled, and wandered the hillsides. The departure time of our train, called *The City of Los Angeles,* was barely two hours away. We had to drive downtown, deliver our car to the dealer who had bought it, and take a taxi to Union Station, but we couldn't leave without both our cats. Suddenly, there was Samantha, having materialized in time. We gently put her next to Gregory inside the big carryall cage we had purchased. Soon, they were liberated in our train compartment aboard *The City of Los Angeles.* Apart from Samantha urinating on me in my upper berth (she was still a very young cat), they and we enjoyed the journey. In Chicago, we had a splendid lunch with friends before departing for New York on the

Broadway Limited. Our cats explored the elegant apartment overlooking Lake Michigan while we drank champagne and munched filet mignon. The next morning at the Dorset Hotel, next to the Museum of Modern Art in New York, the maids took care of the cats and the cats took care of the furniture, while we looked for an apartment.

We found our new home on Park Avenue's Gold Coast at Sixty-fifth Street, for the then outrageous rent of five hundred and fifty dollars a month. Years passed. Days were not always sunny. We had fights. I lost jobs. Helen became—may I say?—catatonic and was afraid to leave the apartment in a scary new city far from her bright, friendly Southern California. There were bad patches, and Gregory and Samantha, in their catlike way, responded to them all. Sometimes nervous, sometimes hissing, they were aware. We felt sure of that. When we went away on long trips, the doorman of the building would feed them; they always sensed our arrival home and were at the door to greet us. After leaving Pacific Palisades, they had become housecats and seemed content to sit on windowsills watching the snow fall over the city, or taking sudden interest in the first birdsongs of spring. We took them out on leashes, but they were clearly unhappy not to be able to move freely.

Then, twelve years later, came another big move, from Park Avenue to the west side of the city. Once again they were in the carryall cage for the taxi journey across town. They entered a penthouse, with four floors to leap through and large terraces on which to get lost, as Samantha did one wintry day. We finally found her, disoriented, and brought her in and warmed her up. Gregory, our male Siamese, died on my sixtieth birthday, four years ago as I write this. Samantha howled for a while early each morning, missing him, we felt certain. We thought of them as brother and sister. They frequently curled up together and lay like dromedary camels in perfect symmetry. Before Gregory died, he went down to our darkest and smallest room and crawled under a couch. I would reach in and gently stroke him and hear his faint purr in response.

One day, while I was gone, our housekeeper, Anna, telephoned to say that he had died. The memory pains me still because he was my cat. Welcoming me, being aloof, staring at me enigmatically with cat's eyes. Understanding more, I felt, than I ever could. He was the more vulnerable, the less bright, the more sickly, and therefore for me the more beloved. Anna buried Gregory in a small park in the Bronx. Now only Samantha was left. She would sleep between us, sometimes on Helen's chest, sometimes beside us, more attentive, as though to make up for the loss and also to spend what she may have perceived as her own last years comforting us and herself. Samantha remained reasonably well until about two months before the end, when she discovered she could no longer make it up the stairs to our bedroom. She had long since lost the strength to bound up onto our bed or windowsill. But she was still alert. In her best days, she was finicky about food, but now it had to be calf's liver or ground sirloin and she would eat little. At one point she seemed particularly weak but we thought she might recover for a spell and she did, as though to say, "Don't put me away yet. I am comfortable. If I have to die, I would like to die at home where I have lived with you." Two weeks later, we left for Cannes, wondering whether we would ever see her again. We asked our housekeeper to have her put to sleep if it appeared she was suffering. As we came home early one morning, just off the plane from Paris, I looked apprehensively to the left of our foyer and there she was, lying on the dining room rug, stretched out, no longer on her haunches but this time on her side. I was certain she was gone but when Helen went over to her, she looked up, her eyes burning bright, and then, with great effort, turned and looked at me. Ever so gently, we stroked her, and she purred but there was a disturbing rattle as though she were trying to say something. Touching her seemed to cause pain. Her tail twitched and she purred again, attempting to tell us, I thought, that she hadn't wanted to leave before saying good-bye. She had waited for us to come home. Later that morning, our housekeeper bundled her into a straw basket with a small blanket under her so that she wouldn't be too uncomfortable. She then covered her with a towel in order that her privacy not be violated by a peering elevator operator or doorman. Anna took her away to be put to sleep, peacefully and without pain.

Our twenty-dollar investment at the Pacific Palisades Pet Shop in 1962 gave us enormous returns in happiness. When we adopted first Samantha and then Gregory, it was after we had lost Duncan, our tricolor collie, whose death was agonizing to me. We had vowed we would never have another dog because of the pain of losing him. Now I knew we would not have another cat. Not soon, anyway. Samantha and Gregory endeared themselves as firmly as Duncan. All that's left of Duncan, Gregory, and Samantha are a few photographs and memories of selfless love.

The Zanuck/Brown Company, which Richard Zanuck and I founded on my birthday in 1972, became one of the most famous independent movie companies because of its successes, *The Sting,*

Jaws, The Verdict, and *Cocoon.* My decision to leave it in the spring of 1988 was very painful for me and for my partner, Richard. We had been together for more than thirty years, going back to Richard's apprenticeship at Twentieth Century Fox. I hope we will always be friends. Helen and I are the godparents of his two sons. My decision to dissolve the partnership and go on alone has been variously attributed to Dick's wife, Lili, having come into the company (which was actually my idea), and paranoia on my part, or wanting to slow down in my declining years.

The facts are these. I like Lili. Before she married Richard, Lili came to see me and stated her desire to work for us. I encouraged her and sponsored her entrance into the Zanuck/Brown company. She was an apt student, bright, gifted, loquacious, funny, feisty, and honest in her appraisal of stories, casting, and individuals. I was her mentor, but finally I found myself with two partners instead of one, and they were sleeping together. This did not work for me as well as it did for them. I harbor no grudges and still love them dearly.

In June of 1988 I started my own company and called it The Manhattan Project. As a soldier in World War II, I had seen orders transferring men to the Manhattan Project and wondered why I couldn't be so assigned. After all, I came from New York. I did not know the Manhattan Project was the code name for the atomic bomb in development at Los Alamos, New Mexico. I liked the name so much that, as the television commercial goes, I bought the company, the one that had succeeded to the name.

Mort Rosenthal was head of the funeral division of Kinney Services, which buried more people than any company alive. Mort was a pleasant, affable man as he faced the decision of having to leave the funeral business, which was the core enterprise of the company that bought Warner Brothers, and, under the direction of a handsome, young, former football player named Steve Ross, expanded it into the mighty show business and media corporation that is now Time/Warner. When I met Mort, funerals were being phased out of this burgeoning conglomerate. It seemed hardly the business to remain in when your aspiration was to build an entertainment company. The day we had lunch Mort was moving over to the branch of Kinney which would include Warner Brothers, the record companies, the publishing division, and *Mad* magazine. He told me he felt rather bad about leaving the funeral business. I asked, "What do you like about body disposal?" He said that you get to know people and their families awfully well. "Why then are you leaving?" I asked. "It isn't what it used to be," he replied. "Young people today have little respect or interest in the ceremonial aspects of death, and that's how we earn our money. As a matter of fact, I believe that in ten years it's quite possible they'll just put their dead outside with the garbage."

"Oh, that cannot be," I said.

He insisted, "Yes. It's possible."

"What about the older people?" I asked.

"They don't die anymore," he replied. "They live forever. And when they do go, there are no bronze caskets. Many people don't go to funerals. Flowers are replaced by charities. We don't have an interest in the flower business, but I suspect that whenever there is a notice that in lieu of flowers a contribution to something or other be made, nobody gives anything. All in all, it looks as though death is on its way out as a profit-maker." Probably not immediately but at least for Mort Rosenthal, founder of Riverside Memorial Chapel and owner of Frank Campbell's, who took a doleful view of death instead of the old-time optimism which prevailed in happier days when death was a fun business for funeral directors. I'm not at all sure he was right. I see an upturn in funeral grandeur. Elegance and ceremony may be returning to the coffin and casket makers, and funeral chapels may once again be a place of corporate joy. Death, after all, has an advantage. As a product, it suffers no obsolescence. However long deferred, it will come. The sale will be rung up.

There was rarely such an outpouring of love as occurred at the wedding of Charles K. Feldman. It was enough to make one believe in an afterlife. Those who were there will never forget it. He was the elegant, moody, and brilliant agent of such stars as John Wayne, Marilyn Monroe, and Joan Crawford. At one time he represented virtually all the directors, producers, and writers at Twentieth Century Fox. He was also a producer of such memorable films as *The Seven Year Itch* and *A Streetcar Named Desire.* Life ended too soon for Charlie, but he went out with style. Told he had terminal cancer, he proposed marriage to his beautiful Clotilde Barot, with whom he had lived for many years, and invited his best friends to attend his wedding and a festive lunch at his Beverly Hills home on Coldwater Canyon Road. Among those present were Ray Stark, Warren Beatty, Billy Wilder, Louis Jourdan, Frank Sinatra, Danny Kaye, Sam Goldwyn, Irving Lazar, Richard Zanuck, Mike Romanoff, Robert Evans, and Jules Stein. A makeup man made Charlie look robust for a few hours but his burning eyes were looking beyond this life. I witnessed his will, which was executed by him immediately after the ceremony. He toasted and thanked us all after promising Clotilde to love, honor, and cherish her until death did them part, which sadly it did not long after.

I don't believe that a man or a woman begins to live until he has some sense of the imminence of death. My friend John O'Hara, one of America's truly great authors, began his most prolific writing period after having been seriously ill and convinced that death could come at any time. He also managed to have his happiest marriage then. He had cut out all the crud.

I was lucky, after two marriages that failed, to have found a woman I *liked* as well as loved. It's incredible to me that after thirty years we can still act and feel like lovers. I don't know what it is that makes our marriage or any other one work. I think a great deal of it may be luck and timing. The luck was being sexually obsessed with a good woman. The timing was right. She was thirty-seven and I was forty-three. I didn't feel threatened by her success, and she had never married and was ready.

When I was asked to sum up the secret of my successful marriage in a word, I said "fear." Yes, I'm afraid of Helen and in a way it keeps me hooked. That sounds dreadful, I know, but it works. I'm afraid of losing her, not to another man, but to uninterest in me. I keep the marriage fresh and frisky. New material every day. She does the same. As the Chinese do, we treat each other as guests. Years ago, I asked Fulton Oursler, a writer of another time, why he thought marriages fail. He thought it was boredom, rather than infidelity or incompatibility. Helen is never boring. She is as unpredictable as a cat. I still don't quite know her. I fear—that word again—she knows me too well. Another thing—Helen and I are separated often enough to make us interesting strangers to each other for a little while. Very sexy.

In a macabre exchange, Helen wanted to know whether I would agree to be buried with her in the hills of the Ozarks in Arkansas, where I've never been. Or, she asked lovingly—what a loving girl she is—would I prefer to be buried in Southampton, Long Island (as I am a Long Islander and love Southampton)? No, I replied, take me to the Ozarks. I want to be wherever you are, and besides, I've always liked to go to new places.

Appendix
Herb Mayes's 100 Best Novels List

Little Women (Alcott)
Pride and Prejudice (Austen)
Le Pére Goriot (Balzac)
The Little Minister (Barrie)
Looking Backward (Bellamy)
The Old Wives' Tale (Bennett)
Lorna Doone (Blackmore)
Four Horsemen of the Apocalypse (Blasco Ibañez)
Jane Eyre (C. Brontë)
Wuthering Heights (E. Brontë)
The Good Earth (Buck)
The Last Days of Pompeii (Bulwer-Lytton)
The Pilgrim's Progress (Bunyan)
Erewhon (Butler)
Jurgen (Cabell)
The Manxman (Caine)
Lucy Gayheart (Cather)
Don Quixote (Cervantes)
The Moonstone (Collins)
Lord Jim (Conrad)
The Last of the Mohicans (Cooper)
The Red Badge of Courage (Crane)
Robinson Crusoe (Defoe)
David Copperfield (Dickens)
The Brothers Karamazov (Dostoevsky)
A Study in Scarlet (Doyle)
An American Tragedy (Dreiser)
The Three Musketeers (Dumas)
Rebecca (D. Du Maurier)
Trilby (G. Du Maurier)
Silas Marner (Eliot)
Tom Jones (Fielding)
The Great Gatsby (Fitzgerald)

Madame Bovary (Flaubert)
A Passage to India (Forster)
Penguin Island (France)
The Man of Property (Galsworthy)
Dead Souls (Gogol)
The Vicar of Wakefield (Goldsmith)
Return of the Native (Hardy)
The Scarlet Letter (Hawthorne)
For Whom the Bell Tolls (Hemingway)
Random Harvest (Hilton)
Green Mansions (Hudson)
A High Wind in Jamaica (Hughes)
Les Misérables (Hugo)
The Ambassadors (James)
Ulysses (Joyce)
Darkness at Noon (Koestler)
Kim (Kipling)
Sons and Lovers (Lawrence)
Babbitt (Lewis)
The Call of the Wild (London)
The Magic Mountain (Mann)
The Late George Apley (Marquand)
Of Human Bondage (Maugham)
Moby Dick (Melville)
Gone With the Wind (Mitchell)
Mutiny on the Bounty (Nordhoff and Hall)
The Octopus (Norris)
Animal Farm (Orwell)
Swann's Way (Proust)
The Cloister and the Hearth (Reade)
All Quiet on the Western Front (Remarque)
Jean Christophe (Rolland)
The Catcher in the Rye (Salinger)
The Story of an African Farm (Schreiner)
Ivanhoe (Scott)
Frankenstein (Shelley)
Quo Vadis? (Sienkiewicz)
The Jungle (Sinclair)
The Grapes of Wrath (Steinbeck)
The Red and the Black (Stendahl)
Tristram Shandy (Sterne)
Treasure Island (Stevenson)
Uncle Tom's Cabin (Stowe)

The Wandering Jew (Sue)
Gulliver's Travels (Swift)
Vanity Fair (Thackeray)
War and Peace (Tolstoy)
Barchester Towers (Trollope)
Fathers and Sons (Turgenev)
Huckleberry Finn (Twain)
The Greene Murder Case (Van Dine)
Twenty Thousand Leagues Under the Sea (Verne)
Candide (Voltaire)
Ben-Hur (Wallace)
Brideshead Revisited (Waugh)
Tono-Bungay (Wells)
The Thinking Reed (West)
David Harum (Westcott)
Ethan Frome (Wharton)
The Bridge of San Luis Rey (Wilder)
The Virginian (Wister)
Look Homeward, Angel (Wolfe)
East Lynne (Wood)
The Caine Mutiny (Wouk)
Beau Geste (Wren)
Native Son (Wright)
Swiss Family Robinson (Wyss)

INDEX

Abbott, George, 43
Adler, Buddy, 40, 49, 50–52, 55, 75, 130, 194
Affair to Remember, An, 156–157
Ali, Muhammad, 227–228
Allen, Jay Presson, 232
Allen, Lewis, 232
Allen, Woody, 87, 101
Alves, Joe, 146, 147, 148
Amazing Stories, 67
Ameche, Don, 45, 135
American Medical Association, 26
American Mercury, 20
American Weekly, 29, 94
Andrews, Julie, 170
Annenberg, Walter, 121, 134, 161
Annie Get Your Gun, 41, 42
Ashley, Ted, 143
Asimov, Isaac, 230–231
Atherton, Robert, 27
Attenborough, Richard, 200
Avildsen, John, 202–203
Axelrod, George, 57
Aykroyd, Dan, 201–203
Bailey, Marjorie, 183
Barot, Clotilde, *see* Feldman, Clotilde Barot
Barry, Philip, 133
Baxter, Leone, 26–27
Beatty, Warren, 196–197
Behn, Noel, 166
Bell, Ulrich, 178
Bellevue Hospital, 70
Belli, Melvin, 46
Belushi, John, 201–202
Belushi, Judy, 202
Benchley, Peter, 145, 148, 150
Benchley, Robert, 243
Benét, Stephen Vincent, 178
Bennett, Joan, 140
Berg, Jeffrey, 212
Berg, Moe, 20
Berger, Marilyn, 32–33
Berger, Thomas, 201
Bergman, Ingrid, 74
Berkowitz, Harold D., 128
Berlin, Ellin, 41, 42, 43
Berlin, Irving, 40–43, 184

Berlin, Richard E., 35, 110, 112
Bernstein, Bill, 168
Beyond the Valley of the Dolls, 128–129
Bible, The, 197
Bigman, Rose, 187
Bill, Tony, 144, 222
Billingsley, Sherman, 187
Birnbaum, Steve, 167–168
Bishop, "Doc," 73
Bishop, Jim, 24
Black, Hugo, 140
Blackburn, Richard, 186
Blazing Saddles, 167
Bloch, Bertram, 35, 203
Bloch, Edythe, 203
Blue Water, White Death, 146, 148
Boshko, Nathalie, *see* Brown, Nathalie Boshko
Boss, Duncan, 203
Boston Strangler, The (Frank), 130
Boyd, Stephen, 76
Bradbury, Ray, 230
Bradshaw, Thornton, 253
Bragg, Melvyn, 74, 162
Brand, Harry, 72–73
Brando, Marlon, 206–207
Brandt, Carl, 37
Brooks, Mel, 167
Brown, Al (uncle), 62
Brown, Bruce (son), 36, 39, 40, 62, 189, 253
Brown, David:
  as book publisher, 30
  Cosmopolitan's cover lines written by, 28, 33, 110
  as editor of *Cosmopolitan,* 27–30, 33, 34, 35, 52, 120
  as editor of *Liberty,* 22, 23, 24–27, 111, 134, 204
  father of, 60–64, 70, 197–198
  Helen's courtship of, 38–40
  as laboratory technician, 70
  military service of, 23–24
  mother of, 60, 63, 64, 69–70
  stepfather of, 64
  stepmother of, 61–62, 63, 198
  at Twentieth Century Fox, 34–38, 73, 81, 84, 85, 96, 107, 111, 122–132, 234
  at Warner Brothers, 143, 144
  as writer, 17, 19, 20–23, 28, 33
Brown, Dennis, 158
Brown, Edward (half brother), 63
Brown, Helen Gurley (third wife), 40–42, 44–45, 47, 70, 83, 96, 102–113, 115–116, 140, 158, 165, 166, 171, 173, 182, 189, 190, 192–193, 231, 242, 248–249, 251–252, 254, 255, 257, 259
  as *Cosmopolitan* editor, 28, 30, 33, 106–113, 249
  David's courtship of, 38–40
  newspaper columns of, 106, 111
  on writing *Sex and the Single Girl,* 103–106
Brown, Kathryn, 87
Brown, Kay, 157
Brown, Liberty (first wife), 47, 185, 251, 252, 253
Brown, Natasha (half sister), 63
Brown, Nathalie Boshko (stepmother), 61–62, 63, 198
Brown, Wayne Clark (second wife), 35, 37, 38, 62, 248, 250–251, 252
Brown's Guide to Growing Gray (Brown), 41
Bruno, Harry, 22
Brynner, Yul, 169
Burns, Jerry, 45
Burton, Richard, 74, 76, 162, 219
Butch Cassidy and the Sundance Kid, 140
Butler, Michael, 153
Buttons, Red, 17, 59

Caldwell, Erskine, 36
Calloway, Cab, 62
Campbell, John, 22–23
Cantor, Eddie, 21, 69, 184
Capote, Truman, 165, 179–180
Carnival in Costa Rica, 91
Cavett, Dick, 138
Century City, 73, 75–76
Cerf, Bennett, 163
Chamberlain, Neville, 185
Christie, Julie, 235
Churchill, Winston, 80
Claire, Ludi, 75
Clark, Wayne, *see* Brown, Wayne Clark
Clarke, Arthur C., 150
Cleopatra, 73–77, 111, 219
Cochran, Jacqueline, 21–22, 23
Cocoon, 134, 135, 209
Cohn, Arthur, 119
Cohn, Harry, 80, 81
Cohn, Sam, 158, 168, 212
Colbert, Claudette, 74
Collier's, 20
Collins, Joan, 75
Cooper, Gary, 177
Coppola, Francis Ford, 225

Cosmopolitan, 27–28, 29, 34, 132, 185, 189, 252
D. Brown as cover-line writer for, 28, 33, 110
D. Brown as editor of, 27–30, 33, 34, 35, 52, 120
H. G. Brown as editor of, 28, 30, 33, 106–113
Costello, Bobby, 120
Costello, Frank, 60, 120–121
Coward, Noel, 34, 70
Crawford, Joan, 44–45
Creative Artists Agency (CAA), 211–212
Crist, Judith, 170
Cronkite, Betsy, 139, 240
Cronkite, Walter, 139, 160, 240
Cronyn, Hume, 135
Cukor, George, 53–56, 86, 176
Cuneo, John F., 25
Curtis, Tony, 103, 185

Daily Mirror, 184
Dali, Gala, 164–165
Dali, Salvador, 164–165
D'Antoni, Phil, 208
Daves, Delmer, 156
David, Saul, 102–103, 105
David Brown Associates, 20
Davis, Bette, 140–141, 187
Davis, Marvin, 77
Deacy, Jane, 225
Dead Solid Perfect (Jenkins), 45
Deems, Richard (Dick), 30, 106–107, 112
Deep, The, 150
de Gaulle, Charles, 193
Delacorte, George T., 111–112
De Laurentiis, Dino, 197
Della Femina, Jerry, 131
De Mille, Cecil B., 74, 204
Dempsey, Jack, 34
Depression, Great, 19, 25, 80
Desert Fox, The, 213
Detective, The, 113–114
Diary of Anne Frank, The, 193
Dietrich, Marlene, 164, 231
Disney Studios, 211, 212
Doctorow, E. L., 100
Dolan, Robert Emmett, 218
Donen, Stanley, 196
Douglas, Kirk, 200
Douglas, Michael, 200
Dozier, William, 36
Dreyfuss, Richard, 146–147, 148, 149
Driving Miss Daisy, 249
du Maurier, Daphne, 90
Durante, Jimmy, 164
Durbin, Deanna, 177
Durocher, Leo, 142
Dystel, Oscar, 105

Eastwood, Clint, 226
Ebert, Roger, 129
Ehrlich, Jake, 46–47
Eiger Sanction, The, 226
Eisner, Michael, 212
Eleanor, The Years Alone (Lash), 139
Elebush, Peter, 60
Ellison, E. Jerome, 23
Eltonhead, Frank, 27
Engel, Samuel G., 168–169
Epstein, Jules, 57
Epstein, Julius, 242
Epstein, Philip, 57
Espy, Willard, 254
E.T., 200, 246
Ettinger, Eve, 36
Ettinger, Margaret, 250, 251
Evans, Charles, 114
Evans, Joshua, 115
Evans, Robert, 113–116

Farago, Ladislas, 225
Farnol, Lynn, 204
Farrow, Mia, 196
FBI (Federal Bureau of Investigation), 22–23, 26–27
Feiffer, Judy, 167
Feldman, Charles K., 95, 217, 258–259
Feldman, Clotilde Barot, 217–218, 258–259
Feldman, Marty, 244
Ferber, Edna, 195
Fields, Verna, 15, 16, 147, 155
Filmmaker's Journey, A, 193, 196
Fitzgerald, F. Scott, 80, 99
Fonda, Henry, 103, 176
Forbes, Malcolm, 141, 175
Ford, John, 156, 204
Forsberg, Frank, 35
Fosse, Robert, 100
Fowler, Gene, 139
Fox, William, 130, 204
Fox Studios, *see* Twentieth Century Fox
Foy, Brynie, 81–82
Frank, Gerold, 130
French Connection, The, 208
Frings, Kurt, 84, 113, 114
From Those Wonderful Folks Who Gave You Pearl Harbor (Della Femina), 131
Fryer, Robert, 129–130
Fuoss, Bob, 35
Fyodorova, Victoria, 236–237

Gable, Clark, 34
Gandhi, 200
Garmise, Burt, 134
Gary, Lorraine, 150, 156
Gary, Romain, 86, 170
Geis, Bernard, 105, 112
Gelbart, Larry, 244
George, Phyllis, 115
Gernsback, Hugo, 67
Getty, Jean Paul, 171–172
Giant, 194, 195, 196
Gilford, Jack, 135
Gilles, Genevieve, 217–218
Gilmore, William G., 15, 145, 148, 156
Gimbel, Peter, 146, 190
Ginsberg, Henry, 195
Girl from Petrovka, The, 221–222
Giuliani, Rudolph, 249
Glamour, 22, 107
Glass, Montague, 198
Gleason, Jackie, 58–59
Goetz, William, 96
Goldman, James, 157
Goldman, Milton, 100
Goldstein, Leonard, 141
Goldstein, Robert, 54, 55, 57, 141, 191, 203
Goldwyn, Frances, 56, 137, 138
Goldwyn, Samuel, 56, 86, 100, 130, 137–138, 204
Gone With the Wind, 86, 87, 89, 90, 157–158, 179
Good Housekeeping, 27, 34, 35, 250
Gottlieb, Carl, 145
Grade, Sir Lew, 43
Grant, Arnold, 96
Grant, Cary, 54, 71, 133–134, 156
Gray, Barry, 186
Greatest Story Ever Told, The, 193–194, 196, 197
Greenwood, Helen, 26
Griffith, D. W., 204
Grossman, Teddy, 154
Guinan, Texas, 36

Hackman, Gene, 141, 236, 237
Hakim, André, 96
Halprin, Margo, 57
Hamilton, Murray, 150, 152
Hamlisch, Marvin, 221
Hammerstein, Oscar, 41
Harper's, 20
Harrison, Linda, *see* Zanuck, Linda Harrison
Harrison, Rex, 76, 196
Hart, Margie, 17
Harvey, Anthony, 115
Harvey, James, 159
Hassan II, king of Morocco, 141
Hatful of Rain, A, 52
Hawn, Goldie, 102, 222, 227, 231
Haydon, Julie, 34, 243
Healy, Robert, 250–251
Hearst, William Randolph, 33, 34, 175
Hearst Corporation, 25
Hecht, Ben, 34
Hedley, Pamela, 40, 102
Hefner, Hugh, 110
Hellinger, Mark, 57, 212
Hello, Dolly, 46, 84
Hellzapoppin, 187
Hemingway, Ernest, 28, 29, 80, 95, 99, 114, 222
Hennagan, James, 53
Hepburn, Katharine, 53
Hewitt, Don, 160
Hewlett, Charles, 66
Hill, George Roy, 207, 221, 222
Hirschfeld, Gerald, 202
Hitchcock, Alfred, 86, 90, 223–225
Hitler, Adolf, 228
Hoffman, Dustin, 232
Hoffman, Irving, 42, 185, 188–189
Holbrook, Hal, 222
Holiday, 133–134
Hoover, J. Edgar, 118, 185, 189
Hotchner, A. E., 29
House Committee on Un-American Activities, 52
Hughes, Howard, 25, 172–175, 195
Hunnicutt, Gayle, 237, 238
Hunter, Paul, 24
Huston, John, 71, 166, 170, 197
Hutchings, Edward, Jr., 24

I'd Climb the Highest Mountain, 216
In Cold Blood, 179
Island, The, 209, 246

Jack Paar Show, The, 138
Jacks, Robert, 178
Jaffe, Rona, 109
Janni, Joseph, 218–219
Jaws, 15–16, 128, 145–150, 151, 155, 156, 206, 246
Jaws 2, 150–156
Jenkins, Dan, 45
Jenkins, Simon, 238
Jergens Journal, 184
Jessel, George, 21, 184
Jessel, Ian, 43
John Brown's Body (Benét), 178
Johnson, Alva, 117
Johnson, Julian, 35, 36

Johnson, Lyndon, 163
Johnson, Nunnally, 36, 37, 162–163, 218
Jolson, Al, 59
Jones, Jennifer, 90
Joplin, Scott, 221

Kael, Pauline, 170
Katzenberg, Jeffrey, 212
Kaye, Danny, 44, 142
Kefauver, Estes, 121
Kelly, Charlotte, 111
Kennedy, John F., 55, 120
Kennedy, Joseph P., 120
Kennedy, Robert F., 119–120
Kerr, Deborah, 156
Khrushchev, Nikita, 175–177
Khrushchev, Nina, 175, 176
King, Henry, 90, 216, 217
King and I, The, 169
Kissinger, Henry, 115
Klinger, Henry, 203
Kluge, John, 122, 164, 175
Kluge, Pat, 175, 227
Koch, Howard, 242
Koegel, Otto, 127
Koster, Henry, 169
Krantz, Judith, 29
Kremlin Letter, The, 166
Kriendler, Pete, 45
Kroll, Lucy, 195
Kubrick, Stanley, 163, 230
Kuhn, Fritz, 185

Ladies' Home Journal, 27
Lancaster, Burt, 185
Lash, Joseph P., 139
Lasky, Jesse, 204
Lazar, Irving "Swifty" Paul, 95, 117, 142, 169–170, 179, 180, 229
Lean, David, 114
Lederer, Charles, 243
Lee, Gypsy Rose, 17
Lehman, Ernest, 19–22, 39, 67, 69, 84, 102, 129, 139–140, 185–186, 228
Lerner, Alan Jay, 42
Letterman, Elmer G., 164
"Letter to Five Wives," 102
Letter to Three Wives, A, 102
Levant, Oscar, 109
Levathes, Peter, 55, 57, 203
Lewis, Ted, 20
Liberty, 22, 23, 24–27, 111, 134, 204
Lieber, Maxim, 20
Lilly, Doris, 109
Liveright, Horace, 34
Loew, Marcus, 101
Logan, Josh, 176
Longest Day, The, 77, 86, 89
Look, 22, 160–161
Los Angeles Times, 106, 111, 158
Louise, Anita, 51, 194
Love Is a Many Splendored Thing, 90
Love Me Tender, 178
Lucas, George, 101, 210
Luce, Clare Boothe, 170
Luce, Henry, 121, 170
Lumet, Sidney, 207, 233, 234, 235, 236

MacArthur, Charles, 34
MacArthur, General Douglas, 144, 226, 238–239
MacArthur, Jean Marie, 144
MacArthur, 238–239
McCall's, 30, 170
McCarey, Leo, 57, 156, 159
McCarthy, Frank, 56, 96
McCormick, Colonel "Bertie," 23
McDermitt, Finlay, 36
MacFadden, Bernarr, 23
MacGraw, Ali, 115–116
Mackay, Clarence, 43
McKenna, Ken, 36
McKuen, Walter, 102–103
McQueen, Steve, 115
Maddox, Brenda, 74
Malloy, Susan, 250
Mamet, David, 207, 232, 233, 235
Mamoulian, Rouben, 75, 76
Man Called Peter, A, 168–169
Mandaville, Molly, 95
Mandel, Johnny, 207
Manhattan Project, The, 257
Mankiewicz, Herman, 80–81
Mankiewicz, Joseph, 74, 76, 101
Mansfield, Irving, 165–166
Mansfield, Jayne, 138
Marcos, Ferdinand, 119
Marcos, Imelda, 119
Marquand, John P., Jr., 29
Marshall, Catherine, 168, 169
Martin, "Doc," 243–244
Marx Brothers, 248
*M*A*S*H,* 92–94, 246
Mason, James, 234, 235, 236
Mason, Jerry, 112
Mattey, Bob, 147
Matthau, Walter, 57
Mayer, Louis B., 56, 87, 130
Mayes, Grace, 30, 32
Mayes, Herbert R., 27–33, 35, 87, 113, 185
  100 Best Novels list of, 261–263
MCA/Universal, 15, 16, 98, 99

Medavoy, Mike, 144
Merman, Ethel, 42–43
Merrick, David, 45–46
Metro-Goldwyn-Mayer (MGM), 130, 204
Meyer, Russ, 129
Michener, James, 49
Midsummer Night's Dream, A, 204–205
Miller, Arthur, 177
Miller, Robert Ellis, 222
Millett, Kate, 110
Mr. Right Is Dead (Jaffe), 109
Mitchell, Margaret, 157
Mizner, Addison, 41
Mizner, Wilson, 41
Moffet, Ivan, 75, 194
Mok, John, 36
Monroe, Marilyn, 50, 53, 54, 55, 176, 177
Morgan, Swifty, 118
Moriarty, Cathy, 201, 202
Moskowitz, Joseph H., 34, 35, 36–37, 203
Move Over Darling, 55
Murdoch, Anna, 121
Murdoch, Rupert, 77, 121–122, 134, 138–139, 161
My Cousin Rachel, 90
My Favorite Wife, 54
Myra Breckinridge, 71, 128, 129

Nathan, George Jean, 242–243
Neighbors, 201–203
Nevin, Robert, 146
Newhouse, Samuel, 22
Newman, Paul, 169, 206, 207, 226, 232, 233, 234, 235, 236
News of the World, 122
New York, 121
New York Daily Mirror, 184
New Yorker, The, 26, 170
New York Herald Tribune, 170
New York Post, 121, 138–139
New York Review, 159
New York Times, 160, 161, 170, 247
  obituaries in, 32–33
Nichols, Mike, 228
Nicholson, Jack, 191
Night at the Opera, A, 248
Nixon, Richard, 100, 118–119
Nizer, Louis, 47, 77
North, Edmund, 225

O'Brien, Bill, 25–26
O'Brien, Bob, 163
O'Connell, John J., 29, 112
Odets, Clifford, 80, 138
Odlum, Floyd B., 22, 23, 25
O'Hara, John, 48–50, 80, 246, 259
One Flew Over the Cuckoo's Nest, 200
Only Game in Town, The, 196–197
Orr, William T., 103
O'Shea, Milo, 233
Oursler, Fulton, 23, 194, 259
Outlaw, The, 174
Ovitz, Michael, 211–212

Paar, Jack, 138
Palance, Jack, 140
Pal Joey (O'Hara), 17, 49
Palladino, Eusapio, 183
Paramount Pictures, 195, 204
Parker, Colonel Tom, 178
Parks, Jacqueline, 103
Parsons, Louella O., 243
Patterson, Captain "Joe," 23
Patton, George, 144, 225, 239
Patton, 225–227, 239
Pearson, Drew, 24
Peck, Gregory, 144, 226
Penn, Arthur, 209, 219, 220, 221, 237
Peters, Jean, 169
Phillips, Julia, 144, 222
Phillips, Michael, 144, 222
Pic, 17, 22, 23, 186
Pillar, E. M., 26
Poe, Seymour, 96
Pollock, Jackson, 248
Pomerantz, Abraham, 127–128
Porter, Cole, 42
Portnoy's Complaint, 128, 129
Power, Tyrone, 72
Preminger, Otto, 101
Presley, Elvis, 178
Proctor, Martin, 20
Prohibition, 64, 68

Rage, 226–227
Rampling, Charlotte, 234–236
Ramsey, Clark, 15
Raphael, Frederic, 219
Raposo, Joe, 253
Ratoff, Gregory, 91–92
RCA, 204
Reagan, Ronald, 240
Rebecca, 90
Redford, Lola, 135
Redford, Robert, 135, 206, 232
Reed, Barry, 232
Reed, Rex, 129
Reynolds, Burt, 101
Rhodes, Shari, 146
Rich, Frank, 247
Right Stuff, The, 231

RKO Pictures, 25, 173–174
Roberts, Esther, 92
Roberts, Flora, 249
Robson, Mark, 114
Rodgers, Richard, 41
Romanoff, Gloria, 117
Romanoff, Michael, 116–118
Roosevelt, Eleanor, 28, 139
Roosevelt, Elliott, 28
Roosevelt, Franklin D., 25, 139, 187
Rosenthal, Abe, 160
Rosenthal, Mort, 257–258
Ross, Steven J., 99, 257
Rossellini, Roberto, 50
Roth, Philip, 165
Rubenstein, Howard, 212
Runyon, Damon, 186
Russell, Jane, 173–174

Sackler, Howard, 145, 150
Sage, G. Byron, 88–89
Saint, Eva Marie, 224–225
St. Johns, Adela Rogers, 33–34
Sandburg, Carl, 194–195
Sarne, Michael, 129
Sarnoff, David, 204
Schaeffer, Jack, 94
Schandorf, Ruth, 38
Schary, Dore, 143
Scheider, Roy, 146, 147, 150, 154–155, 156
Schenck, Joseph, 41, 72, 78
Schenck, Nicholas, 41, 87
Schreiber, Lew, 36–37
Scott, George C., 144, 225–227, 239
Scoundrel, The, 34
Screenwriter: The Life and Times of Nunnally Johnson (Stempel), 218
Selznick, David O., 86, 87, 88, 89–90, 99, 142, 157, 204
Sex and the Office (Brown), 106, 107
Sex and the Single Girl (Brown), 45, 47, 102–106, 107
Sex and the Single Girl (film), 102–103
Shalit, Gene, 167–168, 230
Shamroy, Leon, 76
Shane, 195
Shaw, Robert, 146, 147, 149, 150
Shearer, Norma, 114
Sheinberg, Sidney J., 15, 226
Shepard, Sam, 231
Sherwood, Robert, 100
Sholokhov, Mikhail, 176
Shulman, Arnold, 54
Siegel, Ben "Bugsy," 116
Siegel, Herbert J., 99
Silver, Sam, 82–83
Simon, Norton, 30
Sinatra, Frank, 72, 163, 169, 176, 231
60 Minutes, 160, 238
Skouras, Spyros P., 73, 74, 75, 76, 77, 170, 176, 177–179, 194, 203
Smith, Kate, 42
Smith, Liz, 109
Sokolov, Harry, 84, 165
Something's Got to Give, 53, 54, 55
Sondheim, Stephen, 227
Sound of Music, The, 170
Spelling, Aaron, 230
Spiegel, Sam, 86, 114–115
Spielberg, Steven, 15, 16, 101, 145–146, 148, 150, 151, 210, 227, 246
Spies, Virginia, 26
Stack, Phillip, 186
Staircase, 196
Stanfill, Dennis, 123, 125
Stanford University, 182–183
Stark, Ray, 95, 142–143
Steelyard Blues, 144
Stein, Jules, 100
Stempel, Tom, 218
Stevens, George, 57, 74, 193–197
Stevens, George, Jr., 193, 194, 196
Sting, The, 16, 99, 133, 206, 221, 222, 246
Strauss, Helen, 130
Sturges, Preston, 159, 173
Sugarland Express, The, 227
Sullivan, Ed, 186, 188
Sullivan, Kay, 203
Sun (London), 122
Susann, Jacqueline, 129, 165–166
Swanson, H. N., 16
Sweet Smell of Success, The (Lehman), 185, 186, 188
Swope, Herbert Bayard, Jr., 48
Szwarc, Jeannot, 153, 155–156

Tablet, 233
Tandy, Jessica, 135
Target, 209, 219–220, 221, 236–238
Taylor, Elizabeth, 75, 76, 154, 196–197, 219
Taylor, Ron, 148
Taylor, Sam, 205
Thalberg, Irving, 35, 86–87, 114, 116
Thomas, Bob, 186
Thomas, Michael, 123
Thorp, Roderick, 113–114
Thorson, Marge, 36
Three Faces of Eve, The, 94
Time, 16
Tobacco Road (Caldwell), 36

Todd, Mike, 142
Tora! Tora! Tora!, 238
Traub, Marvin, 138–139
Triangle Publishing, 134
Trotti, Lamar, 216–217
Truman, Harry S., 25, 26, 27, 144
Trump, Donald, 175
TV Guide, 134
Twentieth Century Fox, 50–51, 54, 73, 75–77, 86, 91, 95–96, 137, 160, 162, 170, 194, 201, 204, 238
  Century City and, 73, 75–76
  D. Brown at, 34–38, 73, 81, 84, 85, 96, 107, 111, 122–132, 234
2001, 163

Uhry, Alfred, 249

Vaudeville News, 184
Veblen, Thorstein, 183
Verdict, The, 128, 169, 200, 207, 232–236
Vidal, Gore, 129
Village Voice, 121, 122

Wagner, Lee, 134
Wagner, Phyllis, 163
Wagner, Robert, 163–164
Wald, Jerry, 56–57, 130, 187
Walker, Kathryn, 202
Wallace, Irving, 107, 230
Wallace, Mike, 160, 238
Wallace, Sylvia, 230
Walters, Barbara, 157–158, 160
Walton, Sam, 175
Wanger, Walter, 74–75, 140
War and Peace, 88
Ward, David, 144
Warden, Jack, 207, 236
Warner, Jack L., 53, 99, 101, 102, 103, 141, 170, 195, 212, 240–241
Warner Brothers, 143, 144, 170
Wasserman, Lew R., 98–99, 100, 149, 190–191
Wayne, John, 156
Weinstein, Henry, 55
Weisbart, David, 178
Weisberger, Arnold, 96
Weiss, Walter, 45
Welch, Raquel, 71
Welles, Orson, 96–98, 101, 162, 204
Wells, Frank, 213
West, Mae, 71–72, 164
Weybright, Victor, 120
Whalen, Richard, 120
Whitaker, Clem, 26–27
Whitman, Alden, 32
Whitney, Jock, 87, 179
Wilder, Billy, 101
Williams, John, 15
Will Success Spoil Rock Hunter? (Axelrod), 57
Wilson, George, 183
Wilson, Liza, 26
Winchell, June, 185
Winchell, Walter, 35, 119, 183–188
Wise, Robert, 170
Wolf, George, 60, 120–121
Women's Wear Daily, 17, 19, 20
Wood, Natalie, 103
Woodward, Joanne, 75, 94
Woollcott, Alexander, 34, 51
World War II, 23–24, 25, 238, 239
Wyler, William, 220, 225

Zanuck, Darryl F., 34, 35, 36, 37, 50, 51, 72, 74, 77, 81, 85–86, 87–98, 99, 113, 114, 117–118, 123, 130, 143, 162–163, 170, 172–173, 177, 179, 187, 195, 197, 201, 212, 216–217, 225, 229
  as practical joker, 82–83
  R. Zanuck and D. Brown fired by, 84–85, 96, 123–129, 234
  Welles's eulogy for, 96–98
Zanuck, Ginny, 126
Zanuck, Lili Fini, 209, 257
Zanuck, Linda Harrison, 96, 126
Zanuck, Richard (Dick), 46, 54–55, 57, 97, 99, 113, 140, 143–144, 157, 158, 165, 166, 167, 170, 182, 191, 196, 197, 201, 207, 208, 209, 221, 222, 223, 226–227, 232, 233, 234, 239, 245, 246, 256, 257
  D. Zanuck's firing of, 84–85, 96, 123–129, 234
  Jaws and, 15, 16, 145, 148, 149, 150, 206
  as practical joker, 83, 114–115
Zanuck, Virginia, 97, 116
Zanuck/Brown Company, 99, 128, 143–144, 249, 256–257
Zeckendorf, William, 75
Ziegfeld, Florenz, 100
Zucker, Charles, 253
Zukor, Adolph, 204